NO SMOKING GUN

(The Story of the Kirkheaton Police Killings - 1951)

Patrick E. Robertshaw

Bright Pen

A Bright Pen Book

British Library Cataloguing Publication Data.
A catalogue record for this book is available from the British Library

ISBN 978-0-7552-1484-6

Authors OnLine Ltd
19 The Cinques
Gamlingay, Sandy
Bedfordshire SG19 3NU
England

This book is also available in e-book format, details of which are available at www.authorsonline.co.uk

ABOUT THE AUTHOR

Patrick E. Robertshaw, born 7 July, 1945, in Huddersfield and brought up in the nearby town of Elland where his father was a local shopkeeper. Patrick was educated at Hipperholme Grammar School and Southampton University where in 1967 he was awarded a first class honours degree in law. Called to the Bar in 1968 he practised in the criminal courts of the North-Eastern Circuit until 1994 when he was appointed a Circuit Judge. Until his retirement from the bench in 2010 he presided over criminal trials in the Sheffield, Doncaster, Hull and York Crown Courts. On his retirement he was appointed a part-time member of the Parole Board. Patrick was married to Sally, then a lecturer in drama at the Huddersfield Polytechnic, in 1972. Patrick lives with Sally at Scissett, Huddersfield. They have 4 children and at the last count 8 grandchildren.

ACKNOWLEDGEMENTS

I am grateful to Mrs Doreen Dean, widow of His Honour C. Raymond Dean QC, junior defence counsel at the trial of Alfred Moore, for making available to me her late husband's papers from the case. Without them quite simply this book would not have been possible. And to the late His Honour Arthur Hutchinson QC, son of Alfred Moore's solicitor, who, on many occasions, shared with me both his recollections of the trial, which he witnessed as a schoolboy, and his father's lifelong reservations about the safety of his client's conviction. Finally, Patricia, whose emotions when recalling the events re-told in this book remain as raw today as they were in 1951 when, as a tearful ten-year-old, she was compelled to take the witness stand to testify against her father knowing the inevitable consequence of his conviction. Her ordeal was one no child should have had to endure. She was, nonetheless, generous in speaking to me and providing a wealth of information about the Moore family, her memories of the last visit to the condemned cell and growing up fatherless in the shadow of the events of the next morning when as the clock on the mantelpiece struck nine her mother dissolved in tears. Without her input I fear that this book might not have been of interest to other than lawyers and scholars of the history of our criminal justice system.

CONTENTS

ABOUT THE AUTHOR iii

ACKNOWLEDGEMENTS v

FOREWORD ix

1 - High Farmsteads 1

2 - Deserter, Poultry Farmer – and Burglar 4

3 - A Fatal Move 12

4 - A Saturday in July 15

5 - "It's unlucky to turn back" 19

6 - Bells, Whistles, Shouts and Shots 22

7 – Perverting the Course of Justice 27

8 – Stand-Off 30

9 – No Rest on this Sabbath 34

10 - Settled, Hopeless Expectation of Death 38

11 – Bedside Justice 47

12 – Makeshift Justice 54

13 – Child Witness 62

14 – The Morning After the Weekend Before 72

15 - Remand 80

16 – A True Bill 95

17 – 'I Could Hang Him Myself' 122

18 – 'Albert' and the Judge 130
19 – Proof 140
20 – "I was in the British Navy not the German Navy" 158
21 – "I am going to shock everybody" 173
22 – Burglar not murderer 189
23 – The last word 198
24 – The reporter's gaffe 204
25 – Goddard and Kilmuir 210
26 – Last days 222
27 – And still the argument rages 233

FOREWORD

At the time of writing this foreword the online community has amassed the required 100,000 signatures for a petition to Parliament to debate the reintroduction of capital punishment. It is a development as predictable as is the eventual vote in Parliament not to do so. The death penalty will always enjoy a hardcore of support and the level of support today for the rope (or whatever other means science may devise for extinguishing human life) is, undoubtedly, significant. Nor is it confined to the lynch mob mentality of those who turn up to hammer their fists against the sides of vehicles transporting to and from court those accused (but not yet convicted) of some high-profile crime. But it is a support which is also dwindling fast with the recognition that the criminal justice system, administered by human beings, is not immune from human fallibility. The roll call of the wrongly, or dubiously, hanged is a long one. Even longer is the list of those whose lives over the past half century would inevitably have ended with a broken neck at the end of a rope had hanging been retained but whose innocence is no longer doubted.

Whether Alfred Moore is a name to be added to the list of the unjustly hanged the reader will be able to judge having considered the evidence in the case – as fully rehearsed in this book as is possible without a mere unvarnished reproduction of the trial transcript. What is uncontroversial is that the safety of Moore's conviction was not doubted at the time – nor until many years later; equally uncontroversial is the proposition that the same evidence which convicted Moore would fail to do so today. Recognition of the dangers of relying upon fleeting glimpse identification evidence and the imperatives of a fair trial requiring an effective opportunity to challenge evidence solely and decisively constituting evidence of guilt would ensure at worst a trial ending at the close of the prosecution with a judicially directed verdict of not guilty or at best no trial at all.

In 1951, however, eye-witness identification evidence was actually regarded as being as good as it gets as evidence of guilt. After all, there was nothing 'circumstantial' about it; it was immediate, direct and provided by a source convinced of its rightness, telling it as the truth of a proposition honestly believed to be true and therefore convincing to those tasked with hearing and judging it. The right to a fair trial was considered sufficiently safeguarded by the requirement that the prosecution had to prove its case beyond reasonable doubt. A right to legal representation to challenge effectively disputed evidence was recognised but rather as a sophistication than something fundamental, underpinning the fairness of the proceedings. Alfred Moore was convicted on a fleeting glimpse identification of which circumstances did not allow any effective challenge.

Besides, these were deferential times. Whatever jurisprudence might dictate there was an unconscious assumption that the police did not arrest, let alone charge, those against whom there was not already cogent evidence of guilt. It was an assumption that permeated all strata of the law-abiding classes. Nowhere was it more deep-seated than in the hearts and minds of the affluent, property-owning, middle classes who alone qualified at that time for jury service.

At his best Alfred Moore was not someone to attract instinctive sympathy. Those who witnessed his performance in the witness box describe it as 'arrogant' – though a mere reading of the transcript would not necessarily lead to this conclusion. In truth, however, even before stepping from the dock to the witness box Alfred Moore's fate was sealed. In fact it was sealed once he was identified as the gunman and the identification confirmed by sworn deposition not allowing of further challenge following the death of the deponent a few hours later.

No doubt the jurors on taking their solemn oath to decide the case before them on nothing but the evidence were resolved to do nothing less. Equally no doubt that resolve was sorely tried on the revelation shortly into the trial that the smartly dressed figure in the dock was no respectable, hard-working, farmer but an individual who preyed on his fellow citizens in the course of carefully planned, skilfully carried out, night time burglaries. Worse than that: he had dodged the call to arms in the recent conflict, shirked his duty when other able-bodied young men were making their contribution, sometimes with their lives, to the national effort. Only six years after the cessation of hostilities it is a fair guess that amongst the jury of Alfred Moore's peers would be those who had served their country. To the issue of guilt or innocence his reluctance to engage with the enemy was, of course, an irrelevance. His burgling career was capable of being interpreted as evidence of guilt, the reluctance of a guilty man to engage with the police, but equally consistent with innocence – why perpetrate the one act that inevitably would lead to an army of police officers descending on the farmhouse where the proceeds of numerous burglaries were available to be found?

Alfred really did not have much going in his favour! Except for one unambiguous circumstance – the absence in evidence at the trial of the gun. None was ever found, smoking or otherwise. The whole foundation of the prosecution case was that the gunman, Moore, fled within the cordon of police officers surrounding his farm and not away from it and that, therefore, somewhere within that defined, restricted, area the murder weapon was available to be found. In terms of neither time, nor manpower, nor resources, nothing was spared in the effort to recover it. The only explanation that makes any sense for the failure to do so is that it was not there to be found because the killer fled the scene, away from the farmhouse, taking the murder weapon with him. In short, that the killer was not Alfred Moore.

How could a jury, properly directed, knowing the inevitable consequence of a guilty verdict, take such little time to conclude that this failure of proof did not even qualify for a finding of 'reasonable doubt'? Prepare, readers, to draw your own conclusion. Mine is unequivocally that the wrong man hanged, convicted on questionable evidence buttressed by the prejudices of the age.

Patrick E.
Robertshaw.

1 - High Farmsteads

Few are likely to be puzzled as to the significance and meaning of the 'Kirk' in Kirkheaton. Many might be, however, as to the 'heaton' part of this township's name. It's meaning, 'high farmstead', dates back to ancient times, to the times when this small village, just outside the Parish of Huddersfield, was a Saxon wappentake.

Kirkheaton does not disappoint its quaint, picturesque naming. Known variously over the years as Yetton, Heton and Heptone, Kirkheaton today is a mixture of dwellings dating only from the eighteenth century. Its history, however, goes back over a thousand years. It was in the ninth century that people began to settle in the area and it was one of the 13,418 places mentioned in William the Conqueror's Domesday Book of 1086, used to assess the extent of land and resources in England. But the Kirkheaton referred to there is the original Anglo Saxon settlement at Upper Heaton, over half a mile away from the Kirkheaton of today. In those times people tended to build higher up the slopes. Thus it was that there were two Heatons: Upper Heaton, the original settlement, and Kirkheaton the settlement around the church, the population of which continued to increase albeit at first slowly.

The year 1574 was a significant one for the parish with the birth of Richard Beaumont, later Sir Richard. He, and his successors, for over four hundred years as Lords of the Manor contributed to its growth and, in particular, making it a centre of excellence for the education of boys from both near, who would attend the Grammar School, and afar as well for whom there existed a boarding school. Enlightenment did not of course extend to the education of young girls.

It was only when Kirkheaton became a parish in its own right around

1200 (before that it fell within the parish of Dewsbury) and a church was built convenient for the settlements of population at Dalton, Upper Whitley and Lepton that people began to settle in Kirkheaton itself.

Of High Farmsteads around Kirkheaton there are many. This is a community nestling comfortably high on the Pennine Hills. During the seventeenth and eighteenth centuries many of Kirkheaton's residents would have worked on the land, it being particularly suitable for arable farming and dairy cattle. No doubt many of the farmers kept a few head of poultry as well but it was not until the arrival of a new inhabitant in the twentieth century that poultry as a specialist farming enterprise was ever contemplated.

One of Kirkheaton's High Farmsteads is Whinney Close Farm, often known known locally as Plantation Farm, a rambling building with today obvious add-ons and extensions of varying ages but none of which would remotely qualify it as the original High Farmstead. Quite possibly, however, some former building on the same site lent itself to the naming of the village for it requires a degree of upward exertion to reach it from the hub of the village.

Today Whinney Close Farm with its adjoining tennis courts is a well-appointed dwelling, the home of some local prosperous man of business, rather than a working farm but the fields sloping steeply down from its northern aspect remain much as they were centuries ago, little altered indeed since that dreadful night in the summer of 1951 when the lives of two West Riding police officers were senselessly, and with brutal suddenness, terminated.

The twelve roomed, grey brick, slate roofed, farmhouse continues to nestle comfortably in a dell on the slopes leading to Cockley Hill within the barren grandeur of the Pennine Moors. In all directions the views defy the use of the superlative – spectacular, stunning, splendid all come close; picturesque, scenic only serve to fall short. To the north the whole of the town of Huddersfield, and Halifax beyond it, are in view with the skyline attractively broken by Castle Hill on which perches a Napoleonic beacon tower. To the south the views are less extensive but no less spectacular, rolling fields on the edge of wild moorland country with this time the skyline punctuated by the clean lines of the mast at Emley, the means by which since the early 1970's the area received commercial television; no longer, perhaps, rejoicing in the claim to be the tallest free-standing structure in Europe but still, nonetheless, its higher reaches shrouded in mist on those days when the clouds lie low.

In 1951 it was not cloud but black smoke, belching from the chimneys of the many textile mills on which the prosperity of Huddersfield was founded, that obscured the horizons from view. The Clean Air Act was still two years into the future yet the singular wisdom of Parliament, on this occasion at least, was to rescue the town of Huddersfield from suffocation by smoke, extend the life expectancy of its population, as well as open to view unimagined panoramas.

The only scar on this landscape, acoustically and aesthetically, is the area of artificially created and tiered flats of clay mud marking the site of the former brickworks, used to the annoyance of nearby residents for off-road motor-biking, and to which on that July night the bodies of one dead police officer and another mortally wounded one were stretchered prior to their removal to the town's mortuary and infirmary.

2 - Deserter, Poultry Farmer – and Burglar

Alfred Moore was a Huddersfield man through and through. Born on the 6 June 1915 at Golcar, he was just 35 and approaching the prime years of his life when it was extinguished with no less brutality, or arguably sense – though as to the latter opinions will differ - than were the lives of the two officers. One of his parents' ten children Alfred was a loner, described by his wife Alice as one apart from his four sisters and five brothers. At Golcar Church School he achieved the second highest standard.

Harsh treatment at the hands of his father at home, however, blighted any prospect of academic success and led to Alfred leaving home to live with an aunt, returning to the home of his parents some three years later on his aunt being taken ill.

It was on the 17 July 1933, just a month after his 17th birthday, that Alfred came home from the cinema entering the house through the front door which banged shut because of the draught created by an open back door. "Don't bang the bloody door" yelled his furious father. When Alfred denied that he was at fault the increasingly irate father launched an attack upon his son with the words – "And don't bloody well answer back." The violent struggle between the two was ugly, ending only when mother intervened and ordered Alfred to leave the house for his own safety.

Alfred's return to the parental home brought about only a temporary truce in the hostilities between father and son and on regular occasions the police were called to the house to intervene in the violence erupting between the two. It was courtship and marriage that finally ended those years of attrition and aggression. As Alfred was to tell the prison psychiatrist many years later: "I met Alice shortly afterwards. She hadn't a father and lived with her mother so we decided to get married."

It was in 1939, at the age of 24, that Alfred met the love of his short life. Alice Cox was an attractive, some thought rather flighty, lass from Saddleworth, just across the Pennines. The attraction was mutual and instant, remaining constant to the very bitter end, not all that many years into the future. For her part, to be seen on the arm of this popular, smartly dressed, elegantly mannered youth, to be swirled smoothly by this young Astaire across the dance floors of the many Huddersfield ballrooms of the time made her the envy of other girls and in that she revelled.

Working in the pattern office at Stanley Mills, Golcar, Alfred was just beginning to realise his boyhood ambition, a curious one perhaps, to succeed and prosper as a poultry farmer. Already he was the tenant of a smallholding adjoining Stanley Mill and the proud owner of 600 head of poultry. His ambitions went well beyond that however; not for Alfred, if he could escape it, the constraints of the tenant farmer. Enthusiastically he shared his aspirations for the future with Alice who did nothing at all to dampen them; she encouraged them with the enthusiasm for a future which already they were resolved would be a shared one.

Alfred and Alice married on the 24 February 1940, at the Huddersfield West Riding Register Office, moving to Bottoms Farm at Slaithwaite, still as tenant farmers but with the potential for stock expansion and increased profitability. Poultry farming brought with it another, not unlooked for or unwelcome, advantage. Farming of all kinds was a reserved occupation and when the call came to serve King and Country a virtually automatic deferment was granted. But it was just that - a deferment and only a deferment; and when, for reasons which remain obscure and puzzling given the need of the nation to be self-sufficient in its food resources, the poultry venture faltered and the tenancy of Bottoms Farm had to be surrendered, as an able-bodied young man, fit in mind and body, Alfred once more became liable to service in support of the national effort. Though never claiming the status of conscientious objector, Alfred told Alice that he had an instinctive aversion to killing people.

After a short period working at the David Brown tractor factory at Lockwood, uncongenial to Alfred as was any work to be undertaken other than beneath the skies, and when the demands of military service and his failure to make himself available to do his part, officially designated him as a deserter he decided unilaterally that his war would be spent in the merchant navy. For the next three years he sailed the world's seas, serving on tugs and minesweepers, seeing, being exposed to, but not involved in, military action. His conscience based objection to taking life appeared, at least on the face of it, to represent a principled stand.

Back at home Alice suffered less than many from the privations of war, thanks to a friend and associate of Alfred's, Clifford Mead, small time crook and wheeler dealer, for whom the war opened endless possibilities to turn a fast buck. He was what was euphemistically described as a dealer in 'essential supplies' but bluntly put a black marketeer. Wearing his trade mark white silk scarf he was a regular visitor to the Moore household and it was not merely the apparently effortless ease with which this family, lacking a father figure and bread winner, survived the rigours and deprivations of wartime that was the subject of local gossip.

In the post-war years service in the forces was something that counted much in your favour. It led to many a promotion of the mediocre who were perceived as having enjoyed 'a good war'. And for those seen as having shirked their duty and who fell to be judged by their fellow citizens that judgement was likely to be harsh and unyielding. Only a few became liable to that judgement. Alfred Moore was one of the few.

So: Alfred Moore was a man of many parts; army deserter, aspirant, though hardly yet successful poultry farmer – and, by night, accomplished burglar, his speciality mills and offices. He was the archetypal character of fiction – the personable, gentleman crook. Burglary was an occupation to which Alfred turned in the years of post-war austerity when, his service in the merchant navy having come to an end, he nonetheless faced the day of reckoning for his desertion in the symbolic face of the enemy, symbolic because few servicemen, and fewer women, did actually make eye-ball contact with the enemy.

In those years Alfred was constantly on the move, his contact with his family sporadic and intermittent, keeping just one step ahead of the military police and subsisting on the proceeds of crime. When neither burgling nor planning the devices by which to avoid his pursuers Alfred fettled. He was a compulsive fettler. Already his collection of skeleton keys was impressive and it was being put to regular and advantageous use. To Alfred burglary was a craft and he approached it with the, perverted, skill of a professional. None of his offending was spontaneous, unrehearsed or opportunist. He selected his targets well, studied them closely and paid particular attention to their locks and security, weighing the risk of detection against the likely yield. If he did not already possess a key likely to fit then he would simply make one.

His two years on the run came to an end when, in 1947, he was arrested on suspicion of a burglary at the Scapegoat Hill Equitable Industrial Society Limited (the 'Co-op'). When Alfred was arrested the offence was already of some antiquity, having been committed four years previously.

It was early on the morning of the 20 December 1943, whilst James Wilkinson, the 59 year old manager of the premises, was preparing for the opening of the store, putting coke on the stove used to heat the premises, that he heard the sound of an intruder in the area of the sub-post office. Having first alerted a man by the name of Whitwam, who was stood outside the premises, that something was amiss James Wilkinson went to confront the intruder. It was a brave act but one which resulted in him being, as later newspaper accounts put it, 'grievously assaulted'. He was felled with an iron bar and the intruder, who had evidently been at work for some time and had already opened a supposedly secure safe, made good his escape with shoes, groceries, keys, electrical items, cash and postal orders. The total value of the property stolen was some £89-12 shillings, a highly profitable night's work for the burglar – whoever he was.

Neither James Wilkinson, nor the man Whitwam, were able to provide any useful description of the offender. The conventional police tactic of rounding up the usual suspects, who did not include in 1943 Alfred Moore, repaid no dividends but within a few weeks of the offence a number of postal orders began to be cashed in and around Huddersfield. The person cashing them was Alice Moore whose explanation to the police was that she had received them, honestly and in good faith, from her husband. It was not an explanation that the police had any particular reason to doubt but nor were they in any position either to verify or confirm that which they were being told for Alice professed to have no current knowledge of Alfred's whereabouts. That he was wanted as a deserter was soon ascertained and Alfred was now on two separate wanted lists – that of the civil as well as the military police.

On the 30 May 1947, Alfred, paying one of his fleeting, unannounced visits to the family home, was arrested and, in the absence of what the police considered to be an even half decent explanation, he was charged with burglary, placed before the magistrates' court and, despite an impassioned plea for bail, remanded to Armley Gaol. The explanation proffered by Alfred for his possession of the postal orders was in fact no more than a variant of that with which the police are all too familiar –

'bought it from an unknown man in a pub' – and understandably cynical. Alfred claimed that he had come by the postal orders, in good faith of course, from a fellow merchant seaman in the port of Hull. There was nothing available to the prosecution directly to contradict this explanation, merely the unlikelihood of coincidence that Alfred, a Huddersfield man, should have come into possession in Hull of the proceeds of a crime committed in Huddersfield.

After six days Alfred was returned to court. In the meantime the combined efforts of police and prosecution had failed to strengthen the case against him and, whilst not yet ready to throw in the towel, the objections to bail were this time decidedly muted. Bail was granted with the sole requirement that Alfred return to court in three weeks' time.

All that happened in those three weeks was that the military police were alerted to Alfred's forthcoming appointment at the Huddersfield West Riding Court. No other evidence of his guilt of the burglary had been discovered and, in advance of the court date, the police were advised that the case simply did not run. To a force determined to solve a serious and long-standing felony and convinced of the guilt of their suspect it was unwelcome advice, received with ill-grace and a determination that if this was not to be the day of reckoning for Alfred Moore that day, however long it might take, would come.

The final appearance before the court was, therefore, a formality. The prosecutor informed the bench that he would offer no evidence "for the best possible reason that there is no evidence to be offered". And with that disarmingly frank concession he requested that the case be dismissed. Plainly the court had no discretion to do otherwise and it was certainly not a course of action to which the defence had the right to object (and it would have been astonishing if they had sought to do so) and nor was the consent of the defence required to conclude the proceedings with the formality of the charges being dismissed. That did not, however, deter the defence advocate, Mr J.D. Eaton Smith, from making an impassioned, but wholly meaningless, plea on behalf of his wronged client.

Eaton Smith was the Colossus of local advocacy, a figure appearing daily in the lists of both the Borough and West Riding police courts and a name which came readily to the lips of the local criminal fraternity when arrested by the police. In the guise of seeking the widest publicity in the press "so that the grave injury occasioned to this most unfortunate man can be remedied" but in fact in a blatant exercise in self-publicity

Eaton Smith eloquently held forth on the injustice of what had taken place. The police sitting in court quietly fumed as he reminded the bench of the history of the case and of the six days spent by his client in gaol. He declared that:

> "When he was granted bail and returned to his home he was cold-shouldered by his friends and even his own family. It was felt by them that as he had been kept in prison he must have had something to do with the offence."

Warming to his theme and carried along with the exuberance of his own eloquence he pronounced:

> "If ever an individual was unfortunately charged before any court of justice it has been this man and that charge has been without any foundation."

The longer this pontification went on the more irritated became the police, convinced that far from this being a case of a man wronged by the processes of the justice system this was someone cheating the system, 'bang to rights', escaping his just deserts on the 'technicality' that there just did not happen to be available any convincing evidence of guilt. It was, however, an irritation slightly mollified by the knowledge that just outside the door of the court were two officers of the military police ready to put a prompt halt to any jubilation occasioned by the inevitable discharge, within the next few moments, of the prisoner from the custody of the court.

By now Eaton Smith had reached his peroration:

> "I neither assent to nor dissent from the application that has been made. The prosecution must make up its mind what part it will take in this affair. The prosecutor has told you he can offer no evidence. I will go one step further and tell you there is no evidence which can be offered which in any way can connect the accused with the offence alleged against him. He will leave court free from taint in relation to the offence."

Alfred Moore did indeed leave the dock, as he had entered it, a man unconvicted, of unblemished character, save that is for the little matter of the army desertion. Once outside the door of the court room and, apparently unaware of what was going to happen, he was handcuffed after a brief struggle and led away into military custody.

As a postscript to Alfred Moore's 1947 court appearance the prosecutor was Mr R.C. Linney and the Chairman of the Bench Mr Percy Crowther. It was to be four years before those three players were to meet again and in circumstances far more dramatic.

Inevitably the events of 1943 and 1947 led to the opening of a police file with its inevitable 'mug shot' of Alfred Moore. For the rest of his life Alfred was a focus of interest to the police, the intelligence file on his suspected activities growing more bulky month on month. His discharge did nothing to dent, indeed it fortified, the determination of the police one day to see Alfred back in the dock.

To the charge of desertion Alfred had no defence but his service in the Merchant Navy counted in his favour and the result of the Court Martial, held in the Barracks at Pontefract, was a nominal three days' detention against which his time in police custody was counted. It led, again, to his immediate release but once more to an illusory freedom. There was still the little matter of the outstanding national service to be done. It was served uneventfully in the demob office at Stourport in the Malvern Hills. He was discharged from the army after just eight months.

Though still separated from Alice and his, by now, three young daughters, Patricia, Christine and Sandra, the ending of his years as a fugitive came as a relief to both. Alice was able to set up a rather more permanent home, a bungalow at 37, Gynn Lane, Honley, chosen because attached to it was an acre of land, ideal for fulfilling the dream of former years. Alfred's ambition to succeed as a poultry farmer was only temporarily on hold. On his discharge from army service poultry and huts were acquired and the venture resumed with a will on the part of both that it should succeed and prosper. And it did - to an extent. But by no means sufficiently to meet the needs of his young family, by now expanded by the addition of a fourth daughter, Bronwyn - or 'Bronnie' as the baby of the family became known. They never did produce sons. For his family Alfred was determined that nothing less than the best was good enough.

Facing the eternal middle-class dilemma of making ends meet the means whereby his family should prosper and be seen to prosper were obvious to Alfred. Poultry farming might be a chancy and precarious venture and one where Alfred's ambitions outran his abilities but as to his skills as a burglar there was no doubt; and that already formidable collection of skeleton keys, amassed during his years eluding the clutches of the military police, had not been discarded. In fact it had been augmented. So back to burglary it was to be, poultry farming by day, burglary by night. And in the daylight hours when not about the daily routine of the poultry farm he was busily engaged in his makeshift workshop skillfully, obsessively fettling and filing further and better skeleton keys and paying close study to the mechanics of lock opening.

As a burglar Alfred Moore was adept. He chose his targets judiciously and his activities brought him many of the trappings of prosperity. To the West Riding Constabulary the sight of his four young daughters travelling daily by taxi to their expensive private school was enough to raise suspicion that it was being financed by something rather more than the proceeds of poultry farming. He was suspected of being responsible for hundreds of unsolved burglaries. In fact, for any unsolved burglary Alfred was the prime suspect. They were determined he should be brought to justice and the abysmal clear-up rate for burglary in Huddersfield consigned to history.

3 - A Fatal Move

By the Spring of 1951 the modest success of the Honley poultry venture and the even greater profitability of Alfred's burgling enabled a move onwards, and indeed upwards as well in more than one sense, to Whinney Close Farm. Its adjoining eight acres of land and straggling, broken down, outbuildings and workshops made it ideal for the poultry farmer with an eye to yet further expansion. Its remote location, surrounded on three sides by fields, made it even more ideal for a purchaser with more than half a mind to move to and from it with stealth in the hours of darkness. In the few months that followed Alfred Moore came to know well the numerous tracks and paths giving access to the farm.

Whinney Close Farm was acquired for £1,900 at open auction, a speculative investment for the Moores but a well-judged one. The sale had been forced, the previous owner having begun works of improvement and extension but, as so often happens with these ventures, running out of liquid cash part way into it and being left with no alternative but to stave off his creditors by a hasty sale at an inevitable undervalue. The farm was purchased for cash and Alfred was cautiously confident that the profits from poultry together with what was left over from the proceeds of burgling, and with the absence of a mortgage to service, the enterprise was a potential winner. He was, however, a shrewd man of business and his confidence was tempered with sufficient realism for the farm to be conveyed into the name of Alice Moore placing it beyond the reach of creditors in the event that the venture failed resulting in bankruptcy.

But, all in all, it was a nicely judged business plan and, had events not taken the tragic and unforeseen turn that they did, there is no reason at all to think that Alfred and his family would not have ended their days as affluent and respected, the murky origins of their prosperity long forgotten or dimly remembered only by a few.

It was not only furniture and effects that had to be moved and the transport of Alfred's dismantled poultry sheds across the town from Honley to Kirkheaton called for professional expertise. The choice was a pretty obvious one in those days. In the Huddersfield of the 1950's if you were on the move it was not to the national conglomerate Pickfords that you turned but to the alliteratively named Hansons Haulage of Huddersfield with its virtual stranglehold on the transport business. Hansons even ran their own bus company and that was many years in advance of the privatisation of the buses.

The move was to be made over the course of two evenings in May and on the first of those evenings a curious event took place, the truth and significance of which later came to be the subject of fierce controversy. In the course of fettling his skeleton keys Alfred had acquired a formidable array of tools, of a weight and quantity that the box in which they were being housed simply fell apart when lifted by its handles from the ground. It contained an assortment of rusty old saw blades, nails, screws, a folded air rifle and according to Hanson employee, Joe Baxter, not then but months later, something more deadly and sinister. But as to that he kept his own counsel at the time and, on his return the next evening, the box had been nailed together and whether still containing all of its cargo of the previous evening or no it was safely, and securely, transferred to Whinney Close Farm.

An immediate increase in the livestock of the farm was effected once the move to Whinney Close was complete. It now numbered six hundred head of poultry of which one hundred were 'layers' and the rest 'to the point of lay'. Pigs were acquired in an effort at diversification, three gilts two of which were 'in pig'. For the first time the care of his poultry was a full-time occupation and Alfred devoted those hours not so engaged to work of building improvement and the construction of extensions to the farmstead.

To all worldly appearances Alfred was a successful farmer, his success the product of long-held ambition, gritty determination to overcome the numerous reverses of fortune by which he had been beset for a decade and just pure, simple honest toil. And that was to be his claim. Having at last found his feet in the ways of honest business his burgling days, he was to say, were over. Why risk his liberty and the hard won prosperity of his family when there was no longer the need?

Not that he made any claim to be leading the life of an industrious, law-abiding poultry farmer at the time. That would have been to admit that it was not ever thus! Nor did he take any steps to dispose of his lovingly amassed collection of skeleton keys for which, if his resolve was true, he had no further use.

The villagers of Kirkheaton watched with increasing curiosity and the occasional raised eyebrow the arrival each morning at Whinney Close Farm of the taxi to take the Moore girls, in their neat school uniforms, to their private school across the town and its journey back through the village in the afternoon to return them home. Rumours abounded of the farmhouse being stacked with antiques and what were considered at the time to be luxury items – refrigerators, radiograms and the like - well beyond the means of a modest, small-time poultry farmer. Small-time Alfred might have been but with aspirations to become a country gentleman farmer.

And the local police were as suspicious as ever, almost to the point of paranoia, that this one-man crime machine was a major contributor to the depressing statistical returns made monthly by them to headquarters at Wakefield. Something had to be done.

4 - A Saturday in July

There were to be no holidays this year for the Moore girls but that was no particular hardship. The delights of their new home and the prospect of playing 'hide and seek' in and around its rambling outbuildings meant that this was a long summer holiday to look forward to and a seaside holiday was still, in those years of post-war austerity, reckoned to be a luxury for the few.

There were of course the holiday camps, fun and entertainment made affordable for the masses by Billy Butlin and Fred Pontin, but this was not really an option for a family aspiring to status and gentility. The prospect of the Moore girls recounting the excitement of the hotly contested 'knobbly knees' and 'glamorous granny' contests to their refined chums at their private school when they returned there in September was too awful to be contemplated.

Besides there was poultry to be tended and slaughtered and eggs to be collected and sold daily. This was not work to be entrusted to any locum, the cost of which would have been in any event prohibitively beyond the resources, even illicitly augmented, of Alfred and Alice. The new venture was showing promising, but still modest, returns and every penny, not spent on the children, their schooling, their taxis to school and clothing befitting their new status, was being ploughed back into improvements at Whinney Close.

Saturday the 14 July was an average sort of July day, warm but not uncomfortably so, with occasional light showers of rain, and it had been set aside by Alfred for laying flagstones in the pigsty as well as routine repair work to the hen houses. It was heavy work for one man and Alfred was the only man on the premises. He had brothers however and though estranged from his family in former years he had more recently become reconciled to his brother Charles Henry Moore who lived only a mile or so down the hill in Fernside Crescent at Almondbury.

During the summer months of 1951 Charles Henry had become a regular visitor to Whinney Close Farm. Evidently he found working outdoors, evenings and weekends, a healthy and welcome respite from the noise and dirt of his employment as a 'textile percher' in a local woollen mill and, perhaps as well, from his wife, the formidable sounding Mahala Alice Moore. Mahala's regular tongue-lashings of Charles Henry as a 'dirty stop out' were no deterrent to his visits to his brother at Whinney Close Farm, rather they encouraged them it would seem.

And so it came about that on Saturday 14 July, following a shift paid double time at the mill that morning, Charles Henry, happy to give of his labour to his brother for the rest of the day, took the bus for the short ride to Kirkheaton.

It was a productive day's work and it extended long into the gradually fading light of this evening of high summer in 1951. When there was no more that could be done and, after the time for refreshment and winding down from the labours of the day was over, it was time to face the stern Mahala. It was past 10-15pm, the time of the last bus back to Almondbury. To walk, however, was no hardship; it was anyway all downhill and the evening still warm and pleasant.

The only discussion point was whether Charles should walk alone or whether Alfred would accompany him at least part of the way. This was 1951. The ailing George VI still reigned and the Coronation that was to bring his daughter to the throne - and television sets to the overwhelming majority of homes of middle England - was two years away. There was no home entertainment to keep Alfred indoors and it was soon decided that he would savour the night air and enjoy a companionable stroll with his brother at least part way to his home. Before leaving he told Alice that he expected to be home within the hour.

To have walked down the road to Almondbury would have been to take a route both less pleasant and distinctly less direct. So it was down the steep, and none too safe in the dark, field pathway to the rear of Whinney Close, past the brickworks, and through the local cemetery that the brothers Moore took their late evening stroll before hitting anything that might be termed a road. The route required the negotiation of streams and stiles. Alfred was wearing a tightly belted raincoat and, according to Charles Henry, it gave no appearance of concealing anything which might be described as bulky or unusual. Both were to say that they left Whinney Close shortly before 11 o' clock. But there was neither reason to note the time nor cause to think that it might have to be remembered later as at all significant.

Whilst Alfred and Charles were setting out together the final police briefing was taking place for an exercise, not given any kind of fancy code name as it might today in order to heighten the drama and increase the sense of cloak and dagger, aimed at apprehending Alfred Moore whilst returning to Whinney Close Farm in possession, if the police fell lucky, of the proceeds of burglary.

Whether the exercise was purely speculative based on no more than suspicion and a bitter determination to nail Moore at long last and at all costs or on hard, reliable intelligence that a burglary was planned for that night was never disclosed. If it was based on intelligence it was intelligence that was seriously defective. At all events it was shortly before midnight and under cover of darkness, that ten officers, all dressed in civilian clothes, took up their positions on the roads, lanes and field paths leading to Whinney Close Farm. The prosecution were to assert that the time was quarter to midnight, a time that was to assume crucial, critical, life or death significance.

Whatever the time it was in place the cordon was secure. Though the officers involved were positioned at intervals, they were strategically placed. No one could approach, or leave, Whinney Close Farm without coming to the attention of at least one police officer. Anyone approaching Whinney Close Farm from whatever direction would inevitably hit the police cordon, or at least be capable of being observed and confronted. Every path, track, roadway leading to the farm was covered by officers.

The hope or expectation was that Alfred Moore, returning home in the early hours of Sunday morning with the loot from some burglary, would hit that cordon. So the direction given at the briefing was that Alfred Moore, if observed, was to be confronted. Common sense suggests that those tasked with making that confrontation should have more than a vague idea of the appearance of the person to be confronted and, of course, readily available was the mugshot of Alfred dating back to his days as fugitive army deserter. It is inconceivable that it was not shown at the briefing to all the officers who were to form the cordon.

What none of the officers had been issued with were firearms because no intelligence available to the police concerning Moore had ever suggested a propensity to carry arms. Whether he would be capable of violence if challenged and in possession of that which would incriminate and bring crashing down the mounting, but still no more than tentative, affluence of the Moore household was necessarily an unknown factor. After all he had never before been confronted. But if he were to be confronted that night the police certainly had no reason to believe that he would not succumb peaceably to apprehension and detention. So all that was available to those officers were their standard issue wooden truncheons, torches and whistles. Even communication with force headquarters, should an emergency and the need for reinforcement arise, was by nothing more sophisticated than field telephone. It was all very different to any remotely similar exercise being conducted today.

Over the following days and weeks the area between the farm and the positions taken by the officers forming the cordon was to be the subject of the most meticulous, pains-taking, highly labour-intensive, search. There can be no area of Huddersfield ever before, or since, subjected to anything like it. Its objective was the recovery of a gun. If and when discovered it might not exactly have been smoking still but the mere recovery of a revolver capable of discharging .22 bullets would have been sufficient to guarantee beyond all question of reasonable doubt the outcome of the then pending charges against the Kirkheaton farmer.

5 - "It's unlucky to turn back"

When Charles Henry and Alfred Moore reached Fleminghouse Lane, a few hundred yards short of the home of Charles Henry and Mahala, Alfred declined an invitation "to call in." He had no wish to encounter Mahala having deprived her of her husband for the better part of that day. Possibly because his only wish was to return to his farmhouse and family. Possibly because he had other work planned for the night hours; but for whatever reason he decided it was time to re-trace his steps.

His intention he announced with the words and an accompanying chuckle - "it's unlucky to turn back." He was evidently a man not without superstition and so instead of re-tracing his steps back long Almondbury Rise he continued down Fleminghouse Lane to the main Wakefield Road leading into the town. Charles Henry's last sighting of his brother - as a free man - was of him heading back in the direction of Kirkheaton and Whinney Close Farm.

Charles Henry continued on his weary, slightly but increasingly as he neared home, reluctant, way. When thinking about it later he believed that the unaccompanied part of his walk home lasted something like seven or eight minutes but that was never more than an estimate, albeit one that he had good reason to think about only a few hours later.

In the criminal courts estimates of time given from the witness box are notoriously unreliable. First and foremost because individuals out and about and intent on the comings and goings of daily life do not continuously consult clocks and watches or engage in measuring time. And so, as juries are still regularly reminded, whilst some witnesses may provide an accurate estimate as to the passage of time with many others their evidence is something to be viewed with caution and not accepted at anything like face value. ‘Five minutes’ might just mean ten seconds though to the witness, perhaps describing some unpleasant experience, it might well have seemed as if it was minutes, not seconds, that were being endured.

There are of course occasions when reference to the clock is required and where it becomes known very shortly afterwards that the recorded time is likely to become worthy of later recollection. The next timing of the movement and whereabouts of Charles Henry Moore, and by reference to which the whereabouts of his brother Alfred might be the subject of something more than pure supposition, was one such timing.

As Charles Henry turned the key and entered the home that he shared with Mahala and their family at 23, Fernside Crescent, the sound of the wireless told him that Mahala was still up. He braced himself for the inevitable upbraiding. No words of fond greeting here. Only “dirty stop out”. Mahala did not, and Charles Henry did not expect her, to react kindly to being neglected for the whole of this mid-summer Saturday in July. She accompanied her scolding by reference to the electric clock. It was exactly, she was to say later, 11-35 pm, conceding only the possibility that the clock was within three minutes either way of recording the correct time. Charles Henry was able to corroborate the time shown by the clock but for a somewhat different reason that might be termed the opposite side of the same coin. He told her - “it is *only* twenty-five minutes to midnight.”

Alfred was to maintain that he went straight home taking the same route through the cemetery and up the fields. He had no reason to do otherwise; there was nothing at all to detain him from returning to his family. The suspicion that he may have been out and about on some burglarious activity, equipped with his skeleton keys, looking for some target likely to yield rich pickings, never ever did amount to anything more than suspicion. No evidence was ever offered of any commercial premises in Huddersfield being attacked that night or of Alfred Moore being in possession of any recently stolen property though there was ample evidence that he was in possession of property stolen, and admittedly stolen by him, at some time in the rather more remote past.

Making every possible allowance for human error, and for the electric clock at Fernside Crescent being possibly three minutes slow, the time at which Alfred and his brother parted company and Alfred sought to avoid ill-luck by not turning back, could not have been much earlier than 11-25 pm. Relying upon evidence (that was not to be contradicted) that the time taken to walk to Whinney Close Farm from the point at which the brothers wished each other good-night was 31 minutes, the prosecution were later to contend that Alfred could not have crossed the field leading up to the farm before 11-45 pm. And the one timing that was maintained to be accurate to the second was that at which the cordon was alleged to be in place – 11-45pm.

Whatever the precise time of his walk home Alfred was to say that it was almost entirely uneventful, save that at one point his torchlight let him down and he blundered into a small stream soaking one of his shoes. On his walk through the cemetery and up the fields leading to the rear of the farm he met no-one, encountered nothing out of the ordinary and was wholly unaware of any police activity that might have been taking place. Without being too exact it was just before midnight that he reached the farmhouse. He did not enter immediately for there were the pop-holes in the poultry huts to be closed, the pigs to be checked for signs that farrowing time might be imminent (there were none) and the stables and other outbuildings secured.

Those tasks took Alfred but a few minutes. He entered the house through the French window, paused in the wash kitchen to put to soak in a boiler his trousers, by now contaminated with slurry from the pig sty floor, and went upstairs.

In the bedroom it was not only Alice who was awaiting his return for Patricia, the eldest of the daughters, had sought comfort in the same bed as mummy, as she often did, sometimes to take refuge from some scary dream but at other times just simply to be warm, cosy, enfolded in the arms and love of a parent. Often she would be permitted to stay there all-night but not on this night. The intentions of husband and wife did not allow of the presence of a third party in the matrimonial bed. Patricia was awake but not too alert and in her drowsiness did nothing to resist being carried gently by her daddy to her own bed.

The work of the day finally over, Alfred and Alice Moore settled for the night, comfortable and taking comfort each in the arms of the other. Their lapse into sleep was not immediate but, when it came, apparently untroubled for both by either pangs of conscience or fear as to what the imminent hours of daylight might bring. It was not to be an awakening to the daily routines of a working poultry farm, signalled by the early rising of the sun and the loud, strident crowing of the cockerels. This was to be a disturbed, and disturbing, night, a night to be remembered.

6 - Bells, Whistles, Shouts and Shots

Today a police operation such as that mounted by the West Riding Force on the night of the 14 July 1951 would not only be the subject of detailed, advanced planning but the meticulous logging of times, events, personnel involved. It would be managed not on the ground but remotely from force headquarters by officers of seniority designated for the exercise as the gold or silver command. There would be a dedicated logger seeing nothing but hearing everything and noting it down. Every timing would be exact to the second. And the police helicopter would be on standby to climb into the air so soon as needed to fix its penetrating searchlight onto events on the ground.

In truth there was only one timing that mattered and that was the time at which the cordon was in place around Whinney Close Farm. The police operation was under the control of Chief Inspector Jenkins and it was to be his contention, from which nothing would deflect him, that by a quarter to midnight every approach to the farm was covered by at least one of the ten officers under his command. Any suggestion of the timing being out by a mere millisecond he refused to countenance. By no later than 11-45 pm anyone approaching Whinney Close Farm from whatever direction would be observed and could, would indeed, be confronted. It was never anticipated that such an approach would be made by more than one individual and in the collective police mind the identity of that individual was not in doubt.

The thinking of the Police was that the footpath leading from the cemetery and across and up the fields to the rear of the farmhouse was unlikely to be used by a stranger at that hour of the night. But it might by someone familiar with the terrain and making a surreptitious return to the farm. Posted there were Police Constable Arthur Gordon Jagger and, a short distance away from him, Detective Inspector Duncan Fraser. Both officers were a distance of no more than 350 yards from the farmhouse.

Both the name and accent marked out Duncan Fraser as an unmistakable Scot and in those times a Scotsman exiled to Yorkshire would inevitably be known as 'Jock' or 'Sandy'. Sandy (this being the choice of his police colleagues) Fraser, at 45 years of age, originally from Inverness but now living with his wife and 13-year-old daughter in Ringston Avenue at Dalton, had completed 22 years' service in the West Riding Force and was described as "a commanding figure, a born leader, forthright, straight-dealing and blessed with a charming personality." Having risen through the ranks from Constable to Inspector he was the head of CID for the Huddersfield Division. Not, of course, for the Borough of Huddersfield, only the urban and rural districts surrounding it. The re-organisation of local government was still 20 years into the future and the Borough of Huddersfield had its own force, its own CID and its own Chief Constable. Before joining the Police in 1929 Fraser had served for 9 years with the Queen's Own Cameron Highlanders and his experience as a soldier was to prove invaluable when hostilities commenced just 10 years after his move south of the border to Huddersfield. There was a perceived need for civilian mobilization and Sandy Fraser was appointed A.R.P. Warden's Staff Officer and Instructor for the Upper Agbrigg Division where his commitment and innate good nature endeared him to the communities of the Holme and Colne Valleys.

After the war he served variously as Divisional Safety First Officer; at Wakefield Headquarters as officer in charge of police housing and at the Police Training Schools in both Harrogate and Castleford. It was in 1946 that he was promoted Inspector, returning to Huddersfield the following year as head of C.I.D.

By July 1951 he was looking forward to retirement and the enjoyment of generous pensions from both his military and police service. It was his intention to move back to Inverness and take over the running of his late father's public house. The prospect, however, of a retirement well-earned in no measure diminished, rather it fortified, his determination that before taking it the mounting number of break-ins at mills and offices on his patch, for which no arrests had been made, would be resolved. The cordon thrown around Whinney Close Farm was to Sandy Fraser the means by which he might take his retirement contemplating a job well done and the fulfillment of a long-held and frequently uttered vow: "I'll nail this man if it's the last thing I do".

Although never disclosed at the time the operation mounted on the 14 July was by no means the first attempt at nailing the local burglar. It was in fact a repeat performance of what had taken place the previous night and over two nights the previous weekend. On none of the earlier occasions had Alfred Moore come to the attention of the officers taking part in the operation. Nothing suspicious at or around the farm had occurred and on each night at 3-00 am the cordon was disbanded.

As the cordon party assembled for what was to be one final effort at obtaining a result, for resources simply did not permit of any further expenditure of police time and manpower, it was without undue expectation that it would yield a result.

As with many police exercises this one, as the minutes, and then hours, ticked by, was proving tedious. The hopes of those involved that the concentration of police personnel and resources on this one inhabitant of one small village within the force area would return a dividend were fast fading. No one had approached or been seen anywhere remotely near the farmhouse. Nothing was heard to breach the peace of Kirkheaton. Whether Alfred Moore was out and about burgling or inside the farmhouse asleep was not known. As the hour of 2-00 am approached it rather began to appear that it was the latter and that if ever he was to be brought to account and confronted in possession of the tools of his trade, and if the police were to get really lucky in possession of recently stolen loot as well, it was going to have to be on a night other than this one.

The disagreeable thought was already beginning to form in the mind of Detective Chief Inspector Jenkins that his men might be engaged in more productive duties and those brought to serve, and be paid for, extra hours specifically for this operation sent home. By very definition dilemmas are not easy and this was some dilemma. To call off the operation now might just involve its target being enabled to return to the farmhouse undisturbed and yet in possession of the proceeds of recently committed burglaries. To continue it without anything as yet to indicate that it was likely to prove productive risked the waste of more hours of precious police time.

The dilemma had yet to be resolved when the necessity to address it further dramatically ended. The calm of the hillside above the sleeping village of Kirkheaton was suddenly and without warning pierced by urgent sounds, first of shouting, followed immediately by muffled bangs, then of police whistles and after the lapse of no more than a few minutes the ringing of bells to mark the arrival on the scene of an ambulance and armed police reinforcements. It was the early hours of the 15 July and those officers running towards the sound of the initial disturbance noted the time. It was 1-55 am, just over two hours after the cordon of officers had been put in place.

This was no longer a covert operation. It was not only the peace of the night but the dark as well that was broken. As officers ran towards the positions taken up earlier by Inspector Fraser and Constable Jagger the beams of their torchlights criss-crossed the sky. In those few moments no-one knew what had gone wrong but equally no-one doubted that it was something calamitous; something extraordinary and horrible. In the confusion there were to be inconsistent recollections as to just what the sound was that gave the alert. For some it was the sound of the shots ringing out, five in total. Others, perhaps those nearer, heard the raised voice of Inspector Fraser. Yet others heard first the sound of a police whistle being feebly blown as if by an officer no longer able for some reason to apply to it a full, healthy lungful of breath.

One of the first officers to reach the scene of the catastrophe was Detective Sergeant Herbert Amos Butler. As he ran in the direction of the noise he paused only fleetingly to note that Inspector Fraser was no longer in the position to which he had been posted. The explanation became only too tragically apparent when, seconds later, the officer reached the point where Constable Jagger had taken up his position for the night's watch.

The first thing highlighted by the beam of Butler's torch was the body of Inspector Fraser lying on his back making neither sound nor movement. This was murder and the appearance of the body indicated without the need for more than the cursory flashing over it of a torchlight that the stricken officer was beyond any possibility of hope that might be provided by medical intervention.

Not so however for the other body lying no more than a foot or so away. Constable Jagger was conscious but in shock, lying on his side with his legs drawn up beneath him as if seeking comfort from the pain wracking his inner body by this foetal position. He was able to speak though weakly.

Counsel for the Crown at the trial which followed was to tell the jury, with an air of great piety, that he was not permitted to tell them what had been said by the stricken officer. It was of course hearsay and inadmissible and though the eventual case for the Crown was to be based on the hearsay statement, and little else, of Constable Jagger formally recorded later that day, the jury were not going to be permitted to learn what he had to say as he lay bleeding on the ground. Few law students ever experienced difficulty understanding the hearsay rule but many did the numerous exceptions to that rule and the fine distinctions which they involved. Today almost anything goes. The so-called re-balancing of the justice system, an only thinly disguised attempt to increase conviction rates, led in 2003 to the effective repeal of this particular safeguard of the innocent.

In this instance, however, the safeguard involved was somewhat more illusory than real. Though not told what the officer had said, the jury cannot have been under any misapprehension as to the gist of it for the focus of attention for the remainder of the night was to be Whinney Close Farm and its occupants.

7 – Perverting the Course of Justice

It is a serious crime, contrary to common law, to seek to defeat the ends of justice. It is punishable with up to life imprisonment and triable only at one of the higher courts. More often than not it attracts a sentence of just a few months' imprisonment and involves giving a false name to a police officer when stopped driving in order to avoid liability for some minor motoring indiscretion. But it is an offence that may be committed in many ways and one of its most serious manifestations is the destruction of material evidence. A pre-condition of liability, however, is that there is a course of justice running, the diversion of which has at least a tendency to result in justice going wrong.

By 2-00 am on Sunday 15 July, in the vicinity of Whinney Close Farm at Kirkheaton, there were two strongly coursing streams of justice. One marked 'burglary' which had been running its unproductive course for years. But now a new one was running, relegating the old to mere background history, and marked 'homicide' and, potentially even, double homicide.

Alfred Moore's intentions as hordes of police reinforcements flooded into Kirkheaton was unmistakable and never denied. It was to defeat at least one of those streams of justice.

"What do you think it is, Alfred?" were the words spoken urgently by Alice which, he was to say, roused him from the deep sleep into which he had fallen after his late evening walk and the later pleasurable exertions of the marital bed. As he surfaced to wakefulness the very next sound he heard told him something as to the reason for Alice's question. It was the sound of a whistle.

Today whistles as a means of urgent communication between officers have been relegated to the history of policing. In 1951 the sound of a whistle meant only one thing - urgent police activity; it was the sound signalling alarm and emergency, the means by which one police officer spoke to another to summon immediate assistance. It was, claimed the prosecution later, an unmistakable sound, not one to be confused with the whistles of the trains on the nearby branch line into Huddersfield.

Its urgency, however, does not seem to have penetrated, fully or immediately, Alfred's consciousness for his reaction was to grumble at his sleep being disturbed. As he sat up Alice was already out of bed and peering through the curtains where, after a few moments, she was joined by her husband. The only sight out of the ordinary was a flashing torch light. Their presence at the window did not go unnoticed by the numerous officers whose collective, rigid attention was now focused on the farmhouse.

Whatever was going on needed to be investigated. Alfred hastily threw on some clothing, attempted unsuccessfully to put on his wet shoes, left to dry by the fireplace, and, in his stockinged feet, left the house by the French windows to investigate whether anything was amiss. Though this was only July, high summer in fact, stocks of slaughtered poultry were already in cold storage in anticipation of demand for the Christmas table. The farm had previously suffered the depredations of poultry thieves and this, claimed Alfred, was uppermost in his mind as he went to investigate the strange occurrences outside.

Having satisfied himself that there were apparently no strangers about at the rear, Alfred returned to the house, put on a pair of wellington boots and went outside again to check the sheds. Moments later he returned to the bedroom to assure Alice that all appeared to be in order and settled back into bed, apparently untroubled by whatever it was that was resulting in the still intermittent flashing of lights in the fields below the farm.

Whilst the farmer was untroubled and seemingly incurious, not so the farmer's wife. Every few moments Alice was sitting up in bed and peering through the window at the events outside.

After an hour or so of Alfred's fitful attempts at sleep and with Alice ever more curious as to the cause of the continuing activity in the fields it seems, at long last, to have occurred to one or other, or both, that this was a police matter. How much Alice Moore knew of her husband's illicit night-time activities may have been debatable but she was certainly aware of what was to be found inside the farmhouse should the police outside, taking a watchful and continuing interest in the premises, decide to enter and search. Both were aware of what the consequences would be to their burgeoning prosperity - Alfred's remand into custody on numerous charges of professional, commercial burglary; another appearance at the local court but, this time, no prospect of the same happy outcome of a few years earlier; even a plea bargain resulting in the reduction of the charges to receiving stolen goods was not going to result in Alfred Moore being in any position to resume his poultry farming for years rather than months. Something had to be done.

And thus it was that as morning began to dawn husband and wife set about the task of attempting to pervert the course of justice. It does not appear to have occurred to either that however much time it might be possible to give to the task a total obliteration of the evidence of past criminality was never going to be possible and the best that might be achieved was going to be a reduction in the charges that might eventually be proved. First the skeleton keys, next the gold pocket watches, the cigarette cases, a platinum ring and some old cartridge cases, a relic of Alfred's short period of national service, were dispatched to the cavity of a yet to be fitted window sill.

This was still the age of post-war austerity and Alfred had it in mind that the cartridge cases might one day be capable of conversion into lipstick holders. The cases were 9 mm in size and it was cartridges of that same size that had been discharged only a couple of hours previously into the bodies of the two officers. Not however, it had to be conceded, from the cases secreted by the Moores in their ever more frantic efforts to hide the evidence of Alfred's burgling activities.

The numerous stamps and US dollar bills were capable of a rather more permanent form of obliteration. An old duster was doused with paraffin, placed in the fire grate, lit and the flame fuelled with the proceeds of crime. The resulting smoke billowing from the farmhouse chimney further excited the curiosity of the observers outside. The chimney smoked intermittently for 15 minutes as ever more combustible material was added. It was by now 5-00 am.

8 – Stand-Off

As dawn began to break Whinney Close Farm was surrounded by hordes of helmeted police officers, some of them armed, waiting to move in and make an arrest but uncertain as to how the next move in the game was to be effected. If the police were right, and they had no reason to think that they might be wrong, inside the farmhouse was an armed man, desperate, with nothing to lose and contemplating already the prospect of making a short, final morning walk to the execution shed at Leeds Prison; but also a woman and a number of young children. It was apparent that inside the farmhouse there was much frenetic activity, with lights turning on and off, figures peering out from the upstairs windows and the still intermittent bellowing of smoke from the chimney.

It was a situation with all the makings of a long siege and the very last thing that Detective Superintendent George Metcalfe, the CID chief who had arrived from force headquarters at Wakefield to take control of the operation, wanted was a shoot-out with his men at risk from the sniper fire of a desperate, armed gunman taking pot shots from the relative safety of the upper storey of the farmhouse. For the police simply to move in exposed the officers to a mortal risk that could not be justified.

At one point a very dangerous move indeed was contemplated. Not dangerous for the police because it was intended to shield them from whatever reaction might be the result of confronting the occupants of the farmhouse. Luke Stancliffe and his brother Frank, proprietors of a haulage business with premises adjoining the farm, were approached with a view to them making what was suggested might be 'a neighbourly call' on some pretext that might at least result in the door being opened. In the course of discussion as to what that pretext might be, and with no seeming reluctance on the part of the brothers to lend their assistance to the subterfuge, the idea was abandoned as its potential for yet another catastrophe was appreciated. The prospect of civilian casualties resulting from them being deliberately sent into the danger zone to do the work of the police and the inevitable headlines that would follow was something which, on considered reflection, was too appalling to contemplate.

With a cool gallantry, that later earned him the MBE, George Metcalfe decided to approach the farmhouse, his only back up just one officer, Police Constable Cleaver, discreetly armed with a revolver. Before making any move he surveyed the building first from Cockley Hill Lane and then from the fields by which, some hours earlier, Alfred Moore had returned home. His first sight of the fugitive farmer was of his blurred outline at an upstairs bedroom window, peering out over the shoulder of the more distinct form of his wife Alice, to be seen holding aside the outer edge of the bedroom curtain in a futile endeavour to see but not be seen.

Boldly the Superintendent shouted up to her:

"Come out, we are police officers."

With alert and watchful trepidation the two officers saw, first, a movement towards the opening device of the window; then the window itself being carefully eased open. It was the night-gowned figure of a woman, not the barrel of a gun, that confronted them from the now fully opened window.

"What do you want?"

"I want to speak to Mr. Moore" shouted back the Superintendent.

The response "I will come down" seemed to indicate that the officers were not to be met with armed resistance but this was certainly no time for reduced wariness.

Pausing only to put on a dressing gown and shoes Alice Moore came downstairs and opened the door to the Superintendent. To be seen, shielding himself behind her, reluctant apparently to place himself within immediate reach of the officers, the poultry farmer, dressed as if to start the daily toil of a working farm in grey flannel trousers, open-necked shirt and wellington boots. A few feet behind the Superintendent Police Constable Cleaver nervously gripped the butt of the revolver in his pocket, finger curled around the trigger, observing every slight movement of the pair, fearing the worst but yet hoping for a peaceful outcome to the still unfolding drama of the night.

With an apparently absurd question the Superintendent uttered the first thought that came into his mind:

"Are these your fowls?"

Absurd it might have been but it also proved highly effective in distracting Alfred Moore from possible thoughts that he may be about to be arrested and how he might resist that happening.

The answer was obvious and the farm's proprietor acknowledged his ownership of the farm's livestock.

"Come here."

The words of the Superintendent were curt certainly but authoritative in tone, betraying none of his inner wariness. Alfred Moore's experience of service life may have been brief and ignominious but he recognized an order when it was issued and in instinctive response took a couple of steps in the direction of the officers. This was to be his last exercise of free choice, his last ever movement as a free man.

As the Superintendent took hold of his arms, P.C. Cleaver, already deeming it safe to release the revolver from his grip, whipped out his handcuffs and within moments the farmer's hands were pinioned, not his last experience of such restraint. The danger was over. Any threat that Alfred Moore might have posed was now past and his removal from the scene, the gathering of evidence, the charging and, believed the officers, eventual conviction of the farmer a mere formality. The tragic events of the night had culminated in a triumph of effective, courageous policing.

The drama of the arrest was not, however, quite over. Even before Moore could be frisked for any weapon being carried by him, Alice, the faithful wife, made a rush at the Superintendent and with a mixture of fear and anger in her voice made both protest and demand:

"You're not taking him. Let him go. Is it serious?"

Neither officer responded. Somewhat unfortunately for him, as it turned out, Alfred did.

"It's serious enough."

The words seemed to belie some knowledge of the reason for his apprehension. It was an implied assertion of something, not a response to the request made by his wife for further particulars as to the reason why the officers were apparently about to effect an arrest, the formalities of which had yet to be pronounced.

Though in a state of mounting hysteria Alice Moore had still sufficient wit about her to give thought to the practicalities of the situation and her thoughts turned to the family solicitor.

"Shall I get Eaton Smith for you?"

It was a name that had served Alfred Moore well just a few years earlier and, in 1951, the name on the lips of the criminal fraternity of Huddersfield in times of trouble was that of John Davidson Eaton Smith. The name Eaton Smith still graces today the title of one of the town's law firms.

The caution was the next formality required to effect the lawful arrest of the prisoner. Its warning that there was no obligation on the prisoner to say anything but that if he chose to speak his words 'would be taken down in writing and may be given in evidence' was going to alert Moore to the wartime adage that has fallen into the lexicon of daily usage – "Careless talk costs lives!" The officers paused, sensing that this was not the moment to speak the caution. They waited for Alfred's response to his wife's question concerning the solicitor and were not disappointed in that response.

"Eaton Smith can't help me in this."

Seemingly the arrested man was not merely acknowledging his guilt but also that the evidence proving his guilt was likely to be of such overwhelming proportions that even the forensic talents and formidable reputation of the town's police court advocate would be of no avail to counter it.

The seeming hopelessness and despair of the husband escalated the panic in the wife. As she tugged at the arm of the Superintendent in an utterly futile gesture on behalf of her husband, he at last spoke the words of the caution, informing his prisoner that he was being arrested in connection with the shooting of two police officers at 2-00 am that morning at Cockley Hill Fields, Kirkheaton. The farmer repeated his earlier observation that it was serious, adding – "it's awful."

It was Alice Moore who answered the next question from the police.

"Where is the firearm?"

"Oh, my God! There is a gun upstairs."

The gun was located and seized but it was of no value to this enquiry. Whatever firearm had been used to shoot the two officers it was not this ordinary shotgun which was of a kind that might be expected to be found on any working farm.

The long search for the murder weapon was about to commence. It was a search that was never to enjoy a convincing conclusion.

9 – No Rest on this Sabbath

The day had already dawned as the Kirkheaton poultry farmer was being driven the couple of miles to the West Riding Police Station and Courthouse at Princess Street in the centre of town. Eventful might have been the night but the day was to be no less so. There was a farmhouse and its surrounding fields to be searched for the murder weapon; statements to be taken; a suspect to be interviewed. And at the town's Infirmary a desperate struggle went on throughout the day to save the life of Police Constable Jagger. And if, tragically, that did not prove possible one way or another his testimony had to be secured.

It was to the Infirmary that the bodies of both officers were conveyed. Pronouncing that of Inspector Fraser dead and extinct of life was the merest of formalities but one that needed to be followed later by an autopsy to confirm the cause of death, which was never in any doubt, but also to yield up the bullets which had terminated the life of the Inspector and inform the police search, already under way, as to the make, manufacture and calibre of the firearm being sought.

No less than four shots had been fired at the body of the Inspector, three of them had resulted in bullet wounds to the chest, right wrist and left elbow. A fourth shot, though like the other three fired at close, or even possibly contact, range, had for some reason misfired leaving only a ring of bruising to the abdomen. Two bullets were later recovered from the body of Inspector Fraser and they were found to be a match with both those found at the murder scene and those extracted from the body of Gordon Jagger in what was to be a vain endeavour to save the Constable's life.

With the recovery of the bullets the police knew with some precision what was being sought. It was a revolver. Already, however, the search for a firearm of some description was under way. It began so soon as Moore had been taken into custody and of the many tasks to be undertaken that day the recovery of the murder weapon was confidently expected to happen within the course of the morning. After all, reasoned the police, the identity of the murderer was in no doubt. He had fled immediately from the crime scene to the farmhouse. And from the time that he entered the farmhouse for what was to be the last time to the moment that he was led away from it in handcuffs the building was surrounded and the subject of close, intense surveillance. Therefore, the firearm was either secreted inside the farmhouse which, although appropriately described by the adjective 'rambling,' was easily capable of being searched by the limitless supply of police officers pouring onto the scene, or possibly it had been thrown away by Moore as he made his dash across the fields. Either way the area to be searched was both limited and closely defined.

From the moment that Moore was driven away the farm and its adjoining fields became a scene of great activity. The first finding of significance was actually in the living room downstairs and it explained the puffs of smoke seen emitting earlier from the farmhouse chimney. In the fire grate were the, still faintly red, embers of a recent fire. The remains of a number of partly burnt bundles of paper were rescued and that which continued to glow extinguished. Even to the naked eye it could be seen that it was postage stamps. Subsequent forensic examination served only to ascertain that their number was sixty and that, of course, was only the count of those not totally destroyed by the fire. Evidence of burglary, however, was not evidence of homicide and the finding in the fire grate did little more than confirm that which the police knew already. It was, nonetheless, a satisfying find and one that fortified confidence in the early recovery of the evidence that would convict and hang the poultry farmer.

Word about the dramatic events of the night spread rapidly and it was not merely police officers who flooded into Kirkheaton that Sunday morning but pressmen and scores of sightseers. Dawn had not long broken before police officers of the highest ranks within the West Riding force were on the scene. They included Assistant Chief Constable Mr. H. S. Lofthouse and Superintendents Yarr and Foster of the Huddersfield Division. Their presence was hardly necessary to bring to bear a high level of crime detection intelligence to this particular police investigation.

The only suspect was already in custody and his charging a mere matter of time and formality. That there could be any other suspect or even that Moore, on returning home, might have been in the presence of some accomplice was not within the contemplation of any police officer that Sunday morning. What needed to be done was plain – the firearm recovered and submitted for forensic examination to confirm it as the murder weapon and, as a possible added bonus, take from it anything connecting it to the farmhouse or the farmer.

As the morning wore on, progressive waves of officers from other divisions of the West Riding Force were bussed by coach into Kirkheaton and the search of fields and farmhouse continued and widened. But it continued, so far as the search for the murder weapon was concerned, without a result. In no way did this diminish the confidence of the senior officers in charge of operations that it was there to be recovered. The failure of the search was attributed to the fact that this was July and the fields were a good foot deep in mowing grass.

By mid-morning the searching officers had been joined by two police dogs, an Alsatian and a Labrador, and their keepers. Once more it was to no avail. Neither man nor dog had uncovered anything of even remotely evidential value. A more radical solution was clearly required.

A tractor and mower were brought in to cut down the grass and police officers were to be seen wielding scythes in those corners which the tractor was not able to reach. As this was going on other officers turned over the mown grass with rakes. And in the meantime the search of the farmhouse was ongoing and providing more than ample proof to confirm those suspicions which had led in the first place to the police operation which had ended in the tragedy of a few hours earlier. But, as for a murder weapon, nothing. The farmhouse was a thief's lair undoubtedly but nothing was found there to confirm it as a killer's refuge.

Confidence, however, remained high that its eventual recovery was not going to be other than delayed. By the afternoon the police had been joined by a sergeant and five of his men from No. 36 Regiment of the Royal Engineers, stationed at Catterick in the North Riding of the County, who were now sweeping the fields with the assistance of mine detectors. Their search continued throughout the rest of the afternoon and into the evening until the daylight faded.

It was not all routine criminal investigation for the officers on duty at Kirkheaton that Sunday. In the absence from the farm of Alfred Moore, in circumstances likely to be prolonged if not indeed permanent, there were pigs and poultry to be fed. The task was a novel one for the police but accepted as necessary and perhaps even welcomed as a diversion from thoughts of killing, slain comrades and the still to be recovered murder weapon.

When of necessity, because of failing light, the search for the gun was abandoned for the few hours of darkness that descended on Kirkheaton before the start of a new week, there was an acceptance that, just possibly, the search may be more prolonged than had been anticipated at the start of the day. There was no thought, however, that it would not yield up the weapon that had taken the life of one officer and left another in mortal peril.

Confidence that the murder weapon would, in the fullness of time, be recovered was as high as confidence that the murderer was safely lodged in the cells of the town's west riding police station. In fact, confidence in the murderer's identity was actually based to quite a large extent on confidence that the weapon would be recovered from where it had either been flung or secreted by Alfred Moore.

10 - Settled, Hopeless Expectation of Death

In a criminal trial any assertion of fact made other than by a witness, duly sworn, standing in the witness box answering questions, is simply not evidence. It is hearsay or as it is often pejoratively described – mere hearsay. Whether it is a rule founded on the supposed inability of juries to evaluate statements not made in their presence or upon faith in the power of cross-examination at Court to reveal the truth and uncover falsehood is now something lost in the mists of legal history. For this is a rule going back many centuries.

The rule, however, though simply stated and easily understood, is one mired in complexity because of the scope and breadth of the exceptions to it. It is a rule that exists to this day, though largely in name only as the exceptions to it have become ever wider and more complex. Simply stated the rule would mean that assertions made before a trial by a witness subsequently deceased could not be admitted as evidence. There was one vital witness with an uncertain hold on life whose testimony needed to be preserved before a higher court intervened for all time. So: could an exception be found to meet the circumstances of the case? Already on that Sunday morning and before any charge had been, or perhaps even could have been, laid against Moore, the minds of prosecutors were addressing this very question.

Even before the lawyers had got to work, however, the thoughts of Superintendent Sydney Foster of the Huddersfield West Riding Force, who had accompanied the ailing Constable Jagger in the ambulance which conveyed him from the fields at Kirkheaton to the town's Infirmary, had begun to grapple with the question: where was the evidence to identify the gunman, as to the identity of whom the Superintendent was not in any doubt, going to come from should the only surviving eye-witness lose the fight to save his life?

Some basic grasp of the law relating to the admissibility of evidence at a criminal trial was a necessary requirement for success in promotion examinations within the police force. The exception to the general rule prohibiting hearsay evidence that came readily to the mind of the Superintendent was that involving so-called dying declarations. It had been long-established that at a homicide trial any statement made by a deceased victim as to the cause of his death could be admitted as evidence provided that he was under "settled, hopeless expectation of death".

Nothing less than the absolute extinguishment of every hope of this world is required, for, as a Judge expounding the law over two centuries before made very clear, the situation has to be one "where every motive to falsehood is silenced, and the mind is induced by the most powerful considerations to speak the truth; a situation so solemn and so awful that it is considered by law as creating an obligation equal to that which is imposed by a positive oath administered in a Court of Justice."

The threshold marked "settled, hopeless expectation of death" is both high and stern and the witness who entertains but a faint, wholly unrealistic, illusory, hope of recovery does not cross it. The human psyche is understandably inclined to look optimistically at the prospect for survival and sensitivity to human frailty demands that hope for a future in this world, rather than passing on to whatever it may be that the next might hold, is fostered rather than snuffed out. The best evidence of a state of mind such as that demanded by the law is the statement of the witness himself that he is resigned to imminent death and that would generally require that he be told that his death was both imminent and inevitable.

So, at 3-50 am, shortly after their arrival at the Infirmary, the Superintendent nervously cleared his throat as he prepared to impart, by implication at least, his own doubts as the prospect of his officer surviving much beyond a few hours. There was no way of addressing the issue with tact and the question was asked outright and in unmistakable terms: "Do you know what is meant by a dying declaration?" Came the reply – "yes, sir". Shifting now the onus onto the constable to self-certify the Superintendent asked him if he thought he ought to make one.

Jagger was in no doubt that he should and, taking out a *pro forma* witness statement his superior officer began to write - ' I make this statement with the fear of death before me and with no hope of recovery.' The gloomy wording was read to Jagger who this time made no comment. Even as the taking of the statement continued preparations were underway in the nearby operating theatre to try to save the life as to which the wording of the statement had relinquished all hope of recovery.

As the statement continued the occasional question by way of clarification was asked either by the Superintendent or Inspector Knapton who had arrived in order to sign the statement when completed as a witness. But for the most part its staccato style suggests that it was dictated by Jagger. It was to be over half a century later that the statement next saw the light of day.

It reads:

> 'Saw a man going up a field. I went after him. As I got near him he must have heard me and dashed into the other hedge. I says "Hello." He must have heard me and shouted "I thought it was a cow. Who are you?" I flashed my torch on him. Inspector Fraser came up. The man had both hands in his mac coat pocket. I took hold of his left arm. Insp. Fraser shone his light on him and said "Are you Moore?" He said, "Yes." "Albert Moore?" He said, "Yes." Mr Fraser said, "We're police you're coming with us." Moore said, "No Sir. Oh no Sir." Mr Fraser said, "Yes." Moore pulled what appeared to be an automatic pistol out of his pocket and shot at me. I staggered and fell to the ground. He shot at Inspector Fraser, who staggered and he shot him a second time. While Mr Fraser was on the ground he shot at him again. I think I heard another shot. That's all I know. It would be about two o' clock. He was going towards his home.'

Thus far the statement was pretty well consistent with that to be given later that day by Jagger and no doubt had it rested there it would have been sought to be introduced as evidence of Moore's guilt. Questions, however, remained to be asked concerning the appearance of the gunman confidently asserted to be 'Albert' Moore. Asked for a description Jagger dictated:

'Was wearing what I call a wool gaberdine coat, like the Inspector's here (here indicated Knapton). Think it had a belt. Collar and tie. No hat.'

There was nothing remarkable, or likely to prove controversial, about the description thus far. But what followed was puzzling and just somehow fell short of what a poultry farmer intent on burglary might be expected to be wearing.

'I think he had a white silk scarf.'

Even though the assertion hinted at doubt in the mind of Jagger it was a doubt that Superintendent Foster readily appreciated might easily translate into a 'reasonable doubt' in the minds of a jury.

At 4-25 am the statement was signed by Jagger. The necessary preparations for the surgery to commence were not yet complete and for the next half hour the Superintendent remained with his officer who repeatedly asserted that 'he would fight for it', an assertion duly noted by his superior. In the circumstances it was a brave assertion but one that seriously compromised the statement, recorded moments earlier, being used as evidence. After all, a witness determined to fight with every fibre of his being to cling on to his life could hardly be said to be 'in settled, hopeless expectation of death'. The lawyers, who within hours would be pondering just how evidence to identify Moore as the killer might be put before a court, readily appreciated that some other device was needed.

The fight to save the life of Constable Gordon Jagger now commenced. The removal of the bullets that had entered his body was a matter of mere routine surgery and it was quickly ascertained that no vital organ had been lethally penetrated. Yet the prognosis was by no means optimistic for his survival much beyond the rest of that day.

Sixty years ago MRSA may not have been a peril of admission to a hospital but neither had that range of antibiotics been fully developed which could effectively counteract the onset of infection resulting from the entry into the human body of a foreign object.

However, following surgery the Constable regained consciousness and was described as being not merely conscious but alert and capable of providing testimony so long as the process was as minimally intrusive as possible. Once back on the Ward the wife of the patient was permitted to sit at his bedside and she did so dutifully, throughout the rest of that day and to the conclusion that was to result in the Kirkheaton farmer facing a second capital charge.

Following the booking-in of Moore at the police station he was lodged in a cell and left in isolation to think about his awful predicament. If ever there was a time for Alfred Moore to contemplate his own mortality this was surely it.

There was no obvious urgency on the part of the police either to lay charges or interrogate their suspect. They knew full well that no unequivocal confession of guilt would be forthcoming from the suspect, even though Moore had already demonstrated his capability to frame his denials of responsibility in terms redolent of suspicion that they were the denials of a guilty man. On a capital charge there was no credit for a guilty plea and for the murder of a policeman no prospect of any merciful dispensation from the strict course of the law. If Alfred Moore was guilty he was going to hang and contrition as evidenced by a prompt admission of responsibility and an early guilty plea would count for nothing, except of course that he would hang sooner rather than later. Life was precious and even a hopeless trial might prolong it months beyond the few weeks that would elapse between an early plea and the execution of the inevitable sentence.

None of the officers involved in the investigation thought for one moment that the task of identifying the killer was going to be furthered by a confession. Their hopes of putting guilt beyond further question lay in the search taking place a few miles away in the fields at Kirkheaton. Nonetheless some questions would need to be asked of the suspect at some point.

It was not until 8-15 am that the door was unlocked to admit Detective Chief Superintendent Metcalfe and Detective Chief Inspector Edington to the Spartan accommodation of a police station cell, devoid of furniture save for the wooden ledge raised a few feet above the ground which served as a bed. No table or chairs and only the most crude of sanitary arrangements.

At this time the questioning of suspects was not routine and when carried out superficial, unfocused and entirely devoid of anything by way of safeguards to promote accuracy. The making of contemporaneous notes and the tape recording of interviews, though the technology was there, was a development many years into the future.

Whereas earlier at the farmhouse the ground for arrest had been stated merely to be the 'shooting' of two officers, this time the extent of the calamity was, at least according to the later testimony of the two officers, spelled out. After a cursory reminder of the caution, Moore was told that of the officers keeping observation on his farmhouse that night, one was dead and the other in a critical condition. Though not obliged to respond and in the absence of any legal advice being either available or offered as to the implications of the choice between silence and speech – as would become obligatory a few decades later – Moore evidently considered the accusation was one calling for some sort of response. This time he managed to do so without too much further self-inflicted damage. He stated shortly, but in its essentials, what was to be his defence, a defence that he was to hold to consistently, unwaveringly, to the end and when even he could not have conceived that it was of any avail to him.

"I went to bed with Mrs. Moore and Pat about 12 o' clock, within a quarter of an hour each way."

The defence was to be the one tagged by lawyers, as they are apt to do, with the use of Latin – *alibi*, meaning simply 'not me, it couldn't have been because when it happened I was *somewhere else.*' To many non-lawyers and in everyday usage it does have an ever so slightly different meaning and one no doubt coloured by the regular occurrence in the Courts of patently false alibis, manufactured for the occasion by guilty men and women. And that usage is 'excuse', excuse from responsibility, rather than denial of it.

Even for the innocent, in the defence of alibi lies a trap and it is to embellish the truth with lies. Sometimes it involves calling false witnesses in support of a true alibi, human nature tending towards the pessimistic when facing some accusation of serious wrongdoing and without other support to rely upon. Sometimes it involves a reluctance to reveal an individual's true whereabouts for fear of admitting to some other, but altogether unrelated, wrongdoing or even minor indiscretion. Sometimes it is no more than an attempt, dishonest undoubtedly but hardly venal, to embroider the truth.

"I never got up again, lad" stressed Moore.

He did. He knew that he did and the police knew that he did and it was not merely to answer the door to the police.

"How do you account for the smoke issuing from the chimney at 4 o' clock in the morning?"

It was a question to set Moore's mind working on another topic, his answer just might tend to incriminate him in the felonious activity of burglary. It was a predicament calling out for legal advice but that was not to be available to him that day. He thought for a moment before deciding that prevarication was pointless for he knew full well that numerous officers had seen that about which he was being asked.

"If you must know, I got up to burn some rubbish."

It was a truthful answer. With his farmhouse surrounded by the police, such evidence of his burgling activities as was capable of incineration, was exactly that – rubbish for burning. But truthful as the answer might have been it did beg some fairly obvious further questions.

"What kind of rubbish?"

This time Moore wisely kept his own counsel:

"I am not saying any more about that."

Nor was he any more forthcoming when asked what firearms he possessed but his answer, as recorded by the officers, hinted at guilt and betrayed a mounting realisation of the enormity of the peril in which he now stood:

"Oh! My head is bad. Don't talk about it. It's awful."

The question was repeated but without gain:

"I want time to think. I'm in an awful spot" he told them.

At this point Moore, seated on the wooden cell bed, buried his face in his hands and remained silent. The officers waited pensively. The silent contemplation of the prisoner lasted for what seemed an eternity but in reality was three minutes. At last Moore spoke:

"I'm not saying anything now. I never did trust the police. I think I will have a solicitor."

It was said with an air of resignation bordering on dejection followed, after a brief pause, by the distressed exclamation:

"What is going to happen to my children? Oh! My head. I won't talk to you. I'm not forced to. I have my rights."

The officers retired from the cell, their first task to compile a note of the conversation. They knew from experience that although no confession had been forthcoming the words of the prisoner would leave but one impression with the male (largely), middle-class, middle-aged, property owners who, in 1951, were the backbone of the jury system, and that impression was that his denials were those of a guilty but desperate man; someone selfishly concerned only about his own predicament and without thought for the stricken officers or *their* families. In short, the reaction of not merely a selfish man but one, without doubt, guilty as charged.

For the rest of the morning and well into the afternoon Moore was left alone though observed at regular intervals through the spyglass in his cell door. The depth of Moore's despair had been evident in his words during that brief interview and there was an obvious cause for concern, not that he should cheat death but that he might escape that agony of mind and spirit involved in waiting for death, knowing the date and the precise time that his life would end.

Periodic reports were being received at the police station as to the progress, or lack of it, in the ongoing search of farm and fields a few miles away and, already, legal minds were being brought to bear to the problem of the predicted imminent demise of the prosecution's star, indeed effectively only, witness. The reports from the Infirmary were not optimistic and, whilst confidence in the retrieval of the murder weapon remained high, this was clearly not a case for leaving stones unturned. Amongst the many early visitors to the murder scene to observe the search were the County Prosecuting Solicitor, Mr. Linney, and the Acting Clerk to the town's West Riding Magistrates, Mr. Boardman.

Plainly, and so soon as Jagger had recovered from the effects of the surgery, an identification parade needed to be held. It was going to be no easy task to assemble the necessary number of foils, persons of similar age and appearance to Moore, to constitute that parade. It was Sunday and the streets of the town were largely deserted. Time was of the essence and bobbies, uniformed and plain clothed, armed no doubt with the mugshot of the suspect, dating back to his years as army deserter, were dispatched to search not the highways and byways of the town but the nearby Greenhead Park. Any male roughly fitting the appearance of Moore was approached and no doubt anyone who was approached and invited to volunteer would be eager to oblige. The role might have been minor but the drama was great and its potential for a lifetime of reminiscence as one of the key players in that drama was immeasurable.

Confidence in the ability of the failing constable to make the necessary identification was as high as that invested in the ongoing search for the murder weapon. But in this respect it was a confidence well-placed for, after all, whatever fleeting opportunity might have been available to the witness to observe, over a matter of seconds and in the dark on Cockley Hill Fields, the gunman, there could be no doubt that he had studied at leisure the mugshot available to all officers involved in the surveillance operation that night.

No particular urgency, however, was attached to the task of securing the benefit of legal representation for the suspect farmer and this notwithstanding the ingenious legal strategy that was being devised. It was one that would avoid the inconvenience created by the stubborn will of the surviving witness to cling to life. Securing Jagger's identification of Moore as the killer was not anticipated to be a problem. But once secured how might it be deployed? Evidence of those present at any future identification exercise as to what occurred would be inadmissible hearsay. The legal team already assembled from the county prosecutor's office were beginning to think laterally. There was another avenue available to circumvent the hearsay problem. Not the most obvious but, actually, the more it was thought through, far and away more effective than the declaration of a dying witness. Admissible in evidence, concluded the lawyers, would be the sworn deposition of a dead witness. In effect it was intended that once the identification, confidently expected, had been made, its admissibility as evidence would be secured by moving immediately to open, though not of course conclude, the proceedings to commit the prisoner for trial at the assizes.

11 – Bedside Justice

By the middle of that Sunday afternoon the efforts of the police in Greenhead Park had produced a sufficient complement of men to form the proposed identification parade. They were each taken to the Infirmary and dressed in gabardine raincoats, hastily collected together to ensure that both suspect and distracters were dressed as it was believed the killer was dressed hours earlier. It was intended that for the purposes of the parade Moore would wear the gabardine raincoat in which he had been arrested. Any possible later criticism that the parade was unfair because one member of it stood apart from the rest was to be avoided.

Not that any effective objection to either the holding of the parade or its fairness was ever going to be possible, that is at the time that it mattered. It was not until the foils were being assembled that Moore was first told of the intention to hold the parade.

It was at 3-30 pm that Chief Superintendent Metcalfe and Chief Inspector Eddington returned to Moore's cell. Having informed him of what was proposed, the formality of asking the prisoner whether he wished to be legally represented or to have a friend present at the parade was undertaken.

"I would like Mr. Webb from Eaton Smith's."

Seemingly Moore had appreciated that to track down and obtain the services on a Sunday of the town's great advocate, Eaton Smith himself, was too remote a prospect. He would settle then for his under study – if he could be found. Unfortunately for Moore Mr. Webb proved equally elusive on this fine summer Sunday afternoon. To anyone who knew Brian Webb it would not have been difficult to hazard a guess as to where he might be found – on one of the courts at the town's lawn tennis club.

In many respects Brian Webb was the epitome of a 1950's small town solicitor, always neatly, soberly dressed, in personality understated, in his personal life prim to the point of being strait-laced, with but one passion, lawn tennis, to infuse his life. He was no mere local star but an ace who regularly hit the back page headlines of the *Examiner* with his appearances for the County team.

Though it did not figure in the official version of events at the police station that Sunday Moore later asserted to his solicitor that he suggested to the Police that Mr Webb might be found either at a tennis court or, possibly, the Queen's Hotel in the centre of town.

It ought to have been considered nothing less than essential that Moore be extended the benefit of legal advice, given that the police intentions went well beyond the holding of the parade, the outcome of which they did not for one moment doubt. That no steps had been taken during the, almost, 12 hours that had now elapsed since he had been taken into custody to ensure that he had advice and representation was reprehensible applying even the most crude standard of what fairness demanded in 1951.

Just what efforts were made to secure Mr Webb's attendance at the police station are unknown because the head of the legal team eventually briefed on Moore's behalf was apparently disinclined to probe in any way the conduct of the police investigation. What is known is that it was at 3-50 pm, a bare twenty minutes later, that the officers returned to inform Moore that neither of the solicitors who had been named could be contacted. The efforts of the police can only have been at best superficial, at worst perfunctory. Moore was left in no doubt that the parade was to go ahead though in ignorance still of the turn of events planned on its completion.

"If Mr. Webb cannot come today I would like him tomorrow" he informed the police, evidently resigned not only to the parade taking place but also to its result prolonging, rather than terminating, his stay in the cells at the Princess Street Police Station.

By now confident that no resistance on the part of the suspect to the parade was likely and that even a further request by him for representation would prove as futile as had his earlier ones, he was again asked if he wished to have an alternative solicitor or friend present.

"No, lad. It's damned awful. I'll see Mr. Webb tomorrow."

He was asked to confirm that the gabardine raincoat, Harris Tweed jacket and grey flannel trousers, seized by the police, had been worn by him the previous evening. He readily accepted that that was the case and was asked to put them on. Moore later claimed that he did ask for the opportunity before leaving the police station to shave and brush his hair which was refused and that his unkempt, unshaven appearance rendered him conspicuous in the subsequent line out. If there was substance in the complaint, a solicitor present to ensure fair play would have registered protest at the time and been available as a witness to the unfairness at a later time. Moore was simply told that it was time for the short journey to be made across the town to the Infirmary.

The ground rules for an identification parade required that at this point Metcalfe and Eddington, as the two officers in overall charge of the investigation, should temporarily step aside. To be seen as an independent exercise another officer of senior rank, certainly not below that of Inspector, would take on the entire responsibility for arranging and conducting the parade.

The division between Borough and County Police Forces meant that rivalry between the two was an established fact of police life. In the main it was good-natured but where personalities in the upper echelons of the two bodies clashed it was a rivalry sometimes less than amicable and on occasions even tinged with rancour. When tragedy struck its effect was unifying and this identification parade, crucial to a charge being made against the only suspect ever likely to enter the frame, involved a rare exercise in cooperation. There must be no room for even the hint at some later stage that a parade involving an unrepresented suspect departed from either the letter or spirit of the rules.

In charge of the parade were no less than two senior officers, Sydney Foster, uniformed Superintendent in the County force who had earlier that day taken down Constable Jagger's 'dying declaration' and, to assist him, Detective Inspector Bradley from the Borough.

And for Moore's two minute journey across the town a convoy of police vehicles and outriders were deployed. Nothing less than high profile policing was considered appropriate for a prisoner likely to go down as one of the town's most infamous killers for generations. When the convoy drew up outside the infirmary Moore was hurried swiftly into the building. No attempt was made to conceal his appearance by the traditional use, on these occasions, of blanket over the head. There really was no need to do so. There was only one potential witness to the identity of the killer and in front of that witness the one and only suspect was imminently about to be paraded. Either he would make the identification or he would not, though the possibility of a failed identification was never given serious contemplation. There were no other witnesses whose evidence might be compromised by photographs of the suspect appearing in the newspapers or even on television - though there were few of those about in the Huddersfield of 1951.

Once inside the building Moore was taken to a room just off the main corridor. No time was wasted on pleasantries or introductions. The prisoner was told that a parade would take place, that he might raise objection to any of those selected to take part in it and that he would be at liberty to select his own position on the parade. Whilst this was taking place the eight gaberdined foils selected for the exercise were moved into the corridor outside the room.

As Moore was led out it was to the surreal sight of a group of male figures dressed virtually identically to himself. Whether the resemblance was real or superficial can never be known. No photographic record was kept of either the parade or the foils and the video camera, indispensable to the same exercise being conducted today where a suspect puts in issue the correctness of a visual identification made of him by a witness, was a development many years into the future.

After being asked to view the foils and register any objection and following the most cursory visual examination, made in the sure and certain knowledge that any protest would be futile, that this parade was going to happen and happen imminently, Moore nodded his assent to the officer:

"No. They're all right."

Had he made objection there were no spares held in reserve and it is inconceivable either that the objection would have been upheld or the parade postponed.

Possibly without thought at all, possibly thinking that the best tactic in the circumstances might be to mingle, Moore took up a position in the centre of the line of eight gaberdined figures, four to one side of him and four to the other. In single file at the word of command the nine gaberdined figures marched as if one body of well-drilled men down the hospital corridor and into and through the men's surgical ward. The failing constable was being tended to in a private room just off the main ward. The sight must have been bemusing to say the least to the ward's occupants though one for which they had doubtless been given advance warning.

It was in fact a sight to be repeated no more than moments later as the same nine figures filed out. For all the preparation, for all the build-up, the bedside identification procedure was swiftly completed.

The nine figures having been lined in an arc formation around the foot of the constable's bed he was asked:

"Please indicate the person seen by you at 2 o' clock this morning who shot you and Inspector Fraser?"

No caveat there then that the person responsible may or may not be a member of the line-up. He was there to be pointed out, the only question being just exactly at what position in the parade. As the eyes of the constable scanned the nine men the tension in the room was palpable. After hours of mounting disappointment as the search for the murder weapon stubbornly refused to yield a result the possibility of a failed identification was too awful to contemplate. The Constable slowly raised a feeble hand. His outstretched index finger hovered but to the relief of the officers observing the parade it came to rest pointing in the direction of Alfred Moore.

To make assurance doubly sure the witness was asked to count aloud from the far right end of the parade of men and stop at the figure he wished to identify. With feeble voice and shaking outstretched hand he did so and, once more, it was at Moore that the counting stopped and the outstretched finger came to rest. The exercise had taken an undoubted toll on the precarious and failing health of the patient but its objective had been successfully achieved and the fate of Alfred Moore almost certainly sealed. For the time being at least worries arising from the search for the gun, still ongoing back at the farmhouse, could be set to one side.

Constable Jagger was thanked, commended, assured that justice would be done and the procedure that was to follow explained. The explanation was given with tact and restraint undoubtedly but nothing could disguise the fact that what was intended arose from a prognosis that his prospects of surviving to give evidence personally at the Assize Court were not good.

With thanks for their services and some small monetary recompense for their contribution to the cause of public justice the parade's foils were dismissed. Moore was formally asked if he was satisfied with the conduct of the parade and indicated that he was - though far from satisfied with the correctness of its outcome. To his assent to the question he added by way of apparent afterthought and following moments of hesitation "but it wasn't me." Superintendent Foster, recognizing this to be a futile protest and of no avail to the interests of the suspect, duly noted it down.

The responsibilities of the officers charged with the conduct of the parade having been completed Moore was returned to the custody of Detective Chief Superintendent Metcalfe for the next stage of the unfolding drama. Up to this point Moore's status had been no more than that of suspect, detained for questioning, under arrest on the basis of suspicion (albeit reasonable suspicion), and with the expectation that unless charged his release from custody would need to happen sooner rather than later and, if it did not, the ancient remedy of a writ of *habeas corpus* issuing from the High Court was there to enforce it.

With Constable Jagger's identification of him as the killer all that had now changed. The circumstances giving rise to suspicion had crystallized into evidence of guilt on which a formal charge, the necessary preliminary to court proceedings, might be brought.

At 5-20 pm the prisoner was once more formally cautioned and charged with two offences. First, that "at 2-00 am on Sunday the 15th July in a field adjoining Whinney Close Farm, Kirkheaton, you did willfully murder one Duncan Alexander Fraser." After caution Moore responded with both denial "No" and the not unreasonable observation: "I have as much right to be believed as he has." Certainly Moore had as much entitlement to be heard, listened to and judged as any other witness. All witnesses begin their evidence equal in the eyes of the law. No status, be it that of police officer or accused, gives rise to particular advantage or disadvantage. Witnesses do not of course all finish equal. Some leave the witness stand with their credibility enhanced; others, their credibility undermined or even destroyed. Just how equal, however, the word of an admitted burglar against that of a dead hero was going to rank was quite another matter.

The next charge was that "at the same time and place, you did feloniously wound Arthur Gordon Jagger with intent thereby feloniously to murder Arthur Gordon Jagger". Few doubted that this was other than a strictly temporary charge that would soon be replaced with the full, completed offence. It was nothing less than Moore had expected since his arrest hours earlier and with wearied resignation he doggedly persisted in the refrain that had, by now, become all too familiar to the officers:

"How could it be me? I have told you, I was in bed."

As a postscript to what occurred at the bedside of the failing Constable, in 1991 one of the survivors of that line out, Herbert Woodhouse, told the town's newspaper: "Jagger was obviously a very sick man indeed. He looked like a man who had been hit by a car. When asked to point to his attacker he could not keep his hand steady and his finger kept wavering between myself and Moore."

12 – Makeshift Justice

Almost invariably Courts are convened in court buildings. It was not always so. At a time when the separation of functions between the investigation and the prosecution of crime was still just that little bit blurred, magistrates' courts were often to be found in the very same building as police stations. They were in fact widely known as 'police courts' lending to them the unfortunate impression of being under the control of the prosecutor rather than being a truly independent judicial forum.

Sometimes, regrettably, the impression mirrored reality as when magistrates listing cases for trial would enquire of the prosecuting police inspector whether a particular date was convenient for 'our witnesses'! In their defence it could be said that it was only just over a century earlier that Justices of the Peace had, with the development of a professional police force, lost their function as investigators of crime and old habits, as it is said, die hard.

The Magistrates' Court for the West Riding area surrounding the Borough of Huddersfield was in the same building as the police station. It was in fact directly above it and stairs from the cells in which Moore had been lodged led directly into the dock of the court. It was in many ways a convenient arrangement and certainly for those cases, far fewer then than now, where security was a real issue.

The Princess Street building stands today just as it was in 1951, only its use has changed. Following the merging of the jurisdictions of the county and borough magistrates' courts in 1974 the building was put to use for a number of years as the town's Crown Court. With the drive to economise and centralize the town lost this particular access to local justice in the early 1990's. Following a number of years during which the building stood empty it was re-opened as a social facility for elected members of the Kirklees Council. The bars on the small windows at ground floor level still exist to remind passers-by of its former use. Many when passing think of a particularly notorious occupant of one of the cells behind those windows.

If the sworn deposition route was to be followed, then the taking of the deposition could only be done in the presence of a Justice of the Peace with notice being given to the accused person of what was intended and of his right to be present and to cross-examine the witness. It meant, in effect, the opening of the proceedings to commit the defendant to be tried at a higher court, something which in the normal way would not happen for weeks, or even months, following the formal charging of the prisoner. If, however, this could be achieved the testimony of the witness was secure and could be admitted in evidence should the worst happen and, for whatever reason, the witness no longer be available at the trial for cross-examination.

Gordon Jagger was fading fast and patently in no fit state to be brought to Court and yet his evidence was crucial to any prosecution. Without it there was no case that would have withstood scrutiny or the inevitable defence submission that there was no case for the accused man to answer. But, actually, thinking about it the prosecution lawyers had concluded that there was no requirement in law for the witness to be brought to a building formally designated as a Court.

Often in former times Courts sat in a wide variety of public buildings, most often Town Halls, even, occasionally, public houses. All that was required was a building to which the public had, at least notional, access and a Magistrate, one would suffice, to preside over the proceedings.

And thus it came about that on that Sunday it was not only the murder weapon and foils for an identification parade that were being sought but also a magistrate to attend at the hospital bedside of the witness to preside over the commencement of the proceedings to commit the prisoner for trial and take the deposition of the witness.

The urgency of the situation was obvious and the strategic decisions as to how to proceed wholly justified and beyond sensible criticism. What might be said to be thoroughly reprehensible, however, was the total absence of any sense of urgency in securing for the prisoner the benefit of legal advice and representation. This was a suspect facing a capital charge and a trial at which the crucial evidence of guilt was likely to be Jagger's identification. What was about to take place was likely to be the only opportunity that he, or anybody else, would ever have to challenge that evidence and ask those many questions which, to the legal mind, cry out to be asked to test the true reliability of any witness making a visual identification of a suspect.

Standards of fairness do alter with time. That which to one generation might appear unremarkable to the next may seem to be grossly and obviously unfair. But there are also minimum standards applicable to any age and time. The complete absence of legal advice and representation for Moore on that Sunday, given what was intended to be done, appears, from the perspective of an age in which human rights jurisprudence dominates the conduct of criminal trials, to have fallen seriously below even minimal standards of fairness.

In mitigation time was pressing. There was so much to be done and no scheme in existence whereby the solicitors practicing criminal law in the town made themselves available on a rota basis for those being held at the police station whilst their suspected crimes were investigated. The 'duty solicitor scheme' was a very long way into the future. Nor were any of the perils involved in accepting at face value evidence of visual identification from an eye-witness, and the consequent need to test and probe that evidence so as to evaluate its true worth, even remotely appreciated. Quite the reverse actually. It was regarded as evidence of the best and most reliable kind.

Nor was there any outright denial of the right of the suspect to be represented. The police were quite clearly concerned to avoid any such impression. It was simply that no effort or exertion was deployed in making it happen.

The charge of murder confirmed that Moore would not be returning that night or for a very long time – if at all – to either the hearth of his farmhouse or the comfort of his family. He anticipated a speedy return to his cell at the Princess Street Police Station and no doubt a remand hearing the next morning in the courtroom upstairs. The police, however, had other plans. For the first time Moore was informed that the intention was to take, in his presence, the sworn evidence, called by lawyers the 'deposition', of Constable Jagger. It would be done in his presence and hearing and he would have the right to cross-examine such evidence as may be given.

Cross-examination is the tool whereby evidence is challenged and probed, weaknesses and inconsistencies exposed. It is the means by which the rule that in the credibility stakes all witnesses, prosecution or defence, expert or lay, police or civilian, start equal, results in some finishing less equal than others. In the hands of the skilled advocate, whilst rarely does it lead to the credibility of a witness being altogether destroyed, very often it undermines it sufficiently to guarantee a 'result' for the defendant. The objective of cross-examination is rarely to do more than establish reasonable doubt; if the witness does crumble altogether – which does happen but only very occasionally – it is an unlooked for, but nonetheless welcome, bonus.

Cross-examination, however, is a skill based on intuition and flare rather than preparation and hard graft. It is a gift and unlikely to be found in one whose skills lie in lock-picking and rearing and tending hens.

Yet, on this occasion, not even a token reference was made to legal representation for the prisoner. Though Doctor Wrigley, now in charge of the patient, had pronounced Constable Jagger to have a pulse of 'good volume' and a brain that was 'mentally alert', actually stating immediately before the identification procedure commenced that he was "still as bright as ever", he was in reality fading fast and the pronouncements of the doctor no more than an exercise in lending specious credit to the evidence about to be obtained, inevitably crucial to the case against the police's only suspect and never likely to be tested in a witness box.

A mere twenty minutes after the identification Moore was once more at the bedside of Constable Jagger. This time, in addition to the police and hospital staff, a senior local magistrate, Percy Crowther, the clerk to the local justices and Mr R. C. Linney, Chief Prosecutor for the West Riding Force, were present to record and witness the taking of the evidence without which the bare suspicion to which all the rest of the circumstances of the case gave rise would be insufficient to support the charge that had just been made. For some of the characters involved it was in effect a re-union, their last meeting having taken place four years earlier when Alfred Moore was triumphantly acquitted and discharged from court into the arms of the military police. There was to be no similar vindication of his innocence today. Evidently the problems which had resulted in Alfred Moore being unrepresented as he stood before 'the Court' had in no way hindered the search for the other personnel essential to the proceeding.

With Moore observing the patient intently and his every word being noted down verbatim by the Justices' Clerk, Constable Jagger gave evidence for the last time, in circumstances unique in the annals of criminal justice and to what was to turn out to be utterly *deadly* effect.

He began by taking the oath on the testament that had been brought to the bedside and without which what was to follow would count for nothing. He went on to describe, in answer to questions from Mr Linney, all that had occurred when he was wounded and Inspector Fraser killed:

> 'I first saw the accused at 2-00 am on 15 July. He was walking towards his home. As I got near to him, he must have heard my feet in the grass and he dashed under a hedge. I said 'Hello' and I shouted. He said 'I thought it was a cow.' I shone my torch in his face and took hold of his arm. I saw his face clearly in the light of the torch. As I took hold of the accused's left arm Mr Fraser approached and shone his torch in the accused's face. Mr Fraser said, 'Are you Moore, Albert Moore?' He replied 'Yes.' Mr Fraser said, 'We are police officers and you are coming with us.' He said 'No sir. Oh, no sir.' As soon as the accused said that he whipped his hand, his right hand, out of his overcoat pocket and shot me and Mr Fraser.'

It was an account effectively identical to that given earlier in the day save that, on this occasion, the witness was not asked for a description of the man who had identified himself as 'Albert' Moore. Now that a formal identification had been secured it simply wasn't necessary and, in any event, police and prosecutors preferred that if at all possible any further reference to the white silk scarf be avoided.

In deference to fairness and a recognition that natural justice demanded that Moore should enjoy the right to confront and challenge the evidence by cross-examination he was once more reminded of his right to do so.

To the trained and experienced advocate there were so many areas demanding to be probed. Not least of which was the killer being identified in those fields as *Albert*, a piece of evidence that was to create confusion at the trial almost to the very end in the mind of no lesser personage than the trial judge. Another blindingly obvious area: had the accused seen a photograph of Moore before the confrontation in Cockley Hill Fields and, if so, was this a circumstance leading to bias and pre-judgement in the identification of Moore as the killer? Had he been shown, indeed, a photograph of Moore earlier that day whilst a patient at the hospital? Some probing of the constable's condition at the time – had he fully recovered from the effects of the anaesthetic administered only hours earlier for the purposes of major surgery? All of these questions could well have served to assist the jury in evaluating this evidence for what it might be worth rather than accepting it at face value.

The reality of this identification was that it was based on a fleeting glimpse of a face highlighted in the unsteady beam of a torchlight. But none of this was it possible to underline. The best that the farmer cum burglar could manage was one question and the very one that no trained lawyer would have contemplated for the answer to it was both obvious and inevitably damning.

"Are you quite sure?" asked Moore.

Those present at the bedside, and there were none with any sympathies towards the accused man, viewed the inept question with entire satisfaction appreciating the answer that would be forthcoming. As it promptly was:

"I am quite sure."

There were to be no more questions. The deposition of the witness was complete. The magistrate who was present solemnly certified on its face that Moore was not merely present at its taking but 'had full opportunity of cross-examining the witness'.

The prisoner was quickly returned to the police station where one final effort was made by the police to extract from Moore, judged to be suitably unnerved by events at the Infirmary, an admission of responsibility for the shooting of the officers. The possibility was dangled before him that what had occurred in Cockley Hill Fields a few hours earlier might amount to manslaughter; perhaps Moore had been out shooting foxes and had accidentally shot the officers and manslaughter would not attract the ultimate sentence whereas, he was told, "if it's murder you will be tried and in three weeks they will hang you." The Police knew that any such explanation for what had occurred would be laughed out of court and, needless to say, it never featured in the official version of police – suspect exchanges at the police station.

Moore was deaf to the blandishments of the officers. He requested facilities to write a note of re-assurance to Alice. Pencil and paper were provided, possibly in the hope of something being written providing yet further evidence of guilt, but on terms that it should include a statement that he had no criticism to make of his treatment at the hands of the police. Though the note gives a clean bill of health to his custodians Pat Moore remembers to this day her first visit to see Dad at Armley Gaol following his remand there and being shown bruises stated to be the product of rough handling, if not indeed downright assault, whilst in police custody. Moore was later to tell his solicitor of an incident, shortly after his arrival at the police station, when he was taken from his cell, sat on a bench in the corridor and asked to remove his wellington boots. As he struggled to do so two officers jumped forward, each tugged at a boot with sufficient force to remove not only the boot but leaving the prisoner ignominiously sprawled on the stone floor of the cell corridor.

The note is a curious mixture of proposals for the forthcoming court hearing, plans for the care of his poultry in the meantime, optimism for the future together with expressions of love and affection for the family. It reads:

West Riding Police,
Huddersfield.
Sunday Teatime.

Dear Alice,

I am to have a hearing on Tuesday, but I do not know whether it will be at this court or not.

Please get Mr Webb for me as I wish to make known my case, and want to have someone in court to stand bail. Would you ask Miss M? You see Darling someone has made a rather bad mistake here. I hope you will keep your pecker up, and keep the children as happy as you can and dont forget I am thinking about you all the time. Do try to get Mr Webb here for Monday morning wont you. I know that I have done nothing so vile as this but I shall have to tell Webb what little there is to tell for I am afraid I shall burst into bits.

Please ask Charles to get nest boxes into the BUFF ROCK hut but these are now on point of lay, ask him to leave the other breed out of that hut into the small green one and also put it up with nest boxes that are by the Pullet crates.

Mix 4 parts Cerial (sic) to 1 part fish meal, but mix up different kinds of Cerial. Don't give the pigs too much fish meal 1 bucket of swill upwards a day.

Sorry to be so fussy about the stock Darling but try to keep paying till I get back won't you. You see when the pullets start laying we shall have quite a nice little income.

You know that I still love you Darling don't you and things are bound to straighten out pretty soon. I have been treated quite civilly Darling so don't worry its just that not seeing you that hurts. Love the children for me wont you Darling after all I shall soon be seeing you for keeps.

All my love and Thoughts Darling to you all.

DADDY XXXX
XXX

P.S. Please thank Chas. for helping with the stock.
ALF.

Following the strains of the identification and making his sworn deposition Constable Gordon Jagger was sedated by the doctors and slipped gradually into unconsciousness. Throughout the night his wife maintained a constant, tearful vigil at his bedside, holding onto his hand until his very last breath. It was at 8-15 on the Monday morning that he finally succumbed to his wounds. The case against Moore, securely lodged in a cell at the Princess Street Police Station, became one of double murder. With the evidence against him signed and sealed Moore's grip on life appeared only slightly more secure than that of Jagger when Moore had been led away in handcuffs from his bedside just hours before.

13 – Child Witness

It is now many years since young children were to be seen in the witness box of a court room. It was an unedifying spectacle, resulting too often in the child, overcome by the vastness of the court room, the enormity of the occasion and the sea of expectant faces simply being overcome, dissolving in tears and being unable to continue. Many were the cases lost and some unspeakable criminally abusive conduct unpunished when this happened.

It was often said that for the child the experience was one even more abusive than whatever might have gone before to bring about the appearance of the child in court. And even where the child was able to articulate an account of events calling for some sort of response the challenge which followed was brutal. No holds were barred, no concessions made to the vulnerability of the witness, no civilized restraint exercised. The child witness would be castigated as a liar and for many the one thing worse than being ill-used was the perception of not being believed about being ill-used.

It was a state of affairs that simply could not be allowed to continue if justice in these cases was to be done. It was the increasingly ready availability of the video camera which was the catalyst for change. By the late 1980's the technology had developed sufficiently for the testimony of the child, and many other vulnerable witness as well, to be recorded and played at the trial. It was an innovation which meant also that evidence was secured at a time when events were fresh within the recollection of the witness. No longer would giving evidence be a memory test.

And whilst the video recorded examination of the witness is conducted by police officers and will probe for any weakness or inconsistency, it is done gently, with sensitivity the watchword and there, or at least very nearby, whilst the interview is taking place, will be some relative or friend to lend emotional support to the child.

To ensure that the right to challenge the evidence is preserved the witness is still required to attend court but cross-examination is now conducted via a live television link to the so-called 'remote witness room'. And woe betide the advocate engaging in abrasive, confrontational cross-examination for a rebuke from the bench and an invitation to be more child-friendly swiftly follows.

Things were different in 1951. Even then, however, there were many in Huddersfield who considered that the treatment of the Moore's ten-year-old daughter, Patricia, was utterly shameful. When news of the events in Cockley Hill Fields became known there was generally very little sympathy in the town for Alfred Moore or his family. These were deferential times; two police officers had died as heroes in the line of duty and had fallen in the near vicinity of the farmhouse owned and occupied by the very man who now stood accused of the crime. Few were prepared to doubt his guilt. For those, and there were more than a few, who knew something about his murky past it seemed that justice, long overdue, was at last to catch up with the Kirkheaton poultry farmer.

Yet the use of a young child to give evidence against a father facing a capital charge shocked the conscience of decent, right thinking folk in the town. Nor did they know the full story of how it came about that ten-year-old Patricia Moore came to make an appearance in the witness box of the courthouse in Huddersfield.

As Alfred Moore was led in handcuffs from the farmhouse to the police car that was to convey him to the police station, he was followed by the perplexed, protesting, figure of his wife Alice still dressed in night attire. Stranded outside as Alfred was driven away she attempted to return to the house but was denied entry by the officer who had been left on guard at the door with instructions to allow no-one to enter and no-one to leave. It was an understandable instruction in the circumstances. After all there was every reason to believe that to be found somewhere in the farmhouse was the murder weapon. Equally it was an instruction that required to be followed with common sense and a discretion that this officer evidently believed he did not enjoy. The uniformed constable stood his ground, deaf to the protests of Alice Moore that even if her predicament did not provide a sufficiently weighty case for her to be allowed back inside there were four young children, unsupervised, and almost inevitably disturbed by the clamour of recent events.

When the very same children made an appearance at the bedroom window, peering out, curious and anxious, the intervention of Detective Chief Inspector Jenkins permitted Alice to go to them. It was, however, under strict police surveillance and with instructions to dress the children so that arrangements might be made to remove them immediately from the scene.

For the rest of that day Alice Moore was kept under both the watchful eye of the police and their verbal instruction as to just where and when she was to be allowed to move. She was never formally designated as a suspect in the police investigation but left in no doubt at all that her freedom of movement was now to be under strict police direction. No cause existed to suspect her of complicity in the earlier shooting or being what, in those days lawyers quaintly termed, an accessory after the fact. However, there was a weapon to be found and the only other person in the world, apart from Alfred Moore, who might have knowledge as to where it was to be found was Alice Moore.

The children were hastily dressed for the day whilst discussion took place as to a convenient place of safety to which they might be removed. By now Alice was of the same mind as the police, on this issue at least. She suggested the home of Uncle Charles, the last civilian to visit Whinney Close farm. A police car was dispatched to bring him to Kirkheaton, with instructions to the driver to brief him as to the night's events.

By the time of Charles' arrival at the farm Superintendent Metcalfe had returned from the police station to the now officially designated crime scene and, on being told of the identity of the new arrival and before Charles could enjoy any opportunity to speak to his sister-in-law, the Superintendent took him to one side and sought his assistance in persuading Alice to reveal the whereabouts of the gun used in the shooting.

It was not unreasonable to suppose that she might be privy to that information given that no doubt was entertained that after the shooting the killer had fled immediately to the sanctuary of the farmhouse. So the gun must necessarily be there or in the fields somewhere along the route. The possibility that in the hours between the shooting and his arrest Moore, if still in possession of the gun on entering the house, had enlisted the assistance of his wife in lodging it in some secret place seemed a sensible inference.

Charles was not then, or for some hours, informed of the enormity of what had occurred in Cockley Hill fields, merely that there had been a shooting, that a police officer had been seriously hurt, which was of course entirely accurate but only so far as it went, and that Charles' brother 'Albert' was suspected of being responsible. Evidently it was thought that more by way of assistance to the search was likely to be forthcoming if those from whom it was sought were, for the time being at least, kept ignorant that that which they were being asked to do would have the likely effect of putting a noose around the neck of one of the family.

Charles, who had no reason not to assist the police, promised to speak to Alice. Even without being given the full picture the enormity of what he was told was difficult to grasp. But what did register with him was that the police evidently believed that the name of their suspect was not in fact the name of his brother but someone called 'Albert'. It did not, however, register with sufficient force for him to correct, or even at that time, question it. He came to do so increasingly over the following months. So did many others over the years that followed.

The discussion between Charles and Alice was short. He related to her the police belief that she knew more about the night's events than she was prepared to say. She responded that this was nonsense. It was agreed that for the rest of the day Charles and his wife would take over the care of the children.

The police were now anxious to record Alice Moore's version of the time between the arrival home of her husband, whatever time that might have been, and his later arrest. A wife may not have been either compellable or even competent to testify against her husband but to have her account of events, confirmed by a signature and declaration of truth, before either the suspect, or anyone else on his behalf, had the opportunity to collude with her as to the evidence most likely to favour the interests of the accused, would provide a vital tool for cross-examination should she be called subsequently as a defence witness and deviate from the story she was telling at or near the time of the events in question.

As the little girls and their uncle were being driven in a police car to Almondbury Alice, still in night attire, was instructed by a female police officer that her attendance at the police station to provide a statement was required and that requirement allowed no possibility of non-compliance. Not a hint was allowed that she was free to comply or not; that she was in fact possessed of the inalienable right of all the Crown's subjects, if not under arrest on the basis of reasonable suspicion of an offence, to come and go as they pleased.

These were not times when the instructions of police officers were lightly disregarded and Alice complied, suggesting only that she be allowed back into the farmhouse to dress for the rest of the day. The request was brusquely refused, the only concession being that her coat and a pair of shoes were brought out to her.

At the police station she was told for the first time that one of the officers who had been shot was dead. She suggested that, in the light of this enormity, perhaps she should seek the advice of her solicitor before making any statement but she was told that this would not be necessary. Indeed it may not have been *necessary* but it might have been prudent. However, by now scant regard was being shown for her absolute and unqualified right to decline to make any statement or to walk out of the door of the police station at any time of her choosing.

The only evidence that exists today concerning the taking of this statement is the statement itself. Those present when it was taken are long gone. What is known is what occurred later that day when a statement was taken from Patricia and how senior officers were prepared to bully and browbeat a child into signing a statement against her father. It seems unlikely that the wife of the suspect fared any better. And the statement itself certainly placed beyond any question of doubt her viability as a witness for the defence.

The statement, shown as being taken between 10-00 and 11-30 am by Chief Inspector Edlington with Police Woman Stafford as witness, begins with generalities concerning the purchase of the farm and its livestock. The events of the previous day and her own shopping visit into town on the Saturday morning are detailed. When her husband left the house that evening with his brother she gave him a letter addressed to Post Office Savings to put in the post for her. "My husband said he had a headache and thought the walk would clear him a bit" the statement reads. He left the house about 11-00 pm.

"I went to bed about midnight. I was not concerned about my husband being out so late because it is a thing he often does" the statement continues. In one sentence the potential of Alice Moore to give evidence as defence witness was destroyed. Her husband was not at home at that time when it would be claimed that the cordon was in place and, as a bonus, there was more than ample scope for prejudicial cross-examination as to exactly what the wife thought the husband was up to when regularly away from home in the early hours. Unfortunately for the police Alice could not be moved beyond half past midnight as the time at which Alfred did make an appearance in the bedroom. A description of the disrupted night's sleep followed with a confession from Alice that when her husband removed from the wardrobe and took downstairs "some sheets of postage stamps and foreign paper money" she knew full well that it was the proceeds of burglary that were being destroyed. Nonetheless, she asserted, the police activity in the fields outside did not worry her as she considered it wholly unrelated to either the farmhouse or its occupants.

As to Alfred's activities generally she made no bones: "I know my husband is a criminal and that he was going out at nights and was getting money, which I thought he may have stolen. He never told me where he had been and I never asked him. I do not know whether Alfred had gone out to do a job last night, Saturday, but I don't think he had because he went with his brother just like I've told you."

She was asked about firearms and described an air pistol which fired darts, a toy pistol which fired blanks and a single-barrelled shotgun bought by her husband a month earlier at the 'Model Shop' in Queen Street, Huddersfield in order to kill a fox which had been attacking poultry.

What sort of character was he deep down? she was apparently asked. "My husband does not drink intoxicants but is a very hasty tempered man and gets nasty, but I don't want to say anything more about that side of him. I will say, however, that his parents were always quarrelling and fighting and when he was younger the home conditions were very bad."

The statement concludes bizarrely and one can only conclude that it was a case of a silly answer in response to a silly question: "I have never heard my husband say he would shoot a police officer who tackled him – or anyone else."

It was not until 1-45 pm that Alice Moore was driven back to Whinney Close Farm. She had been interrogated for some 5 ½ hours, her account reduced to the form of a written statement, her signature to it demanded and her request to read over the statement before doing so declined as both unnecessary and a slight upon the integrity of the police who had, they brusquely informed her, accurately, faithfully and in good conscience recorded that which she had told them.

It was with palpable relief that she walked out of the police station to the police car waiting to return her to Kirkheaton and with no thought that she would be returning there within the hour and not for the purpose of a visit to her husband who was, understandably, being denied access to other than the investigating officers.

Back at the farm and under the watchful eye of a female officer Alice was permitted to dress before being driven to the home of Charles and Mahala to be re-united with her girls.

But for one of the girls the police had other plans. Although in her statement no mention was made of any of the children, in the questioning that preceded that statement Alice told the police that Patricia had been an occupant of the matrimonial bed just before the arrival home of her father. Without compunction or compassion, without concession to the vulnerability of childhood, it was determined that she should be questioned and preferably without interference from any adult.

This time, however, events had not been coordinated with the precision intended and the alarming sight that met Alice as she stepped out of the police car in Fernside Crescent was that of Patricia seated in the rear of another police vehicle, a uniformed officer on either side of her, about to be driven away. Alice rushed over and, in barely sufficient time to prevent the removal of her daughter, angrily demanded to be told just what was going on.

To any objectively minded observer there could have been little doubt as to what was going on and what was intended. To put it shortly but without inaccuracy it was the shameful interrogation of a child, vulnerable by reason of age, with the aim of securing evidence on which to hang her father. That was what was going on.

No thought had been given to the provision of what today would be termed an 'appropriate adult' to act as supporter of the child, to ensure that she understood the questions being asked of her, that those questions did not overstep the mark and that her answers were accurately recorded with any ambiguity or apparent inconsistency resolved and not open to later interpretation in a way which might favour the interests of the prosecution or undermine the defence or, possibly, do both.

Even in 1951, however, the furious challenge of Alice Moore could not be denied. A grudging explanation was offered. As the police had reason to believe that Patricia was up and about when her father returned home she was a material witness and it was necessary to obtain a statement from her.

Having been given a reason, it was instinct, but one that did not err, that caused Patricia's mother to challenge whether the police were acting within their rights to remove her to a police station. Of course they were not. English law recognises no right to arrest a material witness, let alone abduct a child from the care and control of a responsible parent. And the police knew this.

With bad grace mother's right to accompany her child was conceded but with the curt instruction to Alice that she would have to "keep quiet."

Patricia remains haunted to this day by her memories of the hours spent by her at the Police Station. She recalls being questioned, initially without her mother in the room, by a large man, a detective she thinks. It began with her being thoroughly unnerved and caused to burst into a flood of tears on being told that her father had shot two policemen. No sensitivity or moderation of language here. No concession that this was mere allegation based only, at this time, on suspicion. No explanation that the allegation had already been denied by her father. That Patricia's father had shot two policemen was already an incontrovertible fact. This detective, she recalls, was interested in one thing only and that was the time of her father's arrival back at the farm and coinciding that event with the sounds of police activity in the fields outside. When she attempted to assert that she had no recollection of the one event following immediately upon the other she was called a liar and physically shaken. It is understandable that the emotions of the police, only hours after the shooting of their colleagues, were running high but high emotion serves only to explain the ordeal to which, without apparent compunction, this ten-year-old was subjected. It does not begin to excuse or justify it.

Eventually Alice was permitted to be present in the room but only once did she intervene to protest at this travesty of an evidence gathering exercise. Only once because she was told that just one more word from her and she would be required to leave. It was enough to cause her to remain silent. The very last thing that she wanted to happen was for her daughter to be left in that room alone and, for their part, it suited the purpose of the interrogators that she should remain as a counter to any later suggestion that the statement of a child taken in the absence of a responsible adult might represent something less than entirely cogent evidence.

The immediate objective of the interrogators was, however, achieved. By a blend of badgering, cajoling and leading questions to which assent was assumed by the briefest nod of the head, the following account, damning of her father, was recorded:

> My father did not come home for a long time and I got worried about it. Then after a long time I heard a police whistle being blown outside. It sounded a fair way off. When I heard the police whistle I was scared because I thought my dad was in trouble and I went and hugged my mother. I went and stood by the window and my mother sat on the edge of her bed looking out of the window. After a little while my mother said something like 'Daddy's coming now'. I saw some lights being flashed in the fields in front of our farm. I then heard a rattle downstairs as though someone had come in through the French window. My father came straight upstairs shining his torch. I don't think he got into bed. He went to his wardrobe and got out some paper. He took the paper downstairs and then came back and took some more. After taking the last lot of paper down he said to mummy 'I'm going to hide'. Just as he was going down I remember mother said 'Don't go Alf.' I think I went to sleep then because the next thing I remember is my mother and a policeman coming upstairs.

Patricia recalls today protesting that, whilst the sound of a whistle she undoubtedly heard, she believed that it came from a passing train. Her interrogators, however, were insistent that it was a police whistle that she heard and a police whistle is the sound recited in the child's statement.

The statement taken, Patricia was asked to sign. No, there was no reason, mother and daughter were told, for her (or her mother) to read it. Such a suggestion was nothing other than an implied slur on the integrity and professionalism of the police. What had been written down was a faithful recital of all that Patricia had said. The sooner the thing was signed the sooner they would be leaving the station. And so the statement was signed, once at its conclusion and a second time after a formal declaration had been added to it telling any later reader that not only was it accurate but the maker had read it and had expressed no wish to alter or add to it in any way.

It was four hours after their arrival at the Police Station that mother and daughter, both of them frightened and exhausted, were permitted to leave, four hours without refreshment for either, four hours during which question upon question, without respite or interruption, was put to the ten-year-old. The possibility that a child, by reason of age alone, never mind the obvious circumstances of coercion, might just be suggestible to the will of the questioner, did not for one moment trouble those firing the questions.

Would it be possible, enquired Alice as she was leaving the building, to see her husband? During the whole time that Patricia's statement was being taken Alfred had been no more than a few yards away in the cell area of the station. Presumably it was thought that to permit this to happen would in some way interfere with the justice process, and of course the search for the gun was ongoing at his time. The request was denied.

No doubt at this time, less than 24 hours after the shooting, the police were confident that it would never be necessary to put the statement of the child to use. The search for the murder weapon was ongoing in the fields and at the farmhouse a few miles away. Confidence that it would soon be yielded up remained undimmed.

14 – The Morning After the Weekend Before

For some caught up in this tragedy Monday was a time for pause and reflection. For yet others a time of intense, increasingly frenetic, activity. Amongst the latter may be counted those labouring in the fields sloping down from the farm towards the cemetery and village of Kirkheaton and taking apart, not perhaps brick by brick but certainly leaving no stone unturned, the farmhouse. Representatives of all divisions of the West Riding Force, as well as military reinforcements with mine sweepers and the local fire brigade, were now involved. The search for the murder weapon continued and widened throughout the day and continued, as on the day before, until night fell, watched by an ever changing band of curious onlookers.

Whilst the farmhouse provided mounting evidence of prolific burgling activity the search for the gun proved as unprofitable as it had the previous day. With the identification of Moore now secured the police were slightly more relaxed about the recovery of the weapon. That the available evidence would convict Moore was not something as to which any real doubts were now entertained; the absence of the gun was likely to serve only to cause a jury to pause for a few moments before returning a guilty verdict. The possibility that failure to recover the gun might lead a jury to conclude that there was a reasonable doubt as to guilt could be discounted. In this calculation the police were not to be disappointed.

Yet the search continued and when all the ground had been trawled where the weapon might feasibly be found, with generous margins being allowed at every extremity, it was gone over again – and again, and yet again. The boundaries of the search were progressively widened. The search went on in fact for the next fortnight but altogether failed to produce a result. It was with extreme reluctance, disappointment and a sense of failure that it was eventually abandoned, all concerned recognizing that it amounted to nothing less than a concession that the gun which *must* be there to be found and found within an area strictly defined and of limited extent was never going to be found. The prosecution of Alfred Moore, in culinary terms, was a rich and highly digestible cake but one which was going to lack icing.

Moore, throughout the search, told those now advising him that whoever the gunman was he must have fled the scene of the crime taking the gun with him. As the days went by the case for the defence which had, at first blush, seemed utterly hopeless began to show some promise and, as it did so, so did the pressure on Moore's legal team mount. For a criminal lawyer in 1951 there was only one thing more stressful than defending a capital charge and that was when the subject of the capital charge might just be innocent.

The death of Gordon Jagger in the early hours of Monday brought at noon that day the inevitable second charge of murder though the rule, at that time, whereby an indictment was not permitted to include more than one capital charge, meant that this was an allegation that would never see resolution by the verdict of a jury. There came to be in existence an indictment alleging that Moore had murdered Constable Gordon Jagger and it still exists somewhere marked, in time-honoured fashion, "not to be proceeded with without the leave of the Court of Assize or the Court of Criminal Appeal."

Inevitably the jury were going to be told that two police officers had been shot dead and of course guilt of one implied inexorably guilt in respect of the other. But the Jagger family would never receive such closure as might be represented by the formality of a verdict. The only resolution that was ever going to be achieved by a jury's verdict was in respect of the charge brought first in time involving the more senior officer who had succumbed immediately to the effects of the bullets which had entered his body in the fields below Whinney Close Farm. Even an acquittal on that charge would not permit the prosecution to proceed with the charge outstanding for an acquittal would imply reasonable doubt as to the identity of the killer and you couldn't bite twice on the same cherry. That would be double jeopardy and an abuse of the process of the court.

To this second charge of murder, Moore, still without the benefit of legal advice which would surely have been by now to say nothing further, responded: "I'm on the spot, I know I am." Not an admission of anything of course but neither was it a reply likely to further the defence of the prisoner.

The formality of the charge meant that no further questioning of the suspect was permitted. Good-humoured banter between gaoler and prisoner at a police station always assists in the passing of the hours of enforced inactivity for both. But Alfred Moore was already marked down as a 'cop killer', a career criminal who had, in cold blood, callously gunned down two brother officers of those now responsible for his comfort and well-being until such time as it was convenient to place him before a Court.

His meals were presented, rather than served, to him in his cell with silent resentment. It was a silence that spoke eloquently of contempt and was just occasionally broken by bitter and lurid predictions as to the likely outcome of all of this for the prisoner. Not that he needed any reminding; he knew only too well the course that events might take and the contemplation of it was terrifying. Monday was a long day for Alfred Moore.

There was no seeming hurry to take the prisoner to the courtroom upstairs and commence, or possibly more accurately re-commence, the court process which had begun the previous day at the hospital bedside and which would end at the Assize Court in Leeds. After all the prisoner was facing the most serious of all charges and had the right to legal representation which he should be given every opportunity to secure before he faced the local bench. It was a solicitude for his rights that was strangely at odds with the lack of urgency to secure those same rights for him the previous, rather more critical, day.

The death of Gordon Jagger at a stroke doubled the work load on that Monday for Home Office Consultant Pathologist, Dr. David Ernest Price. In the Path Lab at the town's Infirmary he painstakingly traced through the bodily cavities of each corpse the tracks of the bullets, in one case the direct and in the other the indirect, cause of death. His findings were meticulously recorded as the surgical exploration proceeded. The conclusion that the cause of the Inspector's death was shock and haemopneumothorax (to the layman a punctured lung) was entirely straightforward. Not really much less straightforward, but requiring more words to explain, was the cause of the Constable's death. It was finally recorded that he too had succumbed to shock but, in addition, toxaemia following peritonitis and retroperitoneal haematoma due to gunshot wound in the abdomen. In the absence of some sufficiently potent antibiotic to counteract infection the death of the Constable could simply, but without essential inaccuracy, be ascribed to lead poisoning.

Another for whom Monday was a day of activity was Alice Moore. Upon her fell the task of both obtaining the services of a local solicitor as well as the somewhat more difficult one of working out the means by which such representation would be funded. Preoccupation with the immediate practicalities at least served in some measure to distract her mind from thoughts of how this catastrophe might conclude.

It was still to the formidable Eaton Smith, who had proved so worryingly elusive the previous day, that the family looked but they were to be disappointed yet again. Both Eaton Smith and his partner, Webb, declined to accept instructions on the ground that they each had some acquaintance with the dead officers. Evidently the stressful task of representing a client facing the prospect of walking to his death on the gallows on the outcome of the case, even a client who would be paying privately and generously to be represented, did not appeal.

Eaton Smith told Alice that he believed the man to take on her husband's case was George Edward Hutchinson, a name not altogether unfamiliar to Alice or to any regular reader of the police court news column of the local paper where it was beginning to feature with increasing regularity as advocate for the defence. Hutchinson, known throughout his life as Ted, practiced as G. Hutchinson & Co. from offices at 15A Westgate, where he combined police court advocacy with the routine work of a provincial solicitor, conveyancing, drafting wills and leases, writing letters on behalf of clients at odds with their neighbours. He was an all-rounder, already carving out a name for himself as an effective performer in the local court. Throughout his long career he practiced alone, his wife, Kathleen, combining the roles of legal executive and managing clerk as well as parent and spouse.

Without qualifications but with a wealth of experience to bring to bear, Kathleen Hutchinson was an essential component in her husband's success. Her task it was to see the clients, take their statements, trace witnesses, all the footwork in fact to enable her husband to present to the courts before which he appeared cases that lacked nothing by way of meticulous preparation. The half mocking designation of such necessary paralegals as 'runners' is neither inaccurate nor inappropriate.

And for his part Ted Hutchinson's obvious competence, easy but matter of fact style, grasp of the real issue in the case (there is usually only one, the art being in identifying it) and refusal to play to the gallery, meant that he enjoyed the respect, more importantly the ear, of the local bench. Not many, in those days, who came before the local bench and challenged the police account of events received vindication. Some of Hutchinson's clients did and many who were found, or pleaded, guilty had cause to thank him for his plea in mitigation of sentence as they left court with their freedom rather than making the journey in the prison bus to accommodation provided by His Majesty at Leeds.

Such is the way in which reputations are forged. It is the customer who is the best judge of the product and amongst the criminal fraternity in Huddersfield the name and reputation of Hutchinson as 'a sound brief' was already well-known. It was known to Alfred Moore and it was known to his criminal associates.

When seen by Alice Moore later that morning and the circumstances explained to him, the essentials of which he was already aware, Ted was no more eager to take the case than had been Eaton Smith and might have deployed the same pretext for declining to act. He was alive to the fact that the cause was likely to be unpopular in the town and incur the bitter displeasure of all ranks of both police forces. As to the latter he was not disappointed in the years that followed. He was, however, moved by the pathetic figure of Alice Moore, by now weeping and desperate, and agreed to act. Having done so there was the delicate matter of finance to be arranged. Alfred Moore was an ostensibly rich farmer, owning his own farm, unencumbered by a mortgage, with his children taxied daily to and from their private school; this was plainly not a client eligible for state aid, or, as it was termed in those days, no doubt in order firmly and further to demean those who sought it, 'Poor Prisoner's Defence.' Unfortunately, however, every penny earned by Alfred Moore, licitly or illicitly, was spent in maintaining the trappings of ostensible wealth. There was no ready, liquid cash to tap and representation in the local court by a local solicitor, let alone representation by one of Her Majesty's Counsel and Junior Barrister at the Assizes, for that was surely where this case was going, would cost thousands of pounds, the equivalent today of tens of thousands.

The solution lay in the farm. Without Alfred, who on the best view of things was not going to be available to tend to his hens for many months, Whinney Close Farm simply could not continue as a viable business. Indeed, without Alfred the prospect of huts full of poultry, unfed and dying from malnutrition, their carcasses fit only to be ground into pet fodder, raised the spectre of a sale that would not even succeed in raising enough to cover a few weeks worth of legal representation.

Whinney Close Farm had to be sold and sold quickly, the second forced sale of the property within the space of a few months. The firm of Hutchinson & Co received instructions both to represent Alfred Moore and arrange the hasty sale of the farm, once, that is, it was no longer receiving the close attention that was being paid to it by the police whilst these arrangements were being made.

The regrettable practical necessities having been attended to, Ted Hutchinson, on the Monday afternoon, walked across the town to his first meeting with the client whose fate was to leave behind a lifetime of disquiet that, on this occasion, justice may have miscarried. There were few during Ted's lifetime who shared that unease but many came to do so in later years.

Now that the charge of double murder had been laid there was no obstacle to the lawyer conferring with his client. On his arrival at the combined police station and courthouse, a building which he frequented daily, and having been provided with carbon copies of the charge sheets he was taken straight through to the cells without further question but also without either disclosure or indication of the case that his client was going to be required in due time to answer. The charge sheets were merely formal documents telling him nothing of which he was not already aware.

The consultation that followed was short. After introductions and assurances from Ted that all that needed to be done would be done to ensure legal representation at the highest level for the remainder of the court process and that his only concern now was to achieve justice for his client, a brief explanation followed of the likely destination of Alfred after his appearance before the court the next morning.

It would be, he was told, a short hearing where the charges would be read, his identity confirmed and an indication given by the prosecution as to when they anticipated being in a position to offer evidence capable of sustaining a case requiring an answer from Moore at the Assize Court.

At this stage of the process the paramount consideration of the prisoner is bail and the reputation of police court advocates amongst the criminal fraternity to make "a good bail shout", in more conventional terms "a convincing argument for bail", a far more effective marketing tool than even an ability to secure an acquittal or a lenient outcome. Many an advocate who is seen to have put up a less than effective performance at this stage of the proceedings has found his services summarily terminated.

Ted Hutchinson knew this but he knew as well that, where a capital charge was concerned, whilst there was no law that said bail was forbidden, and indeed all the presumptions of the common law favour the liberty of the subject, in practice bail was just never granted. Hutchinson was not prepared, even at the risk of losing a high profile, privately paying, client, to irritate the local bench with a hopeless application.

So it was with some slight unease that he told Moore that bail was not a realistic prospect, would not be sought and that the proceedings the next day would conclude with him being remanded to the prison at Leeds. He need not have been over-concerned. Once the realities had been explained Alfred, despite the hopes being expressed in his letter to Alice the previous day, resigned himself to a custodial remand.

This was not a time for taking the client's detailed instructions. The two spoke only briefly about the circumstances that had led to the arrest and charge, the solicitor studiously not asking whether the client had actually done the deed, merely taking his instructions. A client who admits his guilt to his lawyer can only be represented by the lawyer on the basis of a guilty plea with the lawyer's function being limited to a plea in mitigation of sentence. Where the sentence is fixed by law it is a function worse than merely limited. Not that Alfred Moore did not protest his innocence. He did so vigorously. He did so at every subsequent consultation of which there were countless. He did so at his last meeting with Ted when the two said their good-byes.

Sparse though the instructions of the client might have been, the defence that was to be placed before the court was clear enough. It was 'not me – I wasn't there – I was elsewhere'. Although not a claim to have been far distant from the scene of the crime the defence was one of alibi.

All of this was straightforward enough and Ted had heard many a similar protestation from other clients in the past. His concern level was raised markedly, however, when Moore informed him of what had taken place the previous afternoon at the bedside of the now deceased Constable

Gordon Jagger. Already, even before his first meeting with a client facing the prospect of hanging by the neck until dead, the evidence of his guilt had been recorded and was now, literally as well as figuratively, beyond question. Moore's assurance that the ongoing search for the murder weapon would be to no avail, other than to vindicate his innocence, did little to re-assure Ted Hutchinson that the case he had taken on enjoyed any realistic prospects of other than a tragic outcome.

With further re-assuring words and a promise that the two would meet the next morning before Moore's appearance in the courtroom upstairs Ted left his new client to a further long night of dread and foreboding.

15 - Remand

At 10-30 on the Tuesday morning, a full half hour before the Court was due to sit, the throng of people assembled immediately outside the West Riding Police Station and Courthouse in Princess Street, eager for admittance to the public gallery of the court room, was already obstructing the highway. There was real concern that when the doors of the court opened public disorder might break out. Officers emerged from the police station to move the crowd across the road to the Town Hall. There they remained, waiting for the first sign that the Court building was open to the public and about to begin the business of the day.

The mood of that crowd was implacably hostile to the prisoner about to make his first public appearance, so much so that the defence legal team later considered whether to apply to alter the venue of the trial on the ground that their client would not receive a fair hearing from a West Riding jury. In the event no application was made, no doubt because the emotions of any jury would be no different from whatever Riding or County it was drawn.

When the signal came, minutes before 11 o' clock, that the doors of the court were open no more than ten members of the huge crowd outside were admitted. With press, police, advocates and defendants in other cases, it still made for a courtroom packed to the rafters.

Promptly at 11-00 a.m. onto the bench came four of the town's senior magistrates. One of them was already more than familiar with the case to be taken first that day. The Chairman of the Bench was Percy Crowther who had presided over the critical proceedings two days earlier as well as the case years previously resulting in Alfred's vindication and semi-triumphant walk to freedom. With him were Colonel J. P. Norton, the deputy chairman of the bench, Councillor W. Senior and Mr W. A. Woodhouse. From the cells downstairs Moore emerged for the first time onto the public stage. As he did so Alice Moore, accompanied by a female friend, walked into the rear of the courtroom and took her place in a seat reserved for her behind the dock.

To its readers, curious to know more about the man charged with the most heinous crime known to the town in generations, the *Examiner* reported that Moore was "a small man, no more than 5 feet 6 inches tall who entered the dock wearing a fawn pin-stripe suit and red-striped collarless shirt, his thinning hair brushed straight back; he was newly shaved." It was evidently thought the folk of the town would be no less interested in the wife of the accused man: "she wore a grey coat and floral dress."

The proceedings were brief, lasting no more than three minutes. Moore stood throughout, flanked by uniformed constables on either side and behind him. Jumping from the dock and fleeing the building was a not unknown pastime of seasoned criminals familiar with the layout of the building and the surrounding streets. The police were taking no chances.

The two charges of murder were read over by the Justices' Clerk. The prosecutor, Superintendent Foster, head of the uniformed section of the town's West Riding Division, informed the Court as to the age and home address of the prisoner and called Chief Superintendent Metcalfe to give formal evidence that at 5-45 am on the Sunday morning he had arrested the prisoner and later charged him with the offences that had been laid before the Court. The prosecutor applied for a one week remand into custody for the prosecution to continue to prepare its case and, no representations or objections being raised by Ted Hutchinson, Mr Crowther turned briefly to his wingers, flanked on either side of him. Heads nodded in assent. The due process of consultation amongst each member of the Court had been observed and the principle vindicated that, whatever may be represented by the advocates, this was a judicial decision. The mummery complete the Chairman tersely announced:

"Granted."

In truth the prosecution already had the evidence capable of constituting a case for Moore to answer at the Assize Court and the further time sought and granted merely enabled the ongoing search, a few miles away, to continue, to intensify, to become even more careful, more painstaking than hitherto. And it did.

The hearing concluded without one word being spoken by either Moore or his solicitor. Before turning to the other defendants whose somewhat more prosaic cases were listed before the Court that day - the shoplifters, speeders, fine defaulters and petty crooks - the Bench rose to permit the orderly dispersal of those present with no further interest in the business of the day. Over the dock rail Ted Hutchinson briefly spoke to his client with a word of re-assurance that he would visit him shortly at Leeds Prison to begin the task of taking his detailed instructions before the next hearing that had been fixed in seven days' time. Without objection from the officers guarding Moore in the dock they were joined by Alice. It was a brief consultation before Moore was led downstairs and the arrangements put in place for him to be conveyed to His Majesty's Prison at Armley, Leeds.

Over the preceding 48 hours Alice had seen her husband arrested, her young daughter interrogated by the police; she had alone been responsible for the arrangements for her husband's legal representation and the sale of the only asset that would fund that representation. There was now no more that she could do except wait upon the outcome of events. It was a time to pause and reflect upon what that possible outcome might be. She left the court building, handkerchief to her face, blinded by tears. There were many more tears yet to be shed. Over the following months Alice Moore was to view the world through a window of tears.

Outside the crowd of onlookers continued to swell, now waiting with eager anticipation for a glimpse of Moore as he began the journey from Huddersfield to Leeds. They were to be disappointed for the most that even those few in the front line witnessed later that day was nothing more than a brief glimpse of a figure, almost entirely obscured by the two officers sat at either side, crouched in the back seat of a police car as it sped out through the gates of the police station.

Just a couple of hundred yards away, in one of the court rooms at the Borough Court, there were other proceedings relating to the deaths of the two officers. This time before the town's Coroner, Mr S.D. Lister, to inquire into the cause of death. Again the proceedings were brief and formal. For Superintendent Foster it was another public appearance, this time assuming the role of witness rather than advocate. On oath he informed the Coroner as to the identity of the two bodies now within the jurisdiction of the Court and of his qualification to make that identification, namely that he had last seen both men alive at 11-30 on the

Saturday night, no doubt at the briefing before the ill-fated surveillance operation was mounted at the farm. The only other witness was Dr Price who briefly stated his finding as to the immediate cause of death.

An application had been made to the Court by the widow of the murdered Inspector for his body to be removed out of the jurisdiction for burial in his native Scotland. Whatever controversial questions might remain to be answered arising from the deaths of the officers they did not require further *post mortem* examination of the bodies and permission was granted.

The Coroner announced that the Inquest would now stand adjourned and that he would consider at a later date whether it should be resumed. Though not stated in terms the anticipation was that the verdict in the criminal proceedings would answer all outstanding questions surrounding the deaths of the two officers. The Inquest never was resumed.

That evening the editor of the *Examiner,* in a leading article under the headline *The Kirkheaton Tragedy,* paid tribute to the fallen officers and suggested that whilst 'a bobby's job' might have fallen into common speech as a synonym for some easy going occupation it was one that the events of the previous weekend should have laid firmly to rest. If that ever was, as the editor evidently thought, a perception of the work of a constable of the law, it is one that has indeed been laid firmly and fairly to rest for no-one would recognise it today. The editorial pointed out that in ordinary circumstances police officers do not go about their duties armed and are, therefore, "at a serious disadvantage when coping with malefactors who may be armed themselves." Fraser and Jagger had "given up their lives for their country just as truly as if they had died on the battlefield". For many of the readers of that leading article those words would have evoked vivid memories of their own time on battlefields not so many years before and the appeal for public generosity, to supplement the inadequacy of payments to the families under the Police Pensions Act, was one that found a receptive readership.

Adjoining the leading article the anonymous writer of the column devoted each evening to topical musings under the headline "In and About" engaged in extravagant, hyperbolic wordplay to support the claim for public benevolence. This wordsmith had discerned "a shadow over the town more intense than anything that could be caused by the clouds that spread from our native hills." Not merely were the folk of Huddersfield appalled by the events in Kirkheaton, the whole town was "oppressed by the thought of the dreadful crime which cut short two lives in the prime of their manhood and left behind mourning families and colleagues." Not only was the town appalled and oppressed but this was an offence which was an affront to civic pride, a pride built up over the centuries "by its socially minded citizens, its patient craftsmen, its lovers of music and culture, its law abiding people."

The anger and indignation of the columnist, by now at an emotional peak, turned to the perpetrator, expressing nothing less than incredulity that "the town or its environs could harbour anyone capable of so dastardly a crime, sickening to the imagination and a slur upon its escutcheon and repute for worthiness and stalwart reasonableness." The offence was "rank"; a reminder of a "grim underworld of predatory ruffians who talk with gun in hand." The only appropriate response to the Kirkheaton tragedy, concluded this extravagant and elegantly worded exercise in journalistic hyperbole, was zero tolerance, a need to obey the law even in its most trifling aspects.

Doubtless the mood and temper of the town had been expressed and the unarticulated, unexpressed emotions of many readers moulded and formed into words. For those who turned from the front page story of the court appearance of the poultry farmer, on whose land the dastardly crime had been committed, to the fulminations of the columnist, there would be many, and many potential jurors for the West Riding Assize for this West Riding town, for whom the distinction between a person accused and the predatory ruffian depicted by the columnist was ever so slightly blurred.

On the early afternoon of the following day police officers of all ranks, magistrates and representatives of a wide range of public organisations in the town filed into Kirkheaton Parish Church, just a mile away from the scene of the shooting, for the funeral of the murdered Inspector. The local West Riding bench of Magistrates, before whom of course the decision as to whether Moore should stand his trial at the Assizes was still pending, was represented by its Deputy Chairman, Colonel Norton. The Home Secretary of the day, Mr Chuter Ede, who might yet be called upon to decide whether Moore should live or die, was represented by an undoubtedly important local personage, though contemporary records do not record for what he was important, Lieutenant Colonel Sir Frank Brook.

Full police honours were accorded. The hearse carrying the flag draped coffin of Duncan Fraser to the church was headed by a phalanx of uniformed officers, wearing ceremonial white gloves, marching in slow step with heads bowed. The crowds lining the streets were silent, respectful, many visibly moved. Behind the hearse was an additional black funeral vehicle brought into service to carry the huge number of floral tributes that had been received by the Fraser family from near and afar. At the church gate the coffin was slid from the hearse onto the shoulders of six uniformed Inspectors, officers of equivalent rank to the murdered man. It was met by the Rector of Kirkheaton, Dr. G.G. Dawson, two Churchwardens and representatives of the Parochial Church Council.

Inside the Church tribute was paid to a life laid down in the service of the community. The prayers were for justice rather than vengeance though few present had doubts as how they believed that justice could, and should, be achieved. The Rector, leading the eulogies, described Duncan Fraser as a man devoted to his work who bravely and courageously undertook the hazards of whatever task was placed before him.

The Rector was evidently a man of God, but a practical one, and he used the opportunity of his address to echo the call made the previous evening by the *Examiner* for a fund to be established to which the public might subscribe "so that the children of these two devoted men who lost their lives should have the chance in life which their fathers, had they lived, would have given them".

He concluded:

"We know that Duncan Fraser died as he lived – bravely. I don't think anybody could have a better testimonial than that."

The following day largely the same cast of senior police officers and local worthies crowded into the Parish Church at Penistone to pay tribute to Arthur Gordon Jagger. Only Superintendent Foster was absent, travelling to Inverness for the interment of the murdered Inspector. Though living at Longroyde Crescent, Hill Top, Slaithwaite at the time of his death, Gordon Jagger was a native of Penistone; his parents still lived there. Only the family, dignitaries and police representatives were allowed into the Church but even with this limitation of numbers something like 500 persons were in attendance.

Outside it seemed as if the whole village and more had gathered to pay its respects. Hundreds were present outside the church and lining the adjoining streets. Traffic in the roads surrounding the church was halted.

Half a mile from the church the cortege was met by a police escort, including the six officers specially chosen by the Jagger family to bear the coffin into the church. Walking solemnly in slow step, with the bell of the church tolling in the background, the posse of officers preceded the hearse carrying a coffin hardly visible behind dozens of floral tributes.

At the church gate the coffin was met by the local curate, the Reverend N.C. Francis, and carried forward on the shoulders of the selected officers; the silence accompanying the procession was palpable, broken only, as it approached the door of the church, by the voice of the Minister intoning those passages of scripture marking the opening of the funeral rite.

Inside the service was decidedly low key though reverent. No words of tribute were spoken on this occasion and just one hymn was sung, the same hymn that had been sung the day before at Kirkheaton – 'Abide With Me' – still today a funeral favourite, the image of fast falling eventide somehow both reflecting and making its own contribution to the sombre tone of the proceedings.

Following the service the mortal remains of Arthur Gordon Jagger were finally laid to rest, in the presence only of family and those chosen to bear the coffin, in the grave freshly dug at the nearby Netherfield Cemetery. Following the committal to the earth and the lapse of a decent interval after the departure of the funeral party, many of those who had viewed the events of the afternoon, but without any real participation in them, entered the cemetery to stand silently at the grave already filled with the soil dug out days earlier to create it. They were able to view the many wreaths and sprays left on display; among them a simple bunch of roses inscribed 'From the Guides Going to Austria'. Pauline Jagger, the eldest of the two daughters of the murdered officer, was a member of the local Guides and had been due to leave with them the previous day for their annual summer holiday. The holiday party delayed in London where Pauline was able to join them the next day. Her first holiday abroad was one she would never forget; it was memorable, truly so, but for all the wrong reasons.

Today the Chapel adjoining the Netherfield Cemetery is closed and the building converted to housing. The cemetery remains but is neglected, overgrown, all but inaccessible without the use of a scythe. The grave of Arthur Gordon Jagger is marked with a stone bearing the inscription: "Someday. Sometime. We'll Understand." Following her death on the 21 August 1993, at the age of 80, Mary Ellen Jagger was laid to rest beside her husband.

The sombre proceedings in the two churches was not reflected in any pause in the activities of police and army in the fields leading to Whinney Close Farm. The search continued. Its failure to find the gun was by now a cause for concern to those responsible for the conduct of the prosecution of Moore. The response from Police Headquarters to a request from an *Examiner* reporter as to progress was terse: "No further developments."

Following the service at Kirkheaton the body of Duncan Fraser was conveyed to Inverness for private interment in the family vault at Tomnahurich Cemetery. It took place two days later on the Friday. At the graveside pipers of the Queen's Own Cameron Highlanders, Duncan Fraser's former regiment, played a lament as he was lowered to his final resting place in his native earth.

The need for the call by the *Examiner* for public generosity to supplement the meagre provision that the State would provide for the families of the two officers, whose lives had been lost in the service of the State, became only too obvious when it was revealed, a day or so after the funerals, just what that provision would be. The widows would receive a mere one-third of the pension to which their husbands would have been entitled with an additional one-fifteenth for each dependant child. For the Inspector's widow it came to £2-0s-3d per week and for the constable's £1-5s-0d. For the Inspector's daughter 6s-6d (32 ½ pence in new money) and 7s-6d (42 ½ pence) for the constable's two daughters. The value of money might have changed dramatically over the past sixty years but there was no mistaking that what the State was prepared to pay was no more than was barely sufficient to keep two families on the breadline. It amounted in the money of today to about £60 per week for the Frasers, £40 for the Jaggers. These were the years of post-war austerity and the State could do no more.

It was the Lord Lieutenant, the King's representative in the county, who took the first steps towards the practical realisation of the proposal to supplement State parsimony with public benevolence. The Earl of Scarborough, from his home at Sandbeck Park, Rotherham, announced the setting up of the 'Fraser-Jagger Fund' to be administered by trustees "to ensure that the widows and children may in no way suffer from this sudden calamity and enjoy some of the many advantages which the breadwinners would have provided if they had lived." Every donation, however small, should be addressed to the Earl and would be personally acknowledged.

Over the following weeks and months the 'Fraser-Jagger Fund' grew and by no means imperceptibly. The musical traditions of the town are well-known and its Choral Society, Male Voice Choirs, Ladies Choirs, Philharmonic Societies, as well as countless vocal and instrumental soloists, past and present winners of the local, but nationally renowned, 'Mrs Sunderland Competition' contributed their time and talents. At churches and chapels concerts were held. Special fixtures were organised by cricket, football and bowling teams. In pubs and clubs each evening the bucket marked 'Fraser-Jagger Fund' was passed round. The local authorities for the outlying areas of Huddersfield – Colne Valley, Kirkburton, Meltham and Holmfirth – each opened reception centres at which subscriptions might be made and recorded.

Within yards of the home of Charles Henry and Mahala Moore, where Alice Moore and her girls had been afforded temporary refuge, an event was held which raised a modest, but as it was described at the time 'glorious', £12-5s-0d. It was a contribution that received the enthusiastic commendation of the whole town. Healthy children in the fifties were invariably described as 'rosy-cheeked' and thirteen year old Mollie Jowitt of Fernside Avenue was no exception. Whilst at Almondbury County School, attended by Mollie before moving up to Greenhead High, she had been a classmate of Barbara Jagger, daughter of the murdered constable, and she was desperate to do her bit to swell the fund. You seldom hear of Jumble Sales today but in 1951 it was an easy means of raising funds and the means by which poor, but large, families were clothed at minimal expense and, for the unscrupulous prepared to use the cover of the initial rush when the doors opened to sweep the contents of a stall into an open bag, no expense at all. It was a jumble sale that the enterprising Mollie decided to organise.

Only moments following the idea occurring the planning began. The children of the Fernside Estate were recruited to the cause. It was the school six week summer holiday and all the time in the world was theirs. They set about with a will the task of collecting gifts of jumble from the folk of Almondbury and, suitably impressed by their enterprise and charitable instincts, nowhere was a generous response lacking. Those without jumble to give donated cakes and tinned food for auction. Despite an unseasonal belt of rain sweeping across the Pennines and ruining the holidays of many that August the spirit of the Fernside children was never dampened. Let it rain, let it pour, the good work must go on. Despite the weather the children sallied forth daily in a mood that was, paradoxically, festive, joyous, even jubilant, the tragedy that had given rise to the need for the 'Fraser-Jagger Fund' quite forgotten.

The sale was held at an old gun emplacement on the Fernside military camp, a relic of the war years. By 6-30 on the evening of the sale a queue of loyal neighbours waited expectantly for the gates to open whilst inside the Fernside children danced about in delight at their success and basked in the congratulatory pats on the head of the adults. When the gates opened an enthusiastic crowd surged forward. Garments, old books and money swiftly changed hands. All too soon, for the children, the patrons had departed, the trestle tables, minutes before loaded with their efforts, now bare. It was an anti-climax but, as the *Examiner* observed the next evening, "in spirit and in heart this kiddies' jumble sale will occupy a treasured place in the memory of the dependants for whose benefit it was staged."

Somehow the Moore family did not feel able to share the carnival atmosphere of the Fernside jumble sale.

The public's generosity was county wide. On the 30 September, at nearby Halifax, a star-studded concert, organised by the town's borough and county police forces, was held at the Odeon Cinema. It was a sell-out event with 2058 tickets purchased within hours of going on sale, and over £1,000 raised for the fund. A galaxy of top comedians and music hall stars appeared on the stage – Harry Secombe, Al Read (catchphrase 'Right Monkey') and Ken Platt; Norman Evans, performing his celebrated sketch 'Over the Garden Wall'; as well as stars of the music halls soccer ace Stanley Matthews and Blackpool Tower Circus clowns Charlie Cairoli and Paul made an appearance on stage. All gave of their services free; the Performing Rights Society waived its charges and local cafe proprietor, Harry Aldam, donated the interval refreshments. The management of the Odeon entered but half-heartedly into the spirit of the occasion waiving only half of its rental fee. Amongst the audience were the Mayor of the town Alderman Arthur Pickles, brother of local celebrity Wilfred Pickles, and the town's Member of Parliament, Dryden Brook.

Within the first couple of weeks following Lord Scarborough's appeal a staggering (for the time) £4,500 (current day value not far short of £100,000) had been raised. Nightly in the *Examiner* the names and amounts contributed both by individuals and local businesses and organisations was recorded. It became a badge of honour to be listed as having contributed to this most worthy of causes – and if you were prominent in the town a mark of shame not to have done so. From his not over-generous allowance the town's Mayor donated ten guineas. A football match was arranged between a team of West Riding Police Officers and members of the Wakefield and Sandal Rugby Union Team. It was held on the 5 September at the latter's ground in Wakefield. History does not record the result of the game, merely that special permission was given for officers throughout the county to sell tickets whether on duty in uniform or off duty. There were doubtless countless minor misdemeanours overlooked by those upon whom uniformed 'bobbies' bore down with notebook in one hand and tickets for the match in the other!

Whilst all this was going on Alfred Moore was acclimatising to the life and routine of a prisoner on remand facing a capital charge. He was now known and addressed by the number allocated to him. It was a routine different, and in many respects superior, to that of a prisoner remanded and facing a lesser charge. He was visited daily by Alice, sometimes bringing with her the children, and regularly by Ted Hutchinson and his faithful amanuensis, Kathleen. Painstakingly his account of events on the Saturday night and Sunday morning was recorded though, at this stage, what other evidence, apart from the damning bedside identification, the defence might be called upon to meet was unknown. There was no limit to the number of legal visits and Hutchinson & Co were anxious to impress that nothing that could be done would be left undone for a client financing his own defence and facing the gravest of charges.

It was in the hospital wing of the prison that Alfred was lodged. On his arrival there at 5-45 pm on the Tuesday a record was opened which was to monitor in detail the routines of his daily existence. It begins, however, with a comprehensive medical, employment, social history taken down over a period of 1 ¾ hours. It was important for as much information as possible to be recorded by the prison medical officer, Dr. James Walker, at this first meeting for as in all capital cases it was a routine part of his duties to report on whether the prisoner was fit to plead. The use of the rope notwithstanding, this was a civilised and humane society and a civilised and humane society does not put on trial someone so mentally unwell as to be incapable of comprehending the significance of what is happening to him. Not that there was any cause for concern on that score. Dr. Walker was able to report to the Court that the prisoner, during his time on remand, had 'conversed rationally and behaved well; had been quiet, well-mannered and co-operative; spent most of his time reading but had, nonetheless, mixed well with others, shown no signs of temper or aggression, had slept well and been cheerful throughout.' The doctor's report did not amplify on what it was that resulted in the prisoner, confined and in a predicament as cheerless and dire as could be imagined, being 'cheerful throughout'. It can only have been a conviction that when the full story came to be told justice would be done and his innocence, proclaimed all along according to the report of Dr. Walker, vindicated.

The conclusion of the doctor was inevitable. Moore was pronounced 'free from any defect of reason or disease of the mind rendering him incapable of knowing what he was doing or whether what he was doing was wrong'. He was 'of sound mind and fit to plead to the indictment and stand his trial.' There was to be no fallback position for the prisoner. His defence, and his only defence, was going to be, had to be, total innocence, complete absence of any knowledge of the events that had occurred just a couple of hundred yards away on the slopes below his farmstead.

All that, however, was for a future day. At this initial meeting Alfred was assessed as being of good physique and sound health save for 'trivial superficial abrasions r. scapula region – says thinks from bed boards in police cells'. This was not the explanation given by him on the first visit the following day of his wife and eldest daughter when he alleged that his injuries resulted from being aggressively manhandled whilst in police custody. From that day on both his physical and mental condition would be registered daily by Dr. Walker and it would be his task to make positively the final examination of the body of this particular patient.

A requirement of any psychiatric assessment is a full social history sparing nothing by way of either privacy or delicacy and psychiatrists are, of course, notorious for their interest in the sexual side of life. Alfred told Dr. Walker that his sex life was perfectly normal and that the only woman he had 'been with' was Alice. His consumption of alcohol was modest and if he had a favourite tipple it was the occasional glass of rum. Alfred was evidently anxious to put himself forward as a home-loving family man with practical skills employed to the greater benefit of the wider family. No mention was made of the hours spent by him fettling away creating the tools of his trade as burglar but rather – 'says his main hobby when he has time is carpentry and cabinet working; also does the cobbling for the family, says can also sew and cook; spends all his time at home except for an occasional visit to a cinema and holidays'.

No initial assessment would have been complete without the prisoner's reaction to the charge made against him. Alfred's reaction was both unequivocal and predictable. "Something happened near my land you see" he told Dr. Walker "and the man who had had an accident identified me in Huddersfield Infirmary in a ward and that's it. I am definitely innocent. I was in bed at the time the police stated the accident took place. I will say before God that I was not responsible. I have no revolver so couldn't have fired a revolver. I think it's a true case of mistaken identity. I don't think there's anything malicious about it. I asked the man who identified me if he was sure and he said he was but he was very ill at the time."

At the conclusion of the interview Dr. Walker recorded his first impression of the new inmate: 'No evidence of any mental disorder at this interview and he has been perfectly calm and matter of fact throughout. Has told his story without emotion. Only showed emotion when put in the ward. Said then – what a relief you are putting me there; I thought I'd be in the condemned cell. Quite rational and scoffs at the very idea of any mental abnormality. If guilty he is a very cool customer.'

The daily entries that followed were logged by a succession of officers on duty on the wing each with a different 'take' on the prisoner possibly only a few months away from violent, ritualistic death. Some found him 'quiet and respectful'; others 'cheerful and well-behaved'; yet others 'looking worried, fussy type'. Whatever his daily mood, however, there was one consistent theme – 'nothing wrong mentally with this fellow'.

Alfred was evidently no enthusiast in the early days of his confinement for the chores expected of inmates in the hospital wing, expected but not of course enforced in respect of those unconvicted of any crime. The log contains many entries referring to the prisoner as 'not very fond of work, a lazy fellow, spends a lot of time lounging about reading, smoking and playing chess.' The intricacies of the game of chess had been mastered by Alfred long before his arrival at Leeds though, curiously, the less intellectually demanding rules of dominoes he had yet to learn. He did so, and quickly. It was a game favoured by prison officers charged with keeping a 24 hour watch over prisoners occupying the condemned cell and many hours of Alfred's time were to be occupied in playing the game during the weeks following his trial.

Little evidence of any unusual behaviour on the part of the prisoner was noted though one contributor to the record observed 'sometimes he appears to stare into space; quite a showman, slept well.' Even a sense of humour is, on occasions, evident. Following his return to the prison after his appearance at the court in Huddersfield on the 31 July he announced that still no weapon had been found: "there isn't one; the police have a very thin case, if they dig anything up it will probably be something of Julius Caesar's." Only one reference is to be found to any pro-criminal attitude on the part of an undoubted criminal professional – 'gives other patients advice on how to outwit the police' was recorded on the 3 November.

No change was noted in the prisoner's demeanour following his committal to stand trial at the assizes. He remained 'confident and unworried'. If anything his optimism increased the closer drew near the day on which he believed his innocence would be vindicated. He was even planning for the future. On the 19 October he is recorded as saying that on his release he would be assuming the role of manager of a 150 acre farm "with a view to purchase." He was 'without a care in the world'; his 'confidence is amazing'; 'outwardly he does not appear to appreciate the seriousness of the charge'. It was a frame of mind shared by Alice who told medical staff, when interviewed on the 11 October for her input into the psychiatric profile being built up of her husband, that she knew him to be innocent, adding "if I did not think so I'd be really worried."

Meantime police activity was continuing at Whinney Close as Alfred began his time on remand. By the end of the first week there were at least a few who were beginning to nurture, if not exactly harbour, lingering doubts as to the real strength of the case against Alfred Moore. It arose simply from the absence of any result from the search of the fields and meadows surrounding Whinney Close Farm. There was, however, no let up in the search; if anything the hunt was intensifying.

To the Officers of the County Force and the Sappers of the Royal Engineers from Ripon with their mine-detectors were now added an eighty-strong contingent of West Riding Police student cadets who had volunteered to join the search. The curious, there were many, visiting the scene of the tragedy were daily able to view visible signs of the effort being put into the hunt; dozens of bodies in shirt-sleeves, toiling on hands and knees in the hot summer sun, scouring every inch of ground with their finger tips and going over the same ground again and again. There were others armed with hand shears so that every protruding blade of grass might be laid low. And they were followed by yet others with hand brooms to sweep the cut grass to one side.

By the second week the mood was one of decided pessimism; that which had earlier seemed to promise nothing less than 'game, set and match' to the case of the Crown versus the Poultry Farmer cum Burglar, was stubbornly refusing to yield up the murder weapon. How could this be? The unthinkable began to be thought. Might not the murderer have fled the scene away from, not towards, the farmhouse, taking his gun with him? Contemplation of this scenario removed, at a stroke, Alfred Moore from the frame. An alternative theory to explain the failure to recover the gun would have to be found.

Daily the *Examiner's* dogged crime reporter pestered force headquarters for news of any developments in the ongoing search. Daily he was met with a communiqué to the same effect as before and in terms ever more terse. 'No further developments' had marked the end of the first week of searching. It was now a mere 'No developments'.

16 – A True Bill

After two weeks of strenuous effort had stubbornly refused to yield up the murder weapon the search of farmhouse and fields was scaled right down. Some desultory, token forays into the fields were mounted on occasions when there was nothing better to occupy police time but it was done without real expectation of a result, an expectation that was never to be disappointed. To have been able to lay to rest, for all time, any lingering doubt about the guilt of the Kirkheaton poultry farmer would, thought police and prosecutors at the time, have been useful; little did they appreciate just how useful it would have been as over the next half century those doubts multiplied.

But, at the time, no doubts at all were entertained as to the sufficiency of the evidence that was available. The prosecution were confident of an eventual conviction and the defence resigned at least to a finding by the town's magistrates that Alfred Moore had a case to meet at the Assize Court which it would be idle to resist. In the parlance of a few decades earlier, when it was the function of a Grand Jury to examine the available evidence of guilt to determine whether it justified a trial on the proposed Bill of Indictment, it was a 'true bill'. Not 'true' in the sense that the guilt alleged in the Indictment was proved or anything like that but merely that the evidence the prosecution were able to produce was sufficient to justify a trial.

Alice and Alfred were left in no doubt both that a trial at the Assizes by the end of the year was a foregone conclusion and that even to seek to challenge the evidence that the prosecution were intending to place before the examining magistrates would be a counter-productive exercise, giving advance warning to witnesses of the questions they might face at the Assizes and to the prosecutors the arguments they would have to answer.

As the police vacated Whinney Close Farm and the hills and fields surrounding it, permission was given for its second sale by auction that year to go ahead. The property was placed with Messrs. William Sykes and Sons of Holmfirth and the auction fixed to take place on Saturday 11 August. The efforts of the extended Moore family and a few police officers with some reserves of goodwill towards the predicament of Alice Moore had ensured that the farm would be marketed as a going concern. Included in the sale particulars were 500 fowls, feeding stuffs, hen-cotes, wire netting, a garden roller, a lawn mower and a man's bicycle, the latter a reminder that Alfred Moore was neither the holder of a driving licence nor the owner of any mechanically propelled vehicle. He travelled only by foot, pedal cycle or bus - and his children, of course, by taxi. Not least of the questions which Moore's success as a burglar posed for the police was just how he travelled to and from the various premises burgled by him across the breadth and length of Huddersfield. The answer which most obviously suggested itself was that, though presenting as a loner, he did in fact work together with, even possibly under the supervision of, an accomplice with 'wheels'. If he did, it raised yet further questions as to the identity of the figure confronted by the two dead officers and, more importantly, in which direction that figure had fled the scene – towards, or away from, the farmhouse?

On the day of the sale, despite an unseasonal steady downpour of rain, dozens of lorries, shooting brakes, cars and motor-cycles lined either side of Cockley Hill at Kirkheaton. It was the notoriety of the sale rather than the attraction of what was on offer that had brought together the few genuinely interested, the half-interested and the morbidly curious. By the end of the day a sale had been achieved and Alice Moore relieved at least of the anxiety of keeping the poultry venture, begun only a few months earlier with such high hopes, alive. There were far greater issues for her to be anxious about. The proceeds of sale were just about sufficient to pay the legal costs about to be incurred with precious little left over to bring up a family; and there was of course no prospect of public generosity coming to the rescue of the Moore family. For the Moore children the new school year was to bring about a culture shock – education at the expense of the state rather than privately financed from the proceeds of crime.

In the meantime Alfred was making the weekly journey from Leeds to the Princess Street Courthouse, for the first four weeks simply to be told that he was to be remanded back into prison custody, a further warrant for his continued detention being a legal requirement after the lapse of seven days, and for the prosecution to inform the bench that they were not, as yet, in a position to embark upon calling evidence on which to seek Moore's committal to the Assizes. The appearances were brief. Neither objection to his further remand into custody nor complaint about the delay were offered by Ted Hutchinson. The former would have been futile and the latter an exercise in possibly hastening the day that would bring the life of his client to a no less violent end than that suffered by the two officers.

A principal cause of the delay was the debate between police and lawyers as to whether to call to give evidence the ten-year-old daughter. Her contribution to proof of the prosecution case was modest at best and the damage that might be caused to the goodwill of the public towards the police, riding perhaps as high at that time in Huddersfield as it had ever done, was immeasurable but potentially huge. As was the custom at the time the Recorder of the Borough Quarter Sessions, a London based Barrister, George Norman Black, had been briefed to act for the prosecution. The Borough was not considered at the time sufficiently important to justify the appointment of King's Counsel to fulfill its top legal role and Black was still, and would ever remain, amongst the ranks of junior counsel – albeit as the years went by 'a senior junior'. At the Assizes Black would be led by one of His Majesty's Counsel learned in the law, a King's Counsel, but for the purposes of the committal Black had sole conduct of the prosecution case.

Black had no difficulty seeing that which senior police officers, determined to play every note of this particular score, refused to see but Black had neither the presence nor necessary seniority to overrule police insistence that the child be called. It was an appalling misjudgement. It added little or nothing to the case against Moore. No-one, least of all Moore, was in any doubt that the case would go to the Assizes at Leeds – with or without the evidence of Patricia.

Just one month after Moore's first appearance at the Huddersfield Court the prosecution announced that they were in a position to proceed to the committal stage before the end of the month and Monday 27 August was the date fixed, with two days of court time set aside for the hearing. A lapse of just six weeks between first appearance and committal represented an exercise in commendable expedition, that is by the standards of the time when many cases lingered at the local court for months before being ready for committal either to the Quarter Sessions or, for the more serious crimes, to the Assizes to be tried by a 'red judge' (so-called because of his bright scarlet regalia).

Today the case of Alfred Moore, on its first appearance before the local Justices would be sent straightaway to the Crown Court – the modern day equivalent of the Assizes – for preliminary hearing within seven days. But the obvious good sense of a case, only capable of resolution at a superior court being listed before that court at an early stage, did not prevail until 2001. Before this welcome, and obviously needed, reform cases would weekly, and interminably, appear in the list at the local court with the only safeguard for the defendant not admitted to bail the statutory custody time limit of seventy days, introduced in 1987, beyond which he could not "without good and sufficient cause" be further remanded into custody.

Given the intensity of the interest generated by Moore's first court appearance, an interest, no less fervent, was anticipated for this somewhat more significant hearing notwithstanding that over the intervening weeks Moore's weekly return to the Huddersfield Court had attracted a gradually diminishing band of onlookers. The police were certainly prepared for yet another exercise in crowd control, as, apparently, were the two elderly gentlemen observed loitering outside the courthouse as early as 7-15 a.m. on the Monday, a full 3 ¼ hours before the building would be open to the public. Their anticipation that the demand for admittance would outstrip the capacity of the public gallery was understandable, based on solid grounds, but in the event wholly unnecessary because when the doors of the building eventually opened a mere trickle of half a dozen figures filed inside. Public interest in the case, however, had not totally dissipated and over the next half hour their number swelled to about forty, not exactly packed to the rafters, because the court room was vast, but certainly far exceeding the usual handful of 'down-and-outs' who would take refuge from inclement weather either there or in the reading room of the public library opposite.

Doubtless one reason for the waning interest in the case was that, in the course of earlier hearings and in the absence of any restrictions at that time on reporting what was said in the course of remand hearings, there had been a steady drip-feeding to the public of information about the case and the fact of the bedside identification of Moore as the killer was already well known throughout the town. Most felt, apparently, that there was very little more to know; if Moore had been identified as the killer by an eye-witness then that that was that and, if the witness was no longer available for his reliability to be tested, then that made the ultimate outcome of the case more, not less, certain. In that calculation they were not wrong.

The summons that had been issued to compel the attendance at Court of the ten-year-old who was being required to testify against her own father ensured that she was in attendance, brought there by her mother ("wearing a dress of floral design under a grey coat"), though once inside she was handed over to be looked after, pending being called to give evidence, by Kathleen Hutchinson. Alice was intent on a public show of support for her husband in his predicament. In the courtroom her presence throughout the proceedings was deliberately ostentatious and fell sadly and seriously short of that which many interested and respectable onlookers considered to be an appropriate standard of behaviour. It brought about at least one reprimand from the Justices' Clerk and became an unnecessary and unwelcome factor in the worrying decision that would later have to be made as to whether to call to give evidence a witness who had potentially critical evidence of alibi to give. But that was a decision for another day.

On this occasion there was no sign of distress as Alice walked into the gradually filling court room and, instead of retiring to the seats reserved for 'ordinary' members of the public, she proceeded boldly into the well of the court, the area reserved strictly for the professionals, and engaged Ted Hutchinson in animated, apparently amiable, conversation. It was with discomfort bordering on embarrassment that Ted noticed, out of the corner of his eye, his professional opponent, George Norman Black, taking steps that were prudent and tactful to remove himself from earshot of their conversation.

Minutes later as the court room clock approached 11-00 a.m. Moore was brought up into the dock. He was clearly intent on looking his 'Sunday best' for this his positively last appearance in the town. Alfred Moore was no longer the gum-booted, gaberdined poultry farmer arrested weeks earlier. Money may have been tight but Alice had ensured a new suit, delivered by her that morning to the police cells, and it was a dapper, be-suited, colour coordinated figure that climbed into public view, wearing, as the town's newspaper noted that evening, "a fawn suit of herring-bone pattern with light blue shirt and blue tie."

Showing no outward signs of distress or apprehension the prisoner cheerily greeted his wife over the dock rail with a broad smile –

"How are you?"

They continued to chat and smile, Ted Hutchinson looking on until Alice left to check on the well-being of Patricia.

Promptly at 11-00 a.m. those present in Court were ordered by the usher to rise as five of Huddersfield's most senior West Riding Magistrates came onto the bench, once again presided over by Percy Crowther.

After the formality of the magistrates and those on the advocates' benches bowing to each other all took their seats save for Moore who was directed to remain standing. With one hand holding the dock rail and the other casually in trouser pocket he listened, without response, as the Acting Clerk to the Justices, Mr Boardman, read over to him the two charges of murder.

"Be seated" he was told, the necessary formalities for the start of the proceedings over. Alice Moore was observed to slip back into Court and take a seat this time in the public gallery. To those unaware of the identity of the first witness to be called it seemed incongruous that she was clutching a copy of 'The Children's Newspaper'.

G. Norman Black rose to address the Court. The facts as alleged by the prosecution were outlined, calmly, dispassionately, without undue rhetoric. It was, he said, a story easily told. For the first time the public were informed that the dead officers were but two of a much larger group keeping observation on the farmhouse and forming a cordon around it. Those who knew anything about Moore would appreciate why; those who did not were left to engage in speculation and guesswork for the mystery of what the officers were doing there at all was not going to be clarified at this hearing. What Moore might have been doing between parting company with his brother at 11-30 pm and the shooting of the officers two hours later was not, Black told the Court, a matter as to which it would be useful to speculate but he was not, as he had claimed, within the farmhouse at the time of the shooting.

Another mystery to which the facts as related by the prosecutor gave rise, but which was to remain unresolved by this hearing, was why the poultry farmer apparently found it necessary to rise from his bed in the middle of the night and engage in the incineration in the fire grate downstairs of material of some unspecified kind.

Whilst the strengths of the prosecution case were underlined Black was unable to pass over entirely the conspicuous flaw in the prosecution theory of events – the failure to recover the murder weapon despite a search that was both extensive and intensive. The attempt to minimise the impact of the failure was far from convincing but probably the best that could be devised in the circumstances. It was a bold, almost one might say brazen, approach and one that was not to be deviated from at the eventual trial. Black told the magistrates that the failure was "not perhaps surprising in view of the two hours that had elapsed between shooting and arrest and the very broken nature of the ground there." The terrain may have been difficult but for most of the time that elapsed between shooting and arrest it was undisputed that Moore was not at large but inside the farmhouse.

The prosecutor swiftly moved on to stronger ground, proceeding to read the deposition sworn by the dying constable. It was a document with which one member of the Bench was already well familiar. The prosecution opening statement was merely that, a statement and not evidence. On day two of the hearing the deposition was read over again, this time as evidence for the formal record of the proceedings. No objection was raised to this course by the defence. The deposition had been duly sworn and its maker was indubitably beyond providing live testimony. The necessary pre-conditions for evidence to be given by a witness no longer available to be challenged and cross-examined by the defence were satisfied. It was evidence that even standing alone would have placed beyond question the outcome of the proceeding. It did not go unnoticed by those present, though it did actually go unremarked, that the deposition was endorsed as having been taken and sworn in the presence of the accused 'Albert' Moore.

As the police account of the circumstances surrounding Moore's arrest was being told to the Court by Mr Black, the prisoner was observed becoming visibly agitated in the dock and when the Court was told that he had referred to his own position as "serious enough" he stood and shouted "you are a bloody liar." It was his one and only outburst throughout the whole course of the proceedings for he was sternly, immediately reprimanded by the Clerk of the Court:

"Be quiet and don't use language like that."

This was not the only occasion during the hearing that it became necessary for Mr Boardman to issue a rebuke. But it was to the prisoner's wife rather than the prisoner when it occurred. As the hearing progressed Alice had been given a seat in the well of the court immediately in front of the dock. Husband and wife were regularly observed exchanging reassuring smiles. The smiles went unremarked but when the eagle eye of Mr Boardman spotted Alice reading a newspaper, surreptitiously rather than blatantly, he evidently took the view that the dignity of the Court was compromised.

"Mrs Moore please do not read a newspaper in court" he sternly instructed her.

The newspaper was hurriedly folded, put away, not to be seen again. The incident was reported in the local paper that evening and left the decided impression of blasé impropriety in the face of a solemn enquiry into events of tragic enormity and on the outcome of which a third life might be forfeit. It was an unfortunate impression and for those already pondering whether Alice Moore should be called as alibi witness at the eventual, inevitable, trial in Leeds it provided if not grounds for doubt at least food for contemplation.

The introduction to the case over Mr Black turned to the task of calling the witnesses. The hearing was not one to determine the truth of the charges. It was simply to determine whether the evidence was good and sufficient enough to send Moore to be tried at the Assizes or whether he should be discharged there and then. The obligation on the prosecution was no more and no less than to present sufficient evidence on which a jury properly directed as to the relevant law might (not necessarily would) convict. In practice, in the majority of cases, the prosecution would simply adduce a bare sufficiency of evidence to meet this low threshold and serve the balance of their case at a later time under a notice of additional evidence. But, as quickly became apparent, this was not how the prosecution were intending to proceed. This was to be nothing less than a full dress rehearsal for the trial proper. Over two days some thirty-six witnesses were called (one more than would be called at the Assizes) and a total of seventy-six exhibits produced, many of them keys but without clarification of their significance to the case and not possessing any immediately obvious relevance to the shooting dead of two police officers.

The first three witnesses to be called all bore the same surname as the prisoner in the dock for they were his daughter, brother and sister-in-law. The real, perhaps the only, drama of this hearing was the appearance of the child in the witness box to testify, as it turned out unwillingly and tearfully, against her father. She was the first witness. No mention had been made in the opening statement of the intention to call her or of the evidence she might give because the circumstances were such that there was no way of knowing whether she would be emotionally able to give any evidence at all or, if she did speak, what she might say.

In hauling the child before the court the police had taken no chances. On the previous Friday Superintendent Foster had attended before a Justice of the Peace and given sworn evidence that Patricia was unwilling to attend court and a subpoena was requested. In fact all that had happened was that Alice had responded to a police request to bring her daughter to court by stating, not unreasonably, that Patricia would attend if Ted Hutchinson advised that she should do so. Instead of speaking to Ted the police went straight to a magistrate for a court order which was granted.

Mr Black introduced the evidence of Patricia by explaining to the bench that although the anticipated evidence of Patricia would, if a strict chronological approach was adopted, come at a later stage the Court would no doubt understand the concern of the Crown to ensure that a child witness was not detained in the building one second longer than was absolutely necessary. The Justices on the bench and their Clerk, sitting immediately below them in the well of the Court, nodded in unison at this commendable demonstration of sensitivity.

What neither the prosecutor nor the Court, nor for that matter the defence either, had considered was the ability of the Court by statute, which was at that time almost twenty years old, to place an embargo on the publication of anything in the media calculated to lead to the identification of a child appearing before any Court in whatever capacity. The legislation, the Children and Young Persons Act of 1933, was even specific in providing the Court with the power to ban the publication of photographs of children appearing before Courts. It is a power which is today routinely and invariably invoked. Of course, had an order been made it would have effectively prevented publication of any evidence given by Patricia and the public interest in open justice and a free press is a strong one but one which today is generally considered outweighed by the welfare of the child and even when that child is a defendant in the proceedings and guilty of some heinous crime. Patricia was not a defendant; there was no question of 'name and shame' and yet she was not merely publicly identified but her photograph appeared that night in the local press being ushered out of the building, holding the hand of Kathleen Hutchinson, after she had completed her testimony. It is a quaint and pathetic photograph of a forlorn little thing wearing a headscarf and tightly-fitting 1950's style child's coat.

Just as the folk of Huddersfield were relishing the prospect of the opening stages of the legal game that would see the town's notorious police killer receive his just deserts the mood turned to one of sympathy for his child and bewilderment that the prosecution should have considered that this was anything like an appropriate way to proceed. It was a move that damaged, even if only temporarily, the image of police and prosecutors and for Patricia she took into adulthood the burden of having given evidence supposedly adverse to her father as well as the shame attaching to the family of one meeting the end that befell Alfred Moore. Little wonder that Alice considered, in the aftermath of it all, that nothing less than drastic steps were required to place her family as far from the theatre of these events as was geographically possible.

For those in court, not aware of the intentions of the prosecution, it was with astonishment at the cruelty and crassness of it that they observed the child enter the courtroom. As she was guided towards the witness box Alfred, risking yet a further reprimand for disrupting the proceedings, stood in the dock, waved and shouted to his daughter across the court

"Hello Pat."

It did nothing to re-assure her but neither did the prisoner receive any further reprimand for his interruption of the proceedings. Patricia was in tears as she came into Court and tears flowed freely throughout her short time in the witness box. Her earlier statement, extracted after hours of interrogation, had been read to her before she came into court and she had been left in no doubt that should she depart from it there would be consequences, unspecified but certainly consequences. Her evidence did not deviate from her earlier statement but it was extracted only with the utmost difficulty and, it has to be said, skill.

Pat's evidence was the evidence of a child, childish in demeanour and childlike in expression. The prisoner in the dock was now being referred to as 'daddy'. 'Daddy' was cross, she said, when he came home and she was not asleep. Had she heard anything when daddy came home? It was a question that teetered on the very border of being objectionable as leading the witness but what is leading is always a question of fact and degree and this one just managed not to overstep the mark. Yes, agreed Pat, she thought she had heard something. What might it have been? The crucial word that appeared in her earlier statement and the word for which the prosecutor was now probing was, of course, 'whistle'. It was the word that placed 'daddy's' arrival home at the time of the police activity immediately following the shooting. The only response from Pat was tears and sobs – no words.

The process of teasing out the crucial word was going to have to be an incremental one with the dilemma for the questioner being when to call a halt. But this was not the time and the question was put again, ever so slightly re-worded: what sort of noise? After a few further seconds of sobbing it appeared that progress was being made. It might have been a train came the reply. What sort of noise do trains make? Pat's answer, exclusionary rather than inclusionary, made complete sense in 1951 though it might not as readily do so today. It was not a puffing noise. What was it then? Another agonising pause. The question was repeated with an exhortation, kindly in its terms but steely in utterance. Please try to help us. Alice Moore had done all that a mother could to insulate her children from the full horror of their situation and how it all might possibly end but the playground jibes had made that clear enough to ten-year-old Pat. She knew just what it was that she was being asked to help the prosecution achieve. Eventually came the answer – it might have been a whistle.

In the deposition that was being taken down the exchange between advocate and child was recorded as 'I think I heard something. I have never heard a police whistle before.' It satisfied neither prosecution nor defence as an accurate summary of what had just taken place. Ted rose for the first time after the deposition had been read aloud to suggest the insertion of the words 'I think it might have been a train.' The words were added but then Norman Black joined the debate requesting a further addition to the child's deposition 'It was not the puffing noise. It was the whistle.'

The amended deposition was read to Pat. She nodded her agreement to its content and added her signature, not in adult 'joined up' writing but the printed block capitals of the child that she was. Pat exited the adult stage on which she had made her one and only appearance.

To describe the courtroom as merely silent during the evidence of

Patricia would be to engage in understatement. It was hushed, emotionally charged, every ear, every eye, focused on the tearful child, sobbing her way through her testimony. Those present who were responsible for insisting that Patricia be called to the stand had swiftly realised that this was a blunder colossal and calamitous. Resolutions were made that it would not be repeated.

Where issues of death and life are paramount the atmosphere of a courtroom is never other than sombre but on this occasion, as Patricia stepped from the witness box and the court moved on to consider the evidence of Charles Henry and his wife, Mahala, the tension in the air eased perceptibly.

For the rest of the day, and indeed well into the second day set aside for the hearing, the Court embarked on the laborious task of hearing the various witnesses and reducing their evidence to the form of a written deposition. It was a noisy procedure as the court's old style typewriter clacked away, recording the evidence of each witness so that the deposition could be signed before the witness left court. The hearing took place in the full glare of publicity, the unchallenged (at this stage) evidence in support of the prosecution case being made available to be read, pored over, studied by any interested member of the public and of those there were many and many who were potential jurors who might try the case in due course. It was to be another sixteen years before the introduction of restrictions on the reporting of such proceedings and, by then, the committal had become, in most cases, an anaemic, hollow exercise in which the Court rarely heard any "live" evidence but simply pronounced the case committed on the prosecution producing a bundle of statements and the defence conceding that, on paper at least, there was a case to answer.

In 1951 it was necessary for all witnesses relied upon by the prosecution to be called to the stand and give "live" evidence – that is in all but the most exceptional of circumstances. This was an exceptional case because there was one witness, the most important witnesses of all, who was no longer available to give "live" evidence.

It was a long day in Court and continued beyond late afternoon into the early evening and until such time as the advocates were able to guarantee a conclusion to the proceedings the following day. A total of fourteen witnesses were called that first day leaving nineteen to be called the next but of those the majority would give merely short, formal, uncontroversial evidence.

It was not only witnesses as to the events in field and farmhouse that early Sunday morning who were called but the plan drawers and photographers; the doctors and pathologists; the witnesses to the bedside identification; the officers responsible for the arrest, detention and charge of Moore and those who told also of the compromising, if not indeed downright incriminatory, remarks made by him in the cells; the officers who produced the numerous exhibits collected from the farm but not, of course, the one exhibit the public were expecting to hear about and were at least mildly puzzled when the proceedings concluded without reference to the finding of a gun. The hundreds of skeleton keys recovered were laid before the court but without either objection from the defence on the ground of lack of apparent relevance to the identification of the killer or, for that matter, clarification by the Crown as to their significance.

At the conclusion of the evidence of each witness the deposition, noisily typed out as the evidence had been given, was read in full and the witness invited to sign both to attest to its truthfulness and to acknowledge "owing to our Sovereign Lord the King the sum of £5 of good and lawful money of Great Britain to be made and levied on my goods and chattels, goods and tenements, should I fail to attend at the Assize Court."

One item of evidence that did come as a surprise to the defence was the exercise, undertaken by a police officer with the intention of breaking Moore's alibi who had walked and timed the late night stroll of the two brothers. It was claimed that the outward journey would have taken 32 minutes and for Moore's return, up the slopes leading to the farm, only slightly longer at 35 minutes. Not 'about' or 'approximately' but 32 minutes and 35 minutes. It was of course designed to show that had Moore returned to the farm at the time claimed by him he would have hit the police cordon with the inference that he arrived much later, at the time in fact that the two officers were shot, and that he was the killer. On any view the difference between the time claimed by the police for their cordon to be in place and that by Moore for his return to the farm was 'tight' and, given the many variables involved in an exercise of this kind, it could never have been anything like a precise reconstruction. It became a just about useless exercise once any one of the given premises on which it was based was 'out' by but a few minutes. Yet it was solemnly paraded before the Court without objection. The need for caution when considering reconstruction evidence based on timings is underlined by the fact the exercise here was repeated following the committal and the slightly different timings resulting (more favourable to the defence in fact by 1 ½ minutes) put before the jury.

No evidence, however, was offered then, or at any future time, to account for what the burglar farmer might have been doing, if not inside the farmhouse, during the 2 ½ hours or so between parting company with his brother and returning to the farm at the time when the officers were shot.

Throughout the day Ted Hutchinson patiently made notes of the evidence, a largely unnecessary exercise given that the deposition of each witness would be served on the defence at the conclusion of the hearing. At least, however, it gave the appearance of interest and attention to an exercise otherwise lacking entirely in the element of surprise as to its outcome. The defence resolution neither to question nor challenge witnesses was maintained. But at the end of the day when the prosecution formally requested the Court to remand the prisoner overnight Ted rose for the second time that day. Puzzlement as to why was quickly dispelled. It was not to object but merely ask if the remand of the prisoner could be back to the amenities and relative comfort of Armley Gaol rather than the Spartan and hostile environment of the Princess Street police lock-up. It was, Ted told the Court, "Moore's earnest wish that he should not stay here at Huddersfield." To the prison at Leeds Moore was ordered to be returned, spared for the night the taunts and sheer cold loathing of the colleagues of the slain officers.

In the late afternoon of the second day of the hearing Mr Black informed the Court that his case was closed. No more evidence was to be called. The case moved to a swift, unsurprising conclusion. No one expected that the defence would either call evidence or challenge the sufficiency of the evidence adduced by the prosecution to justify the case proceeding to a trial at the Assizes.

It was duly recorded (albeit in the language of another age) that:

> "The witnesses for the prosecution having been severally examined in the presence of the accused and the charge having been read and its nature explained in ordinary language and the accused having been informed of his right to call witnesses and if he desires to give evidence on his own behalf. And the accused having been given clearly to understand that he has nothing to hope from any promise and nothing to fear from any threat which

may have been held out to induce him to make any admission or confession of his guilt, but whatsoever he says may be given in evidence at his trial."

What in fact happened was that Moore was instructed to stand. First the charge was put that he "feloniously, willfully and of his malice aforethought did kill and murder Duncan Fraser against the Peace of our Sovereign Lord the King his Crown and Dignity." The antique wording a reminder that the law of murder required both perpetrator and victim to be under the King's Peace and the felonious act to be *contra pacem domini regis* (against the King's Peace). With the creeping internationalization of our criminal law and the assumption of a jurisdiction to try crimes committed abroad, as well as the commendable shift to the use of plain English in the Courts and a realisation these words meant little more than what was being alleged was a crime, the wording has fallen into disuse. Moore was asked: do you wish to say anything in answer to the charge? You are not obliged to say anything unless you desire to do so but whatever you do say will be taken down in writing and may be given in evidence at your trial? Moore, having been schooled by Ted Hutchinson as to his role and limited speaking part in the final moves of the proceedings, responded:

'I don't wish to say anything today sir.'

It was the standard answer of the prisoner about to be committed for trial at some higher Court, deliberately leaving the impression that there was much that might be said but today it would be pointless to say it but just wait until another day and what will be disclosed is a complete answer to the charge.

The same rigmarole followed with the identically worded charge relating to the killing of Gordon Jagger. This time Moore attenuated his response:

'Not today, sir.'

The formalities were not yet concluded. The prisoner was asked if he wished either to give evidence or call witnesses. His response took no-one by surprise:

'Not today.'

The five justices left the bench to give formal consideration to the sufficiency of the evidence placed before the Court over the previous two days. It was not expected that their retirement would be prolonged and the prisoner was not even removed from the dock. Within minutes the Court reconvened for Moore to be told by Percy Crowther that he would be committed to stand his trial on the two charges of murder at the next assize. It was the expected, inevitable conclusion to the proceedings. In a tone barely audible and in terms hardly appropriate Moore responded to the pronouncement with a deferential – 'Thank you, sir.' The muted tone betrayed a knowledge that, however anticipated this result, it was, nonetheless, a significant step along a path which might lead to a conclusion so awful that the human mind could hardly process it. There was no doubt as to where Moore would be spending this night. Within minutes he was being driven away from Huddersfield for the last time.

Arrival of Royal Engineers

Royal Engineers searching

Search briefing

Searching at Whinney Close Farm

Whinney Close Farm - 1951

Whinney Close Farm today

Crime scene 1951

Crime scene today

Funeral of Insp. Fraser

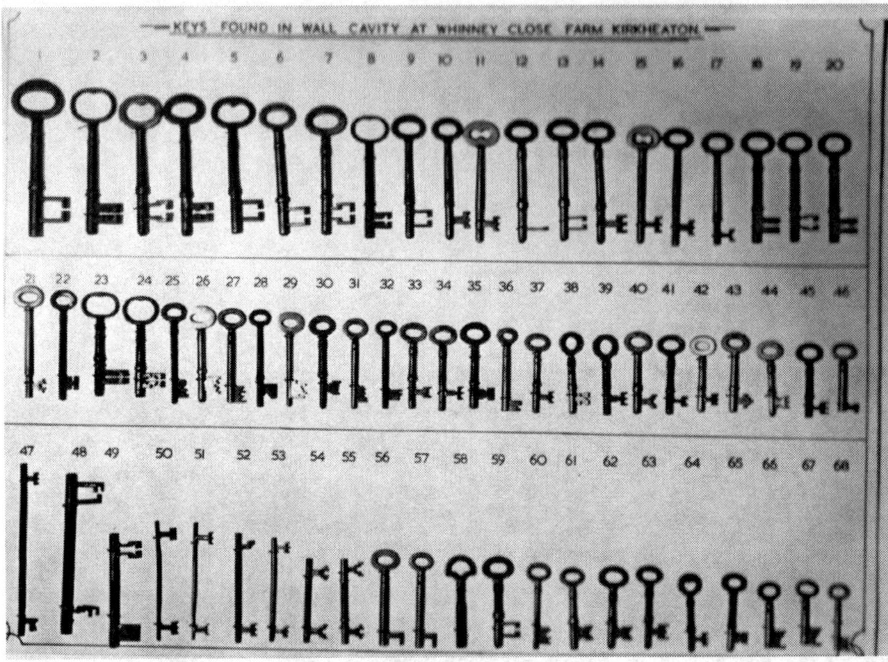

Alfred's keys

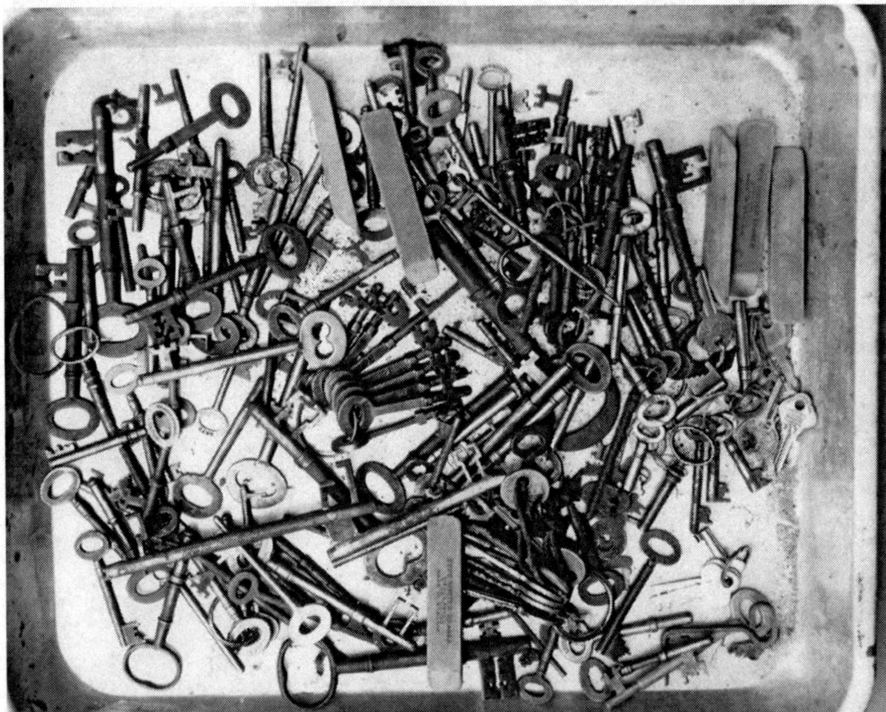

Miscellaneous stolen property

Police Constable Jagger

Alfred Moore

17 – 'I Could Hang Him Myself'

As the summer of 1951 turned to autumn and the days began to shorten and the nights lengthen the lawyers busied themselves with the task of preparing for a trial expected before the year was out. For the prosecution, preparing the Brief to Counsel was simply an exercise in putting together in some semblance of order the various statements and depositions of the witnesses and selecting the King's Counsel to lead Norman Black at the Assize Court. The case allowed of no more investigation. Hope had long been abandoned of any further evidence coming to light; the case lawyers, however, were well satisfied with the sufficiency of the evidence that was now available to them to hang Moore.

Half a century on the concern would be whether the witnesses would attend court and, if they did, whether they would give the evidence contained within their statements. Intimidation of witnesses and special measures to protect them, sometimes as extreme as anonymity and voice distortion, are not quite invariable, but almost so, features of the trials of serious crime today. Those concerns are accentuated where friends, relatives and associates of the accused are witnesses. The trial of Alfred Moore was going to hear from two of his close relatives – the decision that Patricia would *not* be called was the least exacting of the tactical decisions that the prosecution were being called upon to make; no-one, not even this time round the police, was going to risk the sympathies of a jury shifting from the murdered officers and their grieving families towards the prisoner and self-professed and prolific burglar. In any event, these were deferential times and a witness, acknowledging in the face of the magistrates' court an obligation to attend at the assizes when called upon to do so, would not contemplate failing in that undertaking. And, having given a commitment to a particular account of events would not dream of deviating from it. No worries were entertained about the witnesses. In fact no worries were entertained at all. The case was straightforward enough and the evidence of guilt plain.

The Director of Public Prosecutions decided that Counsel briefed to lead for the Crown should be G. Raymond Hinchcliffe K.C., based, as at the time were all Leading Counsel, in Chambers in the Temple in London, the same chambers in fact, at 5 Paper Buildings, as Norman Black. Hinchcliffe was a North-Eastern Circuiteer through and through; born in Huddersfield, son of a local solicitor, he was no great intellect but this was not going to be a trial requiring intellectual stamina but common sense and that instinctive feel for the criminal process which had served Hinchcliffe well throughout his career. It had already led to his appointment to the prestigious Recordership of Leeds and would later result in his elevation to the Queen's Bench Division of the High Court. Following the abolition of Assizes and Quarter Sessions and their replacement with Crown Courts, sitting on a permanent rather than *ad hoc* basis, he became the Presiding Judge of the Circuit, an influential figure with a power he was not slow to exercise to make and break careers. He died in office in the late 1970's.

The defence, of course, were faced with the task of selecting both leading and junior counsel. The profession of barrister at this time was small and the pool of talent from which to choose limited. Ted Hutchinson had already marked down as likely to travel far in the profession young Charles Raymond Dean, product of a local grammar school and Oxford scholarship boy with distinguished wartime service in the Royal Air Force. This was to be Dean's first, but the first of many, briefs in a capital trial. A few years later Dean's talents as lawyer and his economy of style, never more than one word where only one word was required, would lead to him 'taking silk' and assuming the role of leader. After a decade bestriding the Courts of the north-eastern circuit he was, in 1971, amongst the first tranche of appointments to the circuit bench of the newly created Crown Courts. But in 1951 he still had far to travel and much to learn and was to be magisterially, though unfairly, castigated in the course of the Moore case for naiveté.

It was the King's Counsel chosen to lead Ray (as he was familiarly known throughout his life) who issued the rebuke. The money being available to pay for nothing but the best it was to the very top of the profession that Ted Hutchinson looked to brief leading counsel. The choice was obvious – or so it seemed. Harry Braustyn Hylton Hylton-Foster, son of Harry Braustyn Hylton Hylton-Foster (for this highly conservative family neither imagination nor initiative featured in the process of naming its offspring) was, in 1951, succeeding in the high ambitions of both his legal and political careers. Born in 1905, Harry, Sir Harry as he became in 1954, had taken the path marked out for him at birth. Eton, Oxford, the Bar, a fashionable marriage to Audrey Pellew Clifton Brown, daughter of Viscount Ruffside. His unruffled urbanity assured him success at the Bar and, by 1940, he had been appointed to the Recordership of Richmond in the North Riding of Yorkshire, succeeding to that of Huddersfield in 1944 where he had first come to the notice of Ted Hutchinson.

On the Circuit Hylton-Foster was a byword for effortless incisiveness. The anecdote is still related of his appearance before a much-talking judge who had hi-jacked his cross-examination of a witness. He stood patiently, in silence, as question followed question. When the witness was asked by the judge what he was doing at a particular place and replied "Just standing around waiting to do my job" Hylton-Foster observed "I know the feeling well, My Lord."

Conservative both by temperament and political inclination his efforts to enter Parliament began stutteringly. Selected to fight the constituency of Shipley in West Yorkshire, home to countless prosperous wool men from nearby Bradford, he might justifiably have considered his election to the House of Commons little more than a foregone conclusion and his tenure of a safe seat for life secure. In any normal year it would have been. It required nothing less than a Labour landslide for Shipley not to return a Tory but that is just what happened in the General Election of 1945. (History repeated itself in 1997.) Undeterred by this setback Hylton-Foster won the nomination for the constituency of York which returned him to Parliament in 1950. It was a seat he held in 1951 and 1955. His career at the Bar flourished in the meantime; he was elevated to King's Counsel in 1947, following which he figured in just about every trial of significance on the north-eastern circuit. In Parliament he was no less successful. He was appointed a Law Officer of the Crown and knighted in 1954. Three years later he added to the title 'Sir' that of 'Right Honourable' on being sworn to the Privy Council.

But under the veneer of effortless urbanity lay a ruthless streak.

Sensing, wrongly as it happens, a shift away from the Conservative cause in the late 1950's he deserted the marginal seat of York for the rock solid safe seat of Cities of London and Westminster. It was a move that attracted justified criticism in the north for perceived disloyalty but did nothing at all to deflect the upward trajectory of Sir Harry's career. Following the 1959 General Election he was elected to the post of Speaker of the House of Commons. His election was, in the end, unanimous though tinged by controversy. On the Labour side there were protests at a perceived lack of consultation and even on his own side disquiet at a move directly from Government office to the Speaker's Chair. However, the post of Solicitor-General was reckoned to be less politically controversial than most others and his claims to the office of Speaker won through. It was perhaps fortunate for him that Prime Minister, Anthony Eden, chose not to seek the advice of his law officers on the legality of the Suez escapade (as he might be expected to have done), preferring that of his Lord Chancellor, Lord Kilmuir, an indifferent lawyer who could be trusted to tow Eden's line. That would have placed Sir Harry at the very forefront of searing political controversy, the heat of which had but faintly died down two years on.

As Speaker Hylton-Foster was a great success. His immediate successor, Horace King, wrote of him. He

> "ruled the House with urbanity and charm, always calm and unruffled, master of the understatement. He appeared to carry the burden of his office lightly, with the saving grace of not taking himself too seriously."

After the 1964 Election he was re-elected Speaker of the new Parliament with the Labour Party now in office. The following year he presided over the celebrations to mark the 700th anniversary of Simon de Montfort's Parliament but died suddenly in September of that year precipitating a crisis for the Government. Its majority in the House was as thin as the proverbial wafer and the loss of one of its own backbenchers to the Speaker's Chair made inevitable an early General Election.

But to return to 1951. Ted Hutchinson felt well able to assure the Moores that briefing Hylton-Foster would represent the wisest investment of the proceeds of the farm if Alfred was to enjoy any prospect of living out his allotted span. The notion behind the briefing of an advocate independent of the instructing solicitor is to bring to bear to the case that good judgement which arises from emotional detachment and Hylton-Foster brought that all right. It was a detachment born of the aloofness of elitism but, more worryingly, when briefed to defend in a capital case involving the slaying of two on-duty police officers, a conservative enthusiasm for the rope, an unwaivering belief in the integrity of all police officers and a refusal to countenance any doubt as to the credibility of police evidence.

In fact it was not actually detachment at all that Hylton-Foster brought to bear to the case but an instinctive antipathy to the client he was being paid to represent. The 'cab rank rule', requiring barristers not to refuse a brief in any area of the law in which they hold themselves out as competent, meant that once briefed Hylton-Foster had no option but to take on the case. Always more at home when prosecuting than defending this was a brief accepted by Sir Harry with a distinct lack of enthusiasm.

It was a lack of enthusiasm possibly mitigated in part by the 100 guinea fee marked on the back sheet to the brief, plus 2 more guineas for the pre-trial consultation and daily 'refreshers' of yet more money for each day (or part) that the trial lasted beyond that on which it opened. All Barristers' fees at this time, and indeed right up to decimalisation at the start of the 1970's, were calculated in guineas (£1 and 1 shilling in old money, £1-05p in that of today) with the 'bobs' (shillings) 'on the guineas' being the perk of the Barrister's Clerk, in addition to his 10% cut of the brief fee for arranging the affairs of his master. However uncomplicated the case a Leader could only appear with a Junior and his fee was a non-negotiable two-thirds of that of his Leader. Restrictive practices were by no means the prerogative of blue collar trade unions in 1951. With the fees in addition of the solicitor and the firearms expert, instructed to report for the defence but not called to give evidence at the trial, in the money of today the price of Moore's defence works out at a conservative £250,000. Little or nothing was left over from the proceeds of sale of Whinney Close Farm.

Whether Hylton-Foster proved best value for his money may be open to doubt. Ted Hutchinson certainly did. In the hostile environment of the Huddersfield of the late summer and autumn of 1951 the few leads that were capable of being followed were pursued with vigour. Together with Ray Dean, not yet formally retained but with the promise of his first capital Brief to follow, the hills and environs of Whinney Close Farm were traversed over many hours, not in any kind of search for evidence but so that the geographical implications of the evidence which would have to be met at the Assize Court would be appreciated and any shortcomings exposed.

Following the Committal Hearing the Briefs to Counsel were prepared and delivered. Conferences at Armley Goal with the prisoner were a regular feature of Ted and Ray's professional life. Consultation with the London Leader would, as was common practice, await the very eve of the trial. Thus would be avoided any possibility of his professional detachment being compromised. For the Leader even to meet the 'lay client' (so called as not to be confused with the solicitor – the professional client) face to face was a relatively recent innovation and, when it happened, tended to be rather more in the way of an audience granted by a great man who would hold forth on his own greatness, sometimes with thinly disguised derision for the standard of preparation of the case before his own distinguished arrival on the scene.

By the time for the Consultation with Leading Counsel had arrived, however, Hylton-Foster was the thorough master of his brief. He had pored over the ten pages of Ted's analysis of the case, the nine pages of Alfred's proof, the statement of the evidence he was expected to give at his trial, and the further statements of two supporting witnesses with, on the face of it, important evidence to give but who were not called to give that evidence at the trial. The instructions argued the case for the defence, highlighting its strengths, seeking to explain away its weaknesses. It made many points and many good and valid points; it made some that were dubious and others that were downright bad. But for effort it was an alpha plus document. Unsurprisingly the search of fields and farm and the conspicuous failure to recover the murder weapon was rehearsed by Ted in vivid Technicolor:

> *The police remained in possession of the farm for 14 days. They demolished walls (on the land and in the house), cut down trees, mowed the grass, emptied feeding troughs; made with the assistance of the Royal Engineers with their mine detectors a most thorough but unsuccessful search for a weapon. Furniture and crockery were broken in what can only be described as vandalism. A force of at least 50 policemen under the command of almost every officer of high rank in the West Riding constabulary took part. This force was constantly maintained and relays were*

brought three or four times a day. Full arrangements were made for the feeding of the men and a mobile canteen was placed in Stancliffe's yard. The weapon is still missing.

This triumphalist passage in the brief remains unblemished by annotation in the neat, crabbed hand of Hylton-Foster. Not so those paragraphs where instructing solicitor seeks to suggest weaknesses in the Crown's case. Here the natural instincts of a prosecutor are evident. Where the instructions make the point that, apart from the evidence of identification, the case for the prosecution is otherwise "entirely circumstantial" Hylton-Foster's marginal note reads –

No. The statements of the accused.

No doubt a reference to the police account of verbal statements attributed by police evidence to Moore following his arrest. The point that keys found in the fields have not been shown to fit any lock at the farm receives -

But they are skeleton keys.

The suggestion that there is at least a degree of confusion in the deposition of the dying constable –

What is confused about it.

Where the instructions pose the question- if Moore thought he had heard the noise of a cow why did he duck under the hedge?

Oh no. This is meant to be a kind of a joke.

These are all cogent points and mostly well made and Counsel who goes into Court to make bad points that are inevitably and devastatingly going to be exposed as bad points does his case no favours. The concern remains, however, that this advocate would have felt more comfortable prosecuting rather than defending his client and that such was his frame of mind from the moment that the pink ribbon around his brief was untied and its pages first turned. Meeting his client later for the first time did nothing at all to cause Hylton-Foster to warm to the task of saving his client's neck from the hangman's noose.

On the day before the trial was to begin Hylton-Foster travelled north. His junior had already met Moore on a number of occasions at Armley Prison in the presence of Ted Hutchinson when the evidence had been discussed, pored over, the strengths and weaknesses of both prosecution and defence analysed. But this Sunday evening consultation was the occasion for Moore to be introduced to the Great Man himself, the London Silk who would lead for the defence. Ray Dean recounts in his memoir of circuit life and anecdotes, published privately following his retirement from the circuit bench, how he shared a taxi with Hylton on the journey from Armley Gaol into the centre of Leeds after the Consultation and of the revealing conversation between the two of them. Ray was asked by Hylton "What did you make of Alfred Moore?" and responded "He didn't strike me as a villain, still less a violent one." This was not what Hylton expected to hear from a loyal and competent junior. It provoked a truly astonishing, indeed disgraceful and unworthy, outburst. This was hours before his client, paying over the entire assets of the family for his defence, was due to stand trial on the outcome of which his life might be forfeit and four young children orphaned. The mask of aloof professional detachment more than slipped, it clamoured to the ground.

"Dean" (Counsel in those days never addressed each other as 'Mr' and only by a first name where the professional relationship had at least achieved the status of an acquaintanceship) "Moore is a very wicked man. Never allow your emotion to interfere with your judgement. *I could hang him myself.*"

On the eve of the trial Hylton-Foster slept soundly with no concerns about a dreadful outcome for his client, secure in the knowledge that he at least had not permitted emotion, worse sentimentality, to interfere with his judgement. Should, for any reason, the hangman be unavailable he was more than emotionally ready and eager to step into the breach.

18 – 'Albert' and the Judge

You've heard of that seaside place called Blackpool,
It's noted for fresh air and fun,
Mr and Mrs Ramsbottom went there
with young Albert their son.
'Albert and the Lion' - Music Hall Monologue.

It was in November 1951 that the West Riding Autumn Assize, held in the Town Hall at Leeds, opened with the reading of the Ancient Commission of General Gaol Delivery in which the Sovereign directed his "trusty and well-beloved" judges to empty the local prisons. The Commission dated back to an age when imprisonment as a punishment option was not one generally available to a court: those convicted, if fortunate, were destined for a new life in the Antipodes by way of deportation. And so the Commission was to empty, "deliver" that is, the gaols of their prisoners. In 1951 the objective was to fill them up.

Commission Day was one devoted in its entirety to ceremony and pageantry. The Commission having been read, the three judges, two from the King's Bench Division and the third the Probate, Divorce and Admiralty Division of the High Court, retired to be entertained on a scale bordering on the lavish by the High Sheriff of the County. The days of post-war austerity were all but over. The work proper of the Assize would begin the following day. The case listed as 'Rex v Alfred Moore' was not expected to be reached until the closing days of the Assize.

The best that may be said of this trial is that it was conducted according to the standards of the time. Standards change with time and no more so than in the field of criminal justice. This was a trial bearing far more in common with one taking place one hundred years earlier than one fifty years later. The name of the game was proof: was the allegation of murder capable of being proved by the evidence? That was the question and the only question. It was not a question which, in the light of the deposition effectively unchallenged at the time and no longer capable of challenge, only ever realistically allowed of one answer. The forensic exercise marked 'proof' dehumanised defendants, turned them into objects, mere incidental bit-part players in the drama, not as human beings on trial for their life, guilt assumed but requiring the formality of proof.

In almost the final act of this drama, three days into the trial and as defence counsel was about to resume his seat following an impassioned plea to the jury to conclude not that innocence had been vindicated but that the evidence fell short of satisfactory proof, a remarkable exchange occurred between the judge and counsel for the prosecution vividly illustrating the lowly status of the defendant in the trial process -

"Mr Hinchcliffe, as a matter of detail is it right to say that the prisoner's name is Alfred Moore?"

Counsel confirmed that indeed it was and the judge to make assurance doubly sure added -

"Not Albert Moore?"

For confusion as to the name of the prisoner on trial for his life to permeate three days of evidence was an exercise in sheer bad manners on the part of all concerned; for it to be described as 'a matter of detail' one of insensitivity on the part of a judge who was to show later that same day that he was acutely sensitive to the duty demanded of him. To the face of Alfred it brought a wry smile in the midst of his ordeal for in former days, when his passion for poultry vied with that for ballroom dancing, he was a regular at the northern Mecca of the art, the Tower Ballroom at Blackpool and in that same seaside town the same confusion as to his name regularly arose and in the context of the then well-known monologue being quoted at him.

It was a confusion the origins of which it was not difficult to trace. In his death bed deposition Jagger had attributed to Inspector Fraser as he confronted the killer the words -

"Are you Moore, Albert Moore?"

Whoever it might have been who was confronted that night the fact that the killer, immediately before the fatal shots were fired, responded that that indeed was his identity was never sought to be relied upon as grounds to exonerate *Alfred* Moore. That would have represented a threadbare and unrealistic argument. Yet almost to the very end it served to confuse those who ought to have known better.

The gallery of the court had been opened half an hour before the trial was scheduled to begin and within moments had been filled to capacity. A capital trial could always be expected to bring in the crowds, just in the same way that a century earlier public executions had done; crowds drawn from far, travelling on the 'execution excursions' operated by the railway companies, as well as near. That vicarious, ghoulish excitement being denied the next best thing for many was a trial with a prospect of the drama of the black cap. Of course, there were those in that gallery with a genuine, legitimate interest in the trial. Amongst those was Alice Moore, reported that evening in the *Huddersfield Examiner* to be wearing a grey coat and, on a day which saw the first snowfall of the winter, that most fashionable adornment of the 1950's but today worn at peril of vilification, a brown fur cape. To many who read the description it served only to confirm a belief that here was a family for whom crime paid. Others noted not the fur cape but Alice's companions that day, described as "friends of the family" they were identified as Mr and Mrs Norris Bennett, the local Kirkheaton newsagents. The village was already awash with rumours about the apparently increasingly close friendship between the wife of the farmer, removed to Leeds for the past five months, and Mr Norris Bennett; seemingly the rumours had not reached the ears of Mrs Bennett. For the afternoon sitting of the court Alice Moore had been moved by some sympathetic court official to the well of the court in a seat just in front of the dock and immediately behind counsel's row. There she remained for the duration of the trial except, that is, for the endgame when she was not present.

At precisely 10-30 a.m. three knocks on the door leading onto the judge's bench of the number one courtroom signalled the entry into court of the judge, the Honourable Mr Justice Pearson. This was the court room known as the Crown Court, twenty years before the Crown Court replaced nationally the system of Assizes and Quarter Sessions. It was so designated because it was the courtroom in which the criminal business of the Assize was conducted; other courtrooms in the building were reserved for the trial of civil suits. All were commanded to rise and if 'having business to do before His Majesty's Judges of Assize to draw near and give attendance'. The judge wore the red robes of his office and carried the traditional white gloves and, more sinisterly, the square of black cloth that this newly appointed judge of the King's Bench Division of the High Court had not yet had the occasion to don. Many present in court had little doubt that it would shortly come into play.

The calendar of this assize was a particularly heavy one with 188 criminal cases, 88 civil actions to be disposed of as well as 42 defended divorce cases. Three judges had been sent from London to dispose of the work including no lesser personage than Lord Goddard, Lord Chief Justice of England and Wales, a judge renowned for expedition, sternness tempered only by severity and an enthusiasm for the rope and the lash. It was widely believed that a high profile trial involving the shooting dead of two police officers in the execution of their duty would be listed before 'the Chief' but in fact it was to the most recent recruit to the ranks of the King's Bench that it was entrusted. Goddard would still have a role to play but it was not to be at the Assize Court in Leeds.

Colin Hargreaves Pearson was the son of a lawyer as to which nothing surprising there; law was a profession pursued in many families from one generation to another. What was surprising was that he was a Canadian by birth, the family not returning to the mother country until 1906 when Colin was seven years of age. Following an education at the prestigious St. Paul's School he went on to serve his country in the final months of the Great War, a conflict in which his older brother lost his life, before an illustrious career as classical scholar at Balliol College, Oxford. Called to the Bar by the Inner Temple in 1924 he quickly built up a sizeable common law practice and, although never a high profile advocate, he was appointed to the High Court at the relatively young age of 52. To the task, according to the Dictionary of National Biography, he brought a clear mind, profound legal knowledge and unfailing courtesy. After nine years he was promoted to Lord Justice of the Court of Appeal and further promoted in 1965 to the House of Lords as Lord of Appeal-in-Ordinary. But it was as a committee man that Colin Pearson came into his own and his name to wider public attention. Viewed by Government as a 'safe pair of hands' he conducted a wide range of public enquiries, most notably in 1973 a monumental Royal Commission into compensation for personal injury. His enquiry was wide-ranging, collecting evidence both at home and abroad, lasted some five years and made radical proposals for compensation without fault for the victims of road accidents and defective products. He died in 1980 with his recommendations unfulfilled and resignation that the strength of vested interests opposed to change would destine his report to gather dust on some Whitehall shelf. There indeed it remains.

The Autumn Assize of 1951 was his first visit to Leeds but in fact the first of many. His distinctive eyebrows gave him a feline appearance and to the local legal profession he became affectionately known as 'Pussy' Pearson.

The judge in place on the bench the prisoner was brought up into the dock, wearing the same brown suit that he had worn for the hearings in Huddersfield with blue shirt and mottled blue tie. Throughout the trial he listened intently, without any evident show of emotion, to the proceedings, his arms either folded or clasped around his knees. Ted Hutchinson and his young son Arthur, taking an early Christmas break from school but with the excuse that it was good work experience for a career at the Bar for which both he and his fond parents aspired, sat just below the dock and, at regular intervals, the client leant forward to provide whispered instructions then communicated by notes passed to counsel.

Moore was asked by the Clerk of the Assize, Mr Radcliffe, to confirm that he was Alfred Moore whereupon the one charge on the indictment, that on July 15, 1951, in the West Riding Division of the County of York, he murdered Duncan Alexander Fraser, was read and Moore responded 'Not guilty, My Lord'. The plea was recorded in manuscript on the indictment in just one word – 'puts'. A strange word for recording a plea of 'not guilty' but one readily explained by what followed.

The prisoner was next informed of his right to challenge any juror whose name was about to be called. Twelve names were called, no challenges were issued and twelve jurors, ten men and two women, were duly sworn to decide the fate of the poultry farmer. The ancient ceremonials were not yet over however. The jury still needed to be <u>*put*</u> in charge of the prisoner and now they were addressed directly by the Clerk of the Assize, immediately forgetting the name of the prisoner correctly recorded on the indictment read by him moments earlier –

> "Members of the jury, this prisoner, *Albert* Moore, stands charged upon this indictment with murder. Upon this indictment he has been arraigned and upon his arraignment he has pleaded not guilty, thereby *putting himself upon his country,* which country

> ye are. Your charge it is therefore to enquire whether he be guilty or no and to hearken to the evidence."

The stage had been set. The seeds sown for confusion as to the name of the prisoner which was to permeate his trial. His defence team did nothing to seek to set the record straight.

In its report of the proceedings in the local Huddersfield newspaper that evening the fact that the only charge put was the murder of Inspector Fraser was noted but not further remarked upon. At the trial itself no effort was ever made to explain to the jury why it was that they were hearing of two murders but only being asked to deliver a verdict in respect of one. The explanation lies in the 'one felony rule' whereby no indictment might charge more than one murder and was a procedural rule associated with capital punishment and disappeared with its abolition. After all you could only hang somebody once.

The formalities over G. Raymond Hinchcliffe K.C. rose to address the jury, to introduce to them the case they would have to determine. It was he told them a case involving "a most callous and shocking murder." The victim of the charge of murder with which they were concerned was "experienced and distinguished." The fact of the cordon was explained and that which was crucial to the Crown's case, the time at which it was in place, namely, 11-45pm and not a moment later. But it was an opening speech which was to leave many questions hanging in the air at least so far as the jury was concerned.

The defence knew perfectly well why the cordon was in place and would no doubt have wished for this information to go before the jury at the earliest possible stage; the earlier they knew the longer they had to acclimatise to that which did no favours for the prisoner. But the rules of evidence in 1951 effectively prevented the prosecution from introducing evidence of a defendant's bad character in all but the most exceptional circumstances. There is no such squeamishness today; Alfred's night job as burglar would be admitted as 'important explanatory evidence'. In this instance it was to be the shield by which the defence would seek to explain the apparently incriminating remarks made by Moore at and following his apprehension, as well as his efforts at destroying evidence between the shooting dead of the officers and his arrest. When evidence of bad character is introduced today as 'important explanatory evidence' it is to explain something which the defence would prefer remained unexplained. But here the defence were eager for the information about their client's past disreputable criminal conduct to be before the jury and, once it was, their constant refrain became 'burglar yes, murderer certainly not'. It was, of course, something of a double-edged sword and the prosecution would return, with devastating effect, to Moore the burglar's motive for shooting the officers. The defence, however, would not long be denied the opportunity to place this evidence before the court.

Having dealt with the cordon Hinchcliffe went on to describe the lie of the land, pointing out that the footpath across the fields leading to Whinney Close Farm was not the sort of footpath to be used by some stranger to the farm at dead of night. It was not further stated that if it wasn't a stranger then it must have been someone with a connection to the premises and what better candidate than the proprietor. There was no reason for it to be spelled out. The jury could work it out for themselves and the point that juries will always consider to be the strongest is the one that they believe is the sole product of their reasoning and which the professional advocate has completely missed.

The point never made by the defence was that someone, not a stranger to the premises but with business to transact with the criminal occupant of the farm, might wish to approach it under cover of darkness, and not by means of the open highway. There would be no burglars without other criminals ready and willing to 'fence' the proceeds of their offending and if Moore was not the killer and it was indeed someone who after the deed had fled away from the cordon rather than inside it, the obvious candidate would be some criminal associate of Moore – possibly his 'fence', possibly his 'wheels'. Moore never drove a motor-car in his life and someone had to have been available to drive him to and from the scene of his numerous crimes. However, it is not open to counsel to be unduly creative and inventive in their arguments; they may only advance the defence in accordance with their instructions and Alfred's instructions were clear and consistent that not only was he not the killer he had absolutely no idea who the killer might be. So this was a line of argument effectively closed down by Moore himself.

Having briefly described the confrontation between the officers and their killer Counsel turned to the evidence of the officer who did not immediately succumb to his injuries. Evidently there was to be no argument by the defence directed to the unfairness of admitting, as the crucial evidence in the case, that which was beyond challenge and which never had been challenged in any meaningful or effective way. The jury having been told that Jagger remained conscious at the scene they were then told that he was able to speak to another officer, Police Constable Sellick. What he had to say at this point was not, unlike his death bed deposition, on oath and so, with a great show of forensic piety, Counsel informed them: "I am not at liberty to tell you what it was he said because it would not be evidence" then, leaving absolutely nothing to the imagination "but as the result of what he said the officer ran in the direction of the prisoner's farm."

The closing in of the cordon, the smoke emanating from the chimney, the shouted conversation between Superintendent Metcalfe and Alice Moore, with her husband *Albert* cowering behind her, were summarily described before counsel turned to the *piece de resistance* of the Crown's case. And it was some introduction. The jury must have wondered just how and why Jagger did not survive being shot for he was, late on the Sunday afternoon, according to counsel, "as bright as ever" and "mentally alert with a pulse of good volume." And this was no mere assertion by counsel, nor the opinion of any ordinary medical practitioner but that of a "distinguished surgeon."

With this introduction counsel began to read –

Arthur Gordon Jagger says: I am a Police Constable ....

The reading of the deposition halted as Mr Hylton-Foster rose languidly to his feet. Were the jury to be asked to leave Court whilst objection to the admissibility of the evidence was argued? If this was to be the case counsel's timing was surely odd. But no such objection was to be raised and the interjection which followed utterly pointless, serving only on the face of it to indicate that counsel had failed before the trial opened to do that which, if he was minded to do it, he ought already to have done:

> "I did not know my friend was going to read it in opening. I suppose I ought to ask if I might see the original deposition."

Manifestly there never could have been any objection to such a request; the document was handed to defence counsel and a brief pretence at confirming that the formalities were in order followed concluding with Hylton-Foster lamely observing – "I am obliged."

The intervention could only have whetted the appetite of the jury for that which was to follow and they listened with an enhanced anticipation as the damning evidence of the prisoner's guilt, which they now knew lay beyond sensible dispute, was read to them. It would be surprising if minds were not already being made up.

In the course of an unnecessarily detailed description of the entry points of the bullets into the bodies of the dead officers and the recovery from both the bodies and the scene of bullets and cartridge cases, counsel contrived to introduce the most unfortunate omission from what otherwise was proof positive of the prisoner's guilt. It was a throwaway line –

"It remains only for me to tell you that the weapon which fired the bullets that killed the officers has never been found."

It was a bland statement, delivered without explanation of the detailed search which had failed to deliver up the murder weapon; without apology, with no suggestion that in weighing the evidence the jury might just wish to put this fact in the scale marked 'defence'. Not even that it might give them pause for thought. Rather this failure of proof was somehow attributed to the failure of the defendant to reveal its whereabouts –

"In asking yourselves what has happened to the murder weapon you may wish to consider that the prisoner when asked what firearms he possessed replied 'Oh! my head is bad. Don't talk about it. It's awful.' "

It was an observation that was doubly reprehensible for it drove the metaphorical 'coach and four' through the prisoner's unconditional right to remain silent and, worse, far worse, made an assumption of Moore's guilt because only a guilty man would be able to disclose the whereabouts of the murder weapon. The assumption underpinning the very foundations of our criminal justice system, then as now, is that until such time as a jury of twelve pronounce otherwise the prisoner is innocent. Counsel for the defence, who had earlier stood to make a pointless intervention concerning the dying deposition, remained seated.

No such coyness was displayed by Mr Hinchcliffe in describing that which the search did reveal. On the route along which the killer had fled were found a double-ended skeleton key, three keys on a ring and a jack knife, none of them showing signs such as rust to indicate that they had been there for any appreciable length of time. Why the killer might have been in possession of such articles and why, if the killer was the occupant of the farm, he might wish to discard them *en route* rather than secrete them somewhere in a building which the prosecution were later repeatedly to assert was impossible to search thoroughly without taking it apart stone by stone brick by brick, were again questions left hanging in the air.

Of more obvious relevance to the jury's task was the recovery from within a mound of loose bricks in the farmyard of a round of unfired 9 millimetre ammunition and from a cavity wall inside the building two discharged cartridge cases of the same calibre, broken cobwebs indicating that they had recently been placed there. Yet another similar discharged cartridge case was recovered from the tallboy in the bedroom. This time the relevance of the finds was spelled out. All of the discharged cartridges had markings upon them similar to those recovered both from the murder scene and the bodies of the dead officers indicating, according to the prosecution, that all had been fired from the murder weapon.

The opening address concluded without explanation to the jury of some of the fundamentals of the task ahead (as would undoubtedly happen today even in a trial of the most trivial proportions) - that the jury might only convict if, on consideration of all the evidence, they were satisfied so that they felt sure of guilt beyond reasonable doubt; that it was to the evidence that the court was now turning and on that evidence alone, not addresses by counsel, would the jury decide their verdict. Instead an assertion that blandly pre-judged that which was yet to come. The jury would, Mr Hinchcliffe told them, "be satisfied beyond reasonable doubt that it was the prisoner and no-one else who murdered Inspector Fraser."

Before that inevitable conclusion, however, lay the formalities of proof.

19 – Proof

The trial of Alfred Moore proceeded with an expedition that would today be envied by a court administrator coping with an ever increasing workload, trials becoming longer and more complex and diminishing resources available to meet demand. It lasted just three days and heard a total of thirty-three witnesses. A similar trial today might be expected to last many weeks, if not months, with its smooth running interrupted by delays arising from the need to argue points of law and admissibility of evidence in the absence of the jury and ensure that no-one is avoidably inconvenienced; today if counsel has to appear in another court then the court will wait, if a witness or a juror has some prior appointment, then the court does not sit. In the mega trials courts have been known to rise for a month in the summer so that all concerned might take a well-earned break.

In 1951 the only convenience recognised was that of the judge. The paramount concern was that the judges disposed of the list and moved on to the next city on the assize circuit without delay. This trial proceeded without interruption until its completion, the court sitting continuously during each morning and afternoon session. There were no 'comfort' breaks as they are euphemistically termed. At no stage were the jury invited to leave court whilst points of law were argued, indeed no points of law were argued.

The evidence opened with the formalities of calling the drawer of the plan and the photographers to produce the various albums that were to be referred to repeatedly during the trial. No expense had been spared. A number of the photographs of the scene had been taken from an aeroplane chartered for the purpose. In 1951 there was no such thing as a dedicated police helicopter on hand for the task.

When the prosecution sought to place before the jury *post mortem* photographs of the bodies of the two dead officers no formal objection was raised by Hylton-Foster but rather a polite and highly effective enquiry as to whether "at this stage" this was likely to prove of assistance to the jury. Counsel knew full well that nothing was more calculated to inflame passions than the sight of dead bodies laid out on a mortuary slab, life snuffed out, extinct; and the potential of such photographs to prove or even illustrate anything likely to assist the jury in their task is usually at best tenuous. Mr Black, who had temporarily taken charge of the case following the exertions of his leader in his opening address, did not press the point and the judge took the hint, at the same time leaving open the possibility that circumstances might change.

"At some stage they may have some materiality along with other evidence. I am not for a moment indicating what. If they are to be produced they need not be over-stressed. They can be taken very quickly. It is not very pleasant to look at the bodies of wounded men."

The formalities complete Mr Hinchcliffe resumed conduct of the Crown's case turning to the evidence intended to show that Moore, returning home at the time he asserted, must have hit the cordon and, as he did not, he returned home much later – in fact at the time the officers were shot.

Both Charles Henry and Alice Mahala Moore gave their evidence without deviation from the depositions sworn by them earlier at the Court in Huddersfield. Charles Henry recounted the route taken on the walk to Almondbury with estimated times at which the journey began and concluded; the point at which they parted company and the words spoken by Alfred "it's bad luck to turn back" which proved to be anything but prophetic; finally the time of his arrival home to face the indomitable Alice Mahala. Her appearance on the stand was even briefer than when she had testified at the committal hearing, confirming simply the time at which her husband had returned home and that it was by reference to a clock that was correct to three minutes either way.

The real drama of the trial began with the cross-examination of Charles Henry. During the weeks and months since the slaying of the officers, rumour, gossip and mounting speculation was rife as to why a platoon of police officers were keeping watch on a lonely farmstead in the early hours of a July Sunday morning and exactly what the poultry farmer, believed to have been arrested if not in the act itself then almost so, would have to say in his defence. All was now about to be revealed. However, not immediately because the cross-examination began with a piece of dubious forensic artistry. "Have you ever seen your brother with a revolver?" he was asked. "No" came the reply. Charles Henry was then invited to place the air pistol which had been recovered and was an exhibit in the case inside the pocket of the gabardine being worn that night by his brother, to survey the bulge it caused and to agree that on the night no such bulge was visible to suggest that a weapon was being carried. That confirmation being forthcoming it was suggested that the route taken across the fields involved stiles being negotiated which would have accentuated any bulge that there might have been. Charles Henry was not a man to desert his brother in his hour of need and once more he eagerly provided confirmation. No doubt carried away by the success of this line of cross-examination Hylton-Foster then invited the police officer present in court who was in charge of the exhibits to don the gabardine with the pistol in its pocket but it was a forensic step too far –

"The belt will not fasten properly on the officer" observed Hylton-Foster.

It was good theatre but of dubious validity; the air pistol was not the murder weapon and the demonstration depended wholly on the supposition that if brother Alfred had been carrying a gun it would have been in one of the pockets of the garment rather than secreted elsewhere on his person. It was, however, of no less validity than the timings placed before the jury by the prosecution on the supposition that they were accurate to the second to found the assertion that Alfred could not have crossed the fields on his return home at the time he claimed without hitting the cordon.

The demonstration having reached its tame conclusion Counsel turned his attention to the task of disclosing details of the extra curricula activities of the Kirkheaton poultry farmer. There was no reason to suppose that Charles Henry had any prior knowledge of the matters as to which he was being asked (and if he had he was hardly going to admit it) and he was to respond throughout in the negative to the questions that were about to be asked of him. He was no more than the conduit for the defence to reveal at the earliest opportunity open to them the murky secret life of the prisoner, that which ideally the defence would not wish the jury to know but which it was inevitable they should know to begin to make sense of the fact of the police cordon around Whinney Close Farm and the comments made by the farmer following his arrest suggestive of his guilt of the crime of murder.

"To your knowledge did your brother have in his possession, usually kept in the wash kitchen under the sink, a cardboard box in which files and gauges and fragments of keys were kept?"

"I never saw such a thing".

"He is clever with his fingers, is he not, your brother?"

"Well, at woodworking and things like that".

"I meant playing with the works of watches?"

"I do not know".

"You did not know that he had been filing down and making skeleton keys?"

"No".

"And you did not know that on twelve different occasions he had broken into premises and stolen?"

"No, I did not".

Questions are not evidence, only answers and the answers given by Charles Henry proved nothing. However, the information had been adduced and placed before the jury; the tactic had succeeded in its objective and certainly the prosecution were not going to object to the jury knowing that Moore was a 'bad lot', unlikely to be a respecter of the forces of law and order, and certainly not a respectable, land-owning, law-abiding farmer.

Counsel turned finally to a line of questions, this time to establish important facts as evidence in the case. They were designed to show total absence of premeditation in Alfred's decision to savour the night air by accompanying his brother on his walk home. Charles Henry readily agreed that it was very much a spur of the moment decision when he had missed the last bus home and no sooner agreed upon than embarked upon. There was no realistic opportunity, for example, to take arms or, for that matter, the tools necessary to embark upon burgling.

Was anything said or done, Charles Henry was asked, to indicate the thoughts or intentions of the prisoner as to the length of time that he anticipated being away from the farm? Unhesitatingly Charles Henry told the jury that his brother's last words to his wife as they left together were –

"I shall only be about an hour."

A useful foundation had been laid for the proposition that the last thing on Alfred Moore's mind that night was burglary and that evidence, together with concessions that police witnesses were later obliged to make, that no premises in and about Huddersfield had been attacked that night effectively put an end to the idea that the motive for the attack was to avoid being confronted in possession of the proceeds of crime. The whole object of the cordon around Whinney Close Farm was, of course, to confront Moore in just such compromising circumstances. The prosecution were forced into the manifestly less tenuous argument that the motive of the defendant in shooting dead two police officers was to avoid a search of the farmhouse; it was not a motive that survived even cursory critical examination – the police had wholly insufficient grounds on which to enter and search otherwise a warrant would have been sought from a magistrate and the one thing that inevitably would take officers inside the premises was that which the prosecution were busy alleging had occurred. Furthermore, the evidence of Charles Henry, if it did not exactly provide a watertight alibi so far as times were concerned, certainly established that at worst his brother would in all probability have arrived home before midnight. The prosecution never did place before the jury any sensible explanation for what Moore might have been up to over a two hour period if he was not, as he consistently maintained, in bed at home.

Shortly before the mid-day adjournment on day one of the trial the prosecution commenced the task of calling to give their evidence the various police witnesses who had formed the cordon. Though important evidence it was not evidence that the defence, with instructions that their client was not in the fields approaching the farm at any time when the cordon was in place, could do very much to challenge. At most for defence counsel it was no more than an exercise in nibbling away at the edges, seeking any concession which might just advance the time at which it was being alleged that the cordon of officers was in position. It was essentially a fruitless exercise because, of course, each witness had been carefully schooled in the evidence he was to give on that which it had been emphasised was critical to the success of the prosecution.

The first police witness was Police Constable Sellick who was not only able to tell the jury that Jagger had taken up his position about a hundred yards away from Fraser but that it was at two or three minutes before 11-40 pm. Nothing was heard by the witness until at 1-55 am he heard five shots ring out, followed almost immediately by a faint blast from a police whistle. He ran straightaway to the position formerly occupied by Fraser but, finding that he was no longer there, ran in the direction of what he saw to be a faint light. He was the first officer at the scene of the carnage, two mortally wounded officers lying on the ground only one of whom was showing any signs of life. The pantomime of fairness and observance of the rule against admitting evidence of what was said by another, not on oath and away from the courtroom, the rule against hearsay, was duly enacted. Sellick confirmed that Jagger had spoken; and what did he do as a result?

"I ran in the direction of Whinney Close Farm."

So no prizes there for guessing at least the purport of what was said by the mortally wounded officer. Sellick concluded his evidence by recounting the exercise undertaken by him on the 3 September (following, of course, the committal hearing) of walking from the farm to the junction of Waterloo Rise and Fleminghouse Lane – 28 minutes there and 31 minutes back; and from the same junction to the home of Charles Henry and Alice Mahala at 23, Fernside Crescent – 6 ½ minutes.

The remainder of day one brought no surprises. Such cross-examination as took place consisted of cursorily taking the witness through the same evidence given in answer to the prosecution but this time via the medium of leading questions. It achieved nothing, was never likely to achieve anything and, for that matter, it was never anticipated that it would achieve anything. Counsel, however, was being paid, and paid handsomely, to ask questions and so questions had to be asked.

Counsel's efforts were much more effective in dealing with the evidence of witnesses who gave evidence concerning matters going beyond the circumstances immediately touching upon the shooting. One such witness was Police Constable Harry Taylor who appears to have been designated as exhibits officer. There was the little matter of the solitary white hair, just three-quarters of an inch in length, found on the accused's gabardine raincoat and which the evidence of a forensic scientist would pronounce similar to the head hair of Inspector Fraser. It was never claimed definitively to be from the head of the Inspector, merely that it was similar in appearance and certainly not inconsistent with it being a hair from Fraser's head. In reality it was a tenuous piece of evidence but it was, nonetheless, put forward as evidence of guilt and needed to be countered. The line of attack was to suggest the possibility of innocent cross-contamination. That being the chosen battleground

Hylton-Foster made a fair fist of establishing just that and with a witness who could see exactly where cross-examination was leading and ducked and dived in an effort to evade what was shown to be nothing more than a common sense conclusion. Yes, the witness had assisted the task of stretchering the body of Fraser from the scene of the shooting to the brickworks to await the arrival of an ambulance – but only had hold of the handles of the stretcher, not the body lying on it. Yes, the witness was responsible for handling the clothing of the stricken officers and throughout the events of the Sunday was himself wearing the same clothing. Yes, he was also responsible for bagging up the clothing of the prisoner so that it might be sent away for forensic examination – with the exception of the raincoat for some odd, unexplained reason. In re-examination Hinchcliffe sought to clarify when it was that the officer, in charge of the exhibits, had first encountered this most important of exhibits, bearing, as the prosecution asserted, evidence linking Moore to the crime. There followed a most curious answer –

"Just now. I had never seen it before".

Of course, the nearer that any officer on duty that night, especially one coming into close proximity with Fraser following the shooting, came to the gabardine raincoat the greater the likelihood of innocent cross-contamination.

The efforts of police witnesses to distance themselves from the raincoat reached truly ludicrous proportions when Detective Chief Inspector Arthur Leslie Jenkins, the officer in charge of the cordon and sharing responsibility for the exhibits in the case, was cross-examined.

"Did Sergeant Sadler go upstairs and look into the bedroom whilst you were below?"

"Yes. I told him to".

Hylton-Foster's comment preceding the next question was gratuitous, patrician, and unlikely to have impressed this West Riding jury.

"I dare say in the West Riding Police Force they sometimes do what they are told. That is what he did, is it not?"

"Yes".

"He went and brought down a jacket and a gabardine raincoat?"

"I do not remember him bringing a gabardine raincoat down".

Reluctantly the Chief Inspector agreed that he had seen the raincoat in the wardrobe when he himself went upstairs but, thereafter, not again until it was produced in the magistrates' court. And, so far as the jacket was concerned, the Chief Inspector, though reasonably confident that his recall was correct that nothing of any evidential value had been found upon it, nonetheless when questioned in detail decided apparently that the safer course was to distance himself from the jacket as well. He did not now recall this item being brought downstairs, only of seeing it when it was downstairs on the back of a chair and, furthermore, he never touched or came into particularly close proximity to it.

The cross-examination of Police Constable Taylor turned to explore an area of undoubted importance to the case but in respect of which it was an exercise in just that, an exercise in exploration, counsel plainly having no grounds to suppose that helpful evidence was likely to emerge and where the likely antagonism of the witness to the prisoner made it far more likely than not that the opportunity to inflict damage on the defence case would be seized upon.

"To what extent did Jagger know of the appearance of Alfred Moore?"

"He did not know him".

It was a devastating answer, giving an effective quietus to the argument that Jagger's bedside identification was flawed by reason of him knowing Moore prior to the night of the shooting and from his bed pointing out a familiar face, not necessarily the face of the man who had confronted and shot him in the small hours of the same day. The answer having been given Hylton-Foster engaged in damage limitation with a pretence that this was the very answer being sought by the defence, that no better answer to advance the defence case could have been given by the witness –

"He did not know him. I am obliged".

Cross-examination concluded with a series of questions that did no more than feebly go over by now well-trodden ground, underlining that which was familiar to all, the frantic chaos of whistle blowing and torch flashing, the rushing to and fro of police officers immediately following the five pistol shots that had pierced the night air. It was going to take far more than a picture of, understandable, chaos and confusion to cause this jury to doubt the correctness of the identification made by the dying, and now dead, witness.

A procession of officers from the cordon came and went through the witness box that afternoon, but none who could throw light on how the gabardine raincoat with the incriminatory strand of hair arrived into police custody. With some their evidence was not challenged at all and with others questions concentrated on areas of the case known to be safe ground for the defence. There were to be no further voyages of discovery into unchartered waters.

Some useful concessions were extracted from witnesses reluctant to concede anything of arguable value to the defendant and it became clear that the focus of defence interest and attention was to be the murder weapon, the failure to recover it, its availability to be recovered if, as the prosecution asserted, the killer had retreated into the cordon and the absence of any evidence in or about the farmhouse of steps having been taken to dispose of it. When Chief Inspector Jenkins was asked about the ashes in the grate he accepted that it consisted only of the remnants of the destruction by fire of paper and nothing else, absolutely nothing to suggest an attempt to melt down any metal item such as a cartridge or even a gun. It was safe ground because any such evidence, had it existed, would have been led as part of the Crown's case.

Hylton-Foster, having languidly and gratuitously commented that "no doubt a revolver is a tiresome thing to burn in a domestic grate" and "we may take it you would not miss anything of that kind", went on to ask a series of questions the relevance of which to the case was not apparent but as to which neither judge nor prosecution, allowing every leeway to the defence in a capital trial, objected. Despite a promise from counsel that in the fullness of time all would become clear it never did and remains to this day largely enigmatic, although access to evidence available to the prosecution but carefully withheld from the defence at the time, provides some clue.

The change of subject matter from ashes in the grate was abrupt and doubtless intended to unsettle the witness and minimise the time available to him to work out exactly where the defence were going.

"Is there an office at the brickworks?"

"I do not know. I have not been in it. There will be".

Evidently the first guess of the witness as to where it was all leading was a suggestion that the cordon may not have been so secure as was being claimed and that he and others had sought shelter from the rain in this office. That was not to be the suggestion though arguably it might have been.

"Have you reason to think that there was a safe in the office at the brickworks?

"Yes".

"Containing in all probability on that night cash?"

"There might have been, yes".

The questions now appeared to be leading to a revelation of some other aspect of the prisoner's criminal career but once more a sudden, unanticipated shift occurred.

"Did you produce to the wife of the accused on the Sunday afternoon a blue silk scarf?"

"Yes".

"And ask her a question about it?"

"I did".

"Did you in fact find that scarf wrapped round one of the electric lights at the brickworks?"

"No. I did not find that scarf".

"Some other person did?"

"Yes, but about three weeks before".

"Would it be possible to produce that scarf here before the end of this trial?"

"As far as I know it would".

Alice Moore had provided the defence with a statement about the events of the night and it had been included in counsel's brief but it included no reference to a silk scarf blue or otherwise. Evidently she had conveyed this information to Ted Hutchinson at the last minute and counsel had taken the view that there was something in it worthy of being pursued though what it might have been is far from easy to discern. Cross-examination about the silk scarf ended on an enigmatic note with Hylton-Foster observing –

"Its relevance would not have been apparent to the prosecution. Perhaps you could assist me with that before the end".

The Chief Inspector reiterated his belief that the silk scarf could be found and cross-examination turned to a different topic. In fact nothing more was heard about the silk scarf. No doubt in the face of the assurances given it was made available to the defence but apparently the defence had second thoughts about pursuing the matter further. Even with information available today which explains why, on that Sunday, the Chief Inspector might well have been interested in exploring with Alice Moore questions relating to a silk scarf, the relevance of such an item being recovered wrapped around an electric light at the brickworks three weeks before the shooting is impossible to guess.

By the middle of the afternoon the prospect of anything either new or exciting emerging from the evidence of the officers who had formed the cordon around Whinney Close Farm had been firmly extinguished and it was with a sense of relief from boredom that the court turned its attention to the medical evidence, unlikely to prove uplifting or pleasant but at least it was a new topic.

Without further objection from the defence exhibit 6, the album of photographs of the dead officers lying on hospital mortuary slabs, was handed out to the jury. At least they were spared the photographs taken during the course of the *post mortem* examinations and which, in gruesome detail, recorded the exploration made by the pathologist's scalpel through the inner tissues and organs of the bodies in an endeavour to ascertain the track each bullet had taken as it terminated the lives of those bodies.

So far as Constable Jagger was concerned the medical evidence was both *ante* and *post mortem* and it was the *ante* evidence which gave rise to the only real argument that the defence ever made to the admissibility of evidence at this trial. The exchanges were brief but telling and conducted without any suggestion that the jury be asked to withdraw whilst it was considered, a useful precaution it might be thought because there seems little point in ruling inadmissible that which the jury already know. True, the actual evidence was not referred to in terms but what was said made abundantly clear that Mr James Hall Wrigley, the surgeon who had attended Jagger on his arrival and throughout his stay at the Infirmary, was prepared to testify to his medical competency to give a cogent and lucid account of events at the time that his deposition was recorded. It was evidence known to lawyers as 'oath-helping' and it has been long-established that a witness might not be called to give evidence simply to say that another witness is credible or reliable. It is one way of keeping evidence at a trial within reasonable bounds because if witnesses were permitted to say not merely what happened but that the testimony of another witness was creditworthy there would be no end to many criminal trials. In any event, the creditworthiness of a witness is always for the jury, as arbiters of the evidence, to decide and no-one else. The problem here of course was that this jury never did have available to them any of the conventional tools for assessing credibility, the principal of which are appearance and demeanour in the witness box.

Hinchcliffe having confirmed with the witness that Jagger was conscious on his admission continued with a question that was a blatant breach of the 'oath-helping' prohibition –

"Was he able to give a good history of what had happened?"

Before the witness could answer Hylton-Foster was on his feet –

"At this point I think I rightly object, My Lord. I am unable to understand to what relevant issue this evidence is directed. You cannot in a criminal trial give evidence in support of the credit of a witness. That is all this is. This is a witness who was examined before a Justice and who gave evidence on oath. No question arises as to his mental or physical capacity to give evidence on oath – at this stage at all events".

The submission was manifestly well-founded in law but Crown Counsel and future judge of the High Court totally missed the point –

"The only reason this evidence is tendered is as to the state of Police Constable Jagger's mind when he gave evidence before a magistrate".

The trial judge and future Law Lord had the point however and had noted particularly the concluding words of Hylton-Foster's objection ('at this stage at all events'). The defence were not closing the door on the possibility of impugning the credit of the dying constable and so his ruling was terse and to the point –

"I suppose it depends on what line is taken up by the defence. This evidence is in a sense admissible – on a possible line the defence may or may not adopt. It looks to me as if the objection is theoretically sound at any rate. Would it not be right to wait and see what line the defence take. It is to a certain extent bound to be inconvenient".

The convenience being referred to was not that of the prisoner on trial for his life but of the witness who just might have to return to court to give the evidence that, by now, no one in court doubted he was prepared to give, namely, that the Constable whose span of future life was measured in hours was, nonetheless, sound in mind and body and as able as the next man to give sound, reliable testimony.

Hinchcliffe, who had utterly failed to appreciate either what was objectionable about his question or even the proper objection that had been taken to it, now adopted an obsequious acknowledgement of His Lordship's wisdom –

"I quite appreciate what your Lordship says".

The tentative ruling of the judge was now firmed up –

"We shall have to wait and see. The witness might have to be recalled".

When counsel enquired whether his witness might be released for the remainder of the day the judge agreed that he might, but either in anticipation of the defence later attacking the reliability of the evidence given by the dying officer or, just possibly, to flush out the defence the judge added the proviso that the witness should be available to be recalled if required at some later stage. Hylton-Foster promptly hauled up the white flag of surrender –

"To the best of my knowledge, information and belief there will not be any question of needing Mr Wrigley back".

Even with that categoric assurance, effectively closing down even any comment upon the reliability of the critical identification, the judge confirmed with the witness that he would be available to return to court - if required.

By plain inference the jury now knew that were the issue of Constable Jagger's competence to testify from his hospital bed to be raised the prosecution were in a position to counter it and with the best possible evidence, that of his treating physician. The defence knew it as well; they had been placed in the position of being required to make objection, what was acknowledged by the judge to be a proper objection, which resulted in the jury leaving court that day not only with the knowledge that the prisoner had been definitively identified as the killer but with any doubts as to the reliability of the evidence of a mortally wounded hospital patient laid to rest. The court moved on to other evidence. Nothing more was heard on the issue and no further question arose of the witness being recalled.

Evidence of the cause of death was presented by the Pathologist, University Lecturer, Staff Surgeon to the West Riding Constabulary and local eminent expert witness in virtually all murder trials at the time, Dr. David Ernest Price. His evidence was entirely uncontroversial and Hylton-Foster asked only a few questions about a routine examination carried out by him on the Sunday evening at the police station of the defendant 'Albert' Moore (plainly it had been a long day and the concentration of counsel was waning). Dr. Price confirmed that the prisoner showed no signs of significant injury and that he had taken a sample of his head hair. As there was nothing in the prosecution account of events to suggest that the killer, whoever he was, might have sustained injury in the fatal encounter it was, and remains, difficult to understand what the defence might have been seeking to establish and the hair sample served simply to underline that whoever's strand of hair it was that was recovered from the gabardine raincoat the possibility that it might be that of the defendant himself could be eliminated.

The afternoon was drawing to a close but the prosecution were determined that the proceedings for the day should not conclude without the jury hearing for a second time that day the virtual evidence, given from beyond the grave, of the dead constable. The evidence of an officer present when Jagger's deposition was taken was formally called at the conclusion of which Mr Norman Black turned to the Judge and asserted with a confidence, plainly justified, that "the foundation has now been laid for the reading of P.C. Jagger's deposition." It had of course already been read and the further citation by counsel of the relevant Act of Parliament to be found in the relevant paragraph of the current edition of 'Archbold' (the criminal practitioner's Bible) was no more than a public show of learning. The learned judge did not even find it necessary to consult the learned tome beside him on the bench, merely observing and thinking aloud –

"What you say is that this deposition was in substance taken in the ordinary way before a magistrate and that now, owing to his death, which has been proved, that sub-section 13 of section 3 applies? Yes, unless the contrary is argued I should have thought that it did".

There was an invitation there to try to argue to the contrary but also an implicit suggestion that such an argument would need to be highly persuasive and tap something that the learned judge was unable to envisage. Hylton-Foster responded to the invitation, though in enigmatic and halting terms, conceding the point of admissibility –

"Certainly not now. I should have hoped at a much earlier .... it has been read now".

For counsel noted for the polished, eloquent turn of phrase this contribution was anything but. As the law of evidence stood in 1951, without any recognition of a wide, general discretion to exclude evidence on the simple ground that it would be unfair to admit it, that its admission would deprive the defendant of his right to receive a fair trial, there was never the remotest prospect of this evidence being excluded at the committal hearing in Huddersfield, at the opening of the Crown's case at the assize court or at the point reached in the evidence towards the close of day one. The best that may be said of counsel's hedged, reluctant concession is that it was intended, in some way, to send to the jury a coded message as to the unfairness of it all, that if only Alfred Moore had received the benefit of legal advice and representation when this critical strategy was embarked upon by police and prosecution the whole case might have been very different. In that he was undoubtedly correct.

It was always the intention of the Crown that Jagger's deposition should be read to the jury a second time on day one of the trial but that did not prevent a show of deference to the judicial view

"Would your Lordship think it convenient that it should be read again?"

His Lordship saw no objection observing that it was "a very important piece of evidence" and that as it had been read previously but only "as a matter of opening" it could now be read a second time with the different and enhanced status as evidence, the very material on which the jury, earlier that day, had sworn to 'give a true verdict'. Yet further clarification of the judicial view of all of this was sought by Mr Norman Black –

"Would your Lordship think it convenient that I should read the deposition, or should it be read by the learned clerk?"

This time the ruling was terse –

"You may as well read it".

And so following this most elegant of exchanges the deposition was at last read, no doubt, although the transcript of the trial proceedings records nothing other than the words, with some heavy emphasis upon the inept one question cross-examination fortifying the confidence of the deceased witness in the correctness of his identification.

It was by now late in the day and the only remaining police witness available to be called that day was the officer who had taken charge of the murder investigation, Detective Chief Superintendent George Metcalfe. His evidence was not going to finish that afternoon and undoubtedly in the more relaxed regime of today, when judges are not concerned with the need to move themselves and their entourage of clerk, butler and marshal onto the next city in the assize itinerary, the court having heard, after all, a total of fifteen witnesses, would draw stumps for the day, the judge no doubt grateful for the time it allowed to address the many administrative tasks which today, but not in 1951, are a part of judicial life. But this was 1951, the clock had not yet reached the time marking the end of the court day and so the Chief Superintendent was called and duly sworn.

It was a course which suited the prosecution for it enabled them to place before the jury before they left court such explanation as they were able to provide for their total and unexpected failure to produce at court the murder weapon. It may not have been much of an explanation but the prosecution were banking on any explanation sufficing to lay to rest any doubts in the hearts and minds of the jury, doubtless anxious to ensure both that someone paid the price of two lives cut short and to accept the testimony of the now deceased officer. And so, after questions about the officer's arrival at the murder scene at 4 o'clock on the Sunday morning, the circumstances of the prisoner's arrest and the events at the police station that day, where of course the Chief Superintendent had seen the gabardine raincoat for the first time and was quite unable to account for how it got there, questioning turned to the search for the murder weapon.

The witness having confirmed the obvious, that a search was in fact made for the murder weapon, the next most obvious question – was it found? – was not asked in terms, then, or ever, by leading counsel for the Crown. Instead, and with the time available that day fast running out, a series of exchanges between counsel and witness took place to mitigate a failure of proof going to the very heart of the case against Moore, a failure not acknowledged but sought, nonetheless, to be excused.

"Did you find the area about this farm easy or difficult to search?"

The answer "difficult" surprised no-one. The witness was not simply prepared to elaborate; he was positively eager to do so, to explain in graphic detail how an item such as a gun that the police were forced to acknowledge, if their case that Moore was the killer was right, was there to be found within a defined, limited area had, nevertheless, altogether eluded the efforts of hundreds of searchers, many equipped with the state of the art technology of the day, over many weeks.

"The house itself is a converted barn. There were many cavities, some of which were the depth of the house. There were cavities in the window sills. There were cavities in the walls. The chimney stacks were difficult and the drainage was difficult and the house has not been satisfactorily searched to this day. It would have been impossible to search it properly without pulling it down".

Small wonder then that anything at all was recovered! The Chief Superintendent was given no pause for breath before a further gently lobbed question was predictably despatched to the boundary.

"What about the outside of the house? Easy or difficult for searching?"

"Difficult. There was a copse at the back of the house. There were many overgrown hedges, a lot of stone walling; there were dykes and a ditch; there were very considerable tippings in front of the house, many, many tons. Of course, quite a lot of it was moved, but not all of it".

Given the enormous proportions of the search it was desperately unconvincing stuff but in a climate of deference to the authority of the police, sympathy for the dead officers and hostility to the admitted felon sitting in the dock, the prosecution were cautiously confident that it would pass muster.

The first day of the trial, therefore, closed with the prosecution having achieved all that it was going to be possible to achieve to neutralise the weak spot in their case. It was a satisfactory day's work. A total (astonishing by the more measured and leisurely standards of today) of sixteen witnesses had been called. The back of the case had been broken on day one and the target of the jury being sent out to consider its verdict on day three had been achieved.

Mr Hylton-Foster caught the eye of the judge with a look that alone and without words asked a question. The clock in the courtroom was glanced at by the judge by way of confirmation of the unspoken enquiry.

"Whatever you find convenient Mr Hylton-Foster. Would you prefer to wait until tomorrow morning".

Taking nothing for granted, and with a show of courtesy and courtly deference, counsel answered neither that he would or would not prefer any such course.

"If your lordship thought that course acceptable".

Proceedings for the day were closed with the judge turning to the jury box and briefly instructing them:

"In view of the very, very serious charge, you will appreciate you have big responsibilities in this matter and you will not discuss this case with anyone else. I am sure you will understand that".

Today, with a somewhat greater understanding of the various undercurrents, many innocent but some sinister, which are capable of contaminating the pure flow of justice in the form of trial by jury, the exhortation to a jury being sent home at the conclusion of day one is much fuller. It involves a request that anything causing concern to a juror should be reported to a court official so that the judge may be told about it and do whatever may be necessary to address it before a concern becomes a problem. It includes an explanation as to why safeguards need to be observed whilst the jury are away from court, namely, that their oath (or, in an increasingly secular age, affirmation) was to decide the case on the evidence, on what they hear in court, not on anything they might hear away from court. In certain cases the explanation is the subject of elaboration with a warning against the jury seeking to supplement any perceived deficiencies in the evidence presented at court by doing their own out of court research. With the modern day welter of information available on the internet there are cases today in which the computer literate juror may seek and find material, either general or even particular to the case, not presented in evidence because it is either irrelevant or prejudicial. The danger, of course, of warning a jury about the hazards to justice that might be involved in internet research is that it just might awaken a curiosity that would otherwise have lain dormant!

20 – "I was in the British Navy not the German Navy"

Day two began with a general expectation that before it was out the accused would make his one and only appearance in the witness box. But, first, the prosecution still had some way to go.

After the formalities of opening the court and the invocation to all with business to do before His Majesty's Judges of the assize to "draw near and give their attendance" the business of the day began with Chief Superintendent Metcalfe resuming the stand and a question from Hylton-Foster which was a surprising one given that he had already, himself, fallen into that very trap of which he was accusing the witness.

"When you saw the accused in the cells did you refer to him as Albert?"

The question was met with a curt "I did not, sir" and was not pursued further. The purpose of asking it, what line of defence it was thought it might advance or how it might undermine the case for the prosecution remains a mystery.

Hylton-Foster turned to the criminal antecedents of the defendant, first seeking confirmation which was forthcoming that nothing stolen on the night of the murder had been discovered during the search of Whinney Close Farm. However, when the Moore family was still living in Honley there had been a number of breakings and enterings of local mills where the perpetrator had not been detected. Once more the suggestion of counsel was readily confirmed.

With a greater degree of confidence cross-examination turned to the search for the murder weapon. Cross-examination can be a minefield but this was ground over which counsel felt able to tread with the utmost confidence; that almost any question was safe, that there was nothing hidden beneath the surface liable to detonate. For his part the Chief Superintendent had evidently resolved, having already advanced the defence for the failure to recover the gun, to concede graciously at every point for to do otherwise would be, and would appear to be, churlish. It would present the defence with a stick with which to beat the prosecution – a good grumble, something which lawyers without a good defence regard as the next best thing.

First, however, a few questions were required to establish that for two weeks a minimum of twenty officers, working in two teams of ten, were engaged in the search for the weapon. At weekends it was considerably in excess of that figure with the addition of many volunteers, the scale of the effort capable of being judged by the provision of a mobile canteen to refresh the efforts of the labourers in the field.

The search did not lack technology either with the Royal Engineers sweeping the fields with their mine detectors. It was readily acknowledged that grass was mown; dry stone walls demolished; feeding troughs and ditches drained. Were trees cut down, the officer was asked. No, came the reply but with immediate confirmation that this did not represent any failure of thoroughness for, although the trees had been spared, they had been scaled and their branches searched just as thoroughly as the ground below. Nor had the search been altogether in vain because it had yielded up numerous metal objects – its only failure was with regard to the very metal object that was being sought.

Cross-examination turned to the finding of a live bullet in the yard under a heap of bricks which the jury were being invited to infer had been secreted there by Moore in the immediate aftermath of the shooting. It was the perfect cue to undermine the evidence of the previous afternoon that these were premises replete with possible hiding places for incriminating material likely to defy the efforts even of an army to discover.

"It would be a fantastic thing to do, would it not, if you wanted to hide a live bullet, to do nothing more sensible than put it under some loose bricks? There are a thousand and one better places to put it than that?" The answer was ever so slightly grudging: "Well, there may have been better places yes."

Of course, the officer was being asked to comment and comment is not evidence. Questions which invite argument are strictly impermissible for the time to comment upon the evidence is when it comes to final speeches. It is a principle much observed by advocates in the breach. No objection was taken and, emboldened, Hylton-Foster embarked upon another foray into argumentative comment.

"One of the worst things that can happen to you in life is for the police to come upon you when you are in possession of stolen property?"

The question was somewhat over the top and the answer might have been that for the police to accuse you of a crime of such magnitude that your departure from this life is imminent was far worse; or even that the witness could not possibly comment never having found himself in that situation. Instead, the Chief Superintendent parried with –

"I would not say it was the best of times."

In the course of the prosecution's brief re-examination of the witness the judge raised a query as to the accuracy of his own note of the evidence of the Chief Superintendent. For the first and only time in the trial young white wig, Charles Raymond Dean, got to his feet, read out his note. It was a moment of minor triumph, the precursor of many more major ones to follow in the years ahead. The learned judge acknowledged that counsel's note was undoubtedly more accurate than his own.

For the rest of the morning a procession of soldiers and policemen came and went through the witness box, each giving formal, brief evidence of finding individual metal articles. It was evidence necessary to set the scene for the ballistics evidence that was to follow. Amongst the found items was a 9 millimetre cartridge case recovered on the Sunday afternoon from the centre shelf of the tallboy in the bedroom. It had been fired and the obvious question was asked by defence counsel: did you smell it? It was an obvious question and related to a perfectly obvious course of action given the circumstances and the inference that the prosecution were inviting the jury to draw. It was not obvious, however to the witness, Detective Constable John Garnett: "I did not, sir" was the stolid response.

The best, because it is the most effective, question asked by way of cross-examination is often 'why?' Here, counsel settled for the second best question: "Why not?"

The witness was evidently not the imaginative type:

"I could not see any reason for smelling it."

In the course of the evidence of this witness a number of gold cigarette cases and rings were produced; as well, to the astonishment of even those more than well acquainted with the *modus operandi* of the poultry farmer cum part-time burglar, an astonishing total of 157 skeleton keys – many of them double-ended – recovered from various cavity walls.

After the witness had been re-examined by the prosecution Hylton-Foster rose unexpectedly to his feet and sought the indulgence of the court to ask further questions. Leave being granted counsel prefaced his question with the comment:

"I do not think we have got all the incriminating material that I wanted."

Why he was seeking to pile on the agony is unclear. No one was any longer in doubt as to the character of the man or the reason for the police operation culminating in the tragedy that had brought together those present in court. Questions were asked about whether a bag of pearls and a number of watches had been recovered by the officer from the top of a wardrobe. When the officer protested his ignorance of any such items, Hylton-Foster languidly observed that it had been "an unprofitable enquiry."

The court rose and counsel retired for lunch to the artistes' dressing room beneath the stage of the Victoria Concert Hall. Concerts were the main business of the building and the Hall its centrepiece. Around it the various court rooms, used when necessity demanded for the courts of quarter sessions and assize, were but peripheral. When not being used by the artistes their dressing room was used variously as the barristers' luncheon room and even as a jury retiring room.

Following the luncheon, or short, adjournment the mystery of the recovery of the incriminating gabardine raincoat was to an extent resolved though not without raising yet further issues. Police Sergeant Goodwin Sadler told the court that he it was who recovered and took the garment to the police station where, for the first time, it was parcelled but then, in the course of that Sunday, unparcelled, parcelled again and delivered to and taken back from various senior officers at their request. It was certainly not an exhibit of unblemished integrity and, when the officer gave evidence that its recovery was made in the presence of a Police Constable Hopping, notes made by counsel and the judge of the evidence given by that officer the previous day were consulted to confirm a clear recollection that in plain terms he had told the court that he had absolutely no knowledge of any gabardine raincoat. He was of course one of the officers who attended the dead Inspector immediately following the shooting and so with a clear motive, the cynic might say, to put clear blue water between himself and the garment. With Sergeant Sadler defence counsel was able to establish that which he had failed to establish earlier in the day – the recovery of yet more incriminating material, the pearls and watches.

The prosecution case was drawing to its close. The one area remaining to be dealt with related to the ballistics. Before, however, the expert could be called some factual evidence to set the scene and place in context that which was to follow was required. Into the witness box stepped Hansons removal man, Joe Baxter. This was to be his ten minutes of fame and he had every intention of enjoying it to the full. It was going to be an experience that would mark him out, define him for the rest of his life as the man whose evidence secured the conviction of the Kirkheaton Cop Killer. The failure to recover the murder weapon was no doubt puzzling and troubling and might prove an insuperable obstacle to a conviction but Joe Bater travelled to court that morning confident that he would be the key witness in the trial, able to provide the next best thing, evidence of earlier, but not that much earlier, possession of it.

Most witnesses take the witness stand with trepidation but not Joe Baxter. He was not overawed by the occasion and took hold of the testament before the usher could place it in his hand, held it high and recited the words of the oath without prompting or stumble. The presence a few feet away of fashionable London counsel, scrutinising him as he did so, held no terrors for the Hansons of Huddersfield removal man.

Joe Baxter told the court about the time in May when he had been sent by his employers to a job involving a removal from Honley to Kirkheaton. It was one undertaken over two evenings and he had good cause to remember what was no conventional house removal, involving, as it did, hen huts and poultry in crates.

The scene having been set, into court was carried exhibit 28, a large black tool box. Joe confirmed that it was an item he had no difficulty recognising as one of the objects the subject of removal that first evening. He described how he and Moore picked up the box by its handles whereupon it came altogether apart. Though attempted it was not possible to effect a repair that would enable its removal that evening and Moore said that he would nail it together so that it might be removed the next evening.

Thus far the evidence of the removal man was uncontroversial. Nothing had been said with which the defence had cause to disagree. The area the defence would need to tackle head on, and dent the confidence, growing by the minute, of the witness came with the next question.

"When it broke did you have the opportunity of seeing what was inside it?"

"Yes. Rusty old nails and saw blades and one thing and another and what appeared to be a German automatic Luger revolver just thrown in a top corner of the box."

The answer was expressed in terms of an opinion, and opinions other than those of experts on topics as to which the jury would be unlikely to have knowledge of their own, are inadmissible. And so counsel turned to the expertise of the removal man to assert not only that there was a weapon of some description in the tool box but one bearing the precise description attributed to it by the witness.

"In the last war did you serve in the navy?"

"Yes."

"Did you have small arms training when you were in the service?"

"Yes."

Do you know the difference between a revolver and an automatic pistol?"

"Yes. This was a revolver with a rotating cartridge barrel."

The witness was then shown the various weapons recovered from Whinney Close Farm and confirmed that none of them matched the description of that seen by him in the broken tool box. The examination of the witness by Mr Hinchcliffe concluded with Baxter confirming that when he returned the following evening the fractured box had been repaired and was transported on Hanson's wagon to Kirkheaton together with the remainder of the worldly goods of the Moore household.

Hylton-Foster rose slowly to his feet, adjusted his silk gown across his shoulders, turned to the witness as if to ask a question but then turned to the judge with a request to be allowed to see the original deposition of the witness. Joe Baxter viewed the performance impassively. This might be his first appearance in a court of law but he recognised the tactic of delaying the anticipated opening question with a suggestion that to be found in the original deposition was something impugning that which he had just said. He recognised it for what it was and it concerned him not at all.

Having taken his time to consult the deposition counsel first sought confirmation that, apart from himself and Moore, also present giving assistance to the removal on the first evening was a Mr Alfred Pogson, someone who was not a Hanson employee. The question seemed to confirm the impression of the removal man that he was not to be challenged on anything as to which he was not equal to the challenge. With easy nonchalance he answered:

"There was another fellow there on the first day but I do not know that name."

A few more gentle questions followed concerning the way in which the tool box had broken open and the position of one of its internal trays. Joe Baxter had no problem with any of that and, increasingly at his ease, added that "Moore said that he could not be bothered with it that day; he would leave it until the next day and fasten it up in the morning."

Questioning turned perceptibly, but only just perceptibly, and in a tone of almost kindly curiosity, to the object seen by the witness on the first evening –

"This was a Luger, was it, this weapon you saw?"

Joe recognised the question for what it was, a blatant attempt to tie him down in an area where he sensed it might be wiser to keep options open –

"I said it *appeared* to be a luger automatic revolver."

The witness was now confident that he was impressing by both his expertise and expressions of care and caution, the hallmark of the impressive witness, and what followed began with a piece of outrageous massaging of the ego of the witness –

"You know about these things; you have been in the navy."

There was, however, steel in what followed:

"Could you tell me why it was a Luger?"

It was a simple question, apparently an innocuous enquiry, but instinct told Joe Baxter that it was a question being asked for a purpose which was not necessarily one that would enhance his recently achieved status as firearms expert. In fact he was thoroughly rattled and his reply, with its air of flippancy as ill-judged to the occasion as could be imagined, not merely undermined, it totally destroyed at a stroke, his credibility as a witness.

"I said it appeared to be a Luger. I have seen Luger revolvers before and it just appeared to be of a similar type to a German revolver. I was in the British Navy, not the German Navy."

It was never a response to win a standing ovation, perhaps in a context other than that of a capital trial it might have elicited a few smiles but on this occasion the silence which followed was palpable and it was one that the experience of learned counsel knew how to exploit. Let the answer hang in the air for all to savour and for the witness to contemplate its effect. The rebuke following the silence was mildly spoken but devastating nonetheless.

"This is a serious matter you know?"

"I know."

"How did you think that observation helped us?"

To that question there was no answer and none was attempted but the endgame of this cross-examination concluded with a chastened witness, earlier bravado vanished, earnestly hoping for the moment when he might retreat back into the obscurity from which he had been plucked. The victorious return to Huddersfield to which he had looked forward was not going to happen. His reminiscences about his appearances at the assizes would be no more than a grumbling diatribe about 'clever bloody lawyers trying to trip you up.'

Hylton-Foster had not, however, quite finished his business with Joe Baxter.

"Where have you seen a Luger revolver?"

Playing for time Joe repeated the question before giving his answer.

"Where have I seen one? In Devonport."

"When have you seen one?"

"During my time in the Navy."

From this exploration of the by now decidedly uncertain expertise of the removal man counsel returned to the tool box.

"Was this object lying surrounded by other bits of metal?"

The show of defiance which the question evoked was both petulant and pathetic and did nothing to restore lost face:

"I cannot hardly say. I went there to remove the man, not to pry into his business."

But after a few more questions he conceded:

"It was lying in and amongst other bits of metal."

"All kinds of shapes and sizes?"

"If you want to put it that way, yes."

Hylton-Foster was never going to allow the witness to escape with what was no more than a grudging concession:

"Put it another way if you like, if that is not the right description?"

"Nails and drills and things."

More irritability followed suggestions by counsel that what he had seen in the tool box was nothing more lethal than a broken and folded air rifle.

"I have told you what I saw in the box."

Counsel's suggestion that the witness had seen some weapon but not that which he claimed effectively put an end to at least one of the dilemmas faced by the defence team. Included in counsel's brief was a short statement from the third man present on the occasion of the tool box breaking and no doubt he was on stand-by to travel to Leeds to give evidence. But there were a couple of good sound reasons why the defence might not wish to call as a witness Alfred Pogson, a Dyer's labourer living at Petty Royds in Golcar. First, because of the rules of procedure at that time once the defence called to give evidence any witness in addition to the defendant they lost the precious right of having the last word with the jury. This was not a right easily to be given away in a capital trial. But, secondly, what Alfred Pogson had to say was of somewhat limited value in any event. His recollection was not that there was no weapon to be seen in the tool box or, if there was it was not one matching the description attributed to it by the removal man. His evidence would have been that the tool box did not in fact break open sufficiently for anything inside it to be seen at all. What he said in the short proof of his evidence taken by counsel's instructing solicitor was:

'I could not see a revolver or automatic pistol as described by Baxter and I am quite sure he didn't because if he had seen such a thing I am sure I would have done.'

The suggestion put to Baxter that he may have seen a folded air rifle put an end to any prospect of calling Pogson as a defence witness.

One last chance was extended to Joe Baxter to withdraw his evidence but it was offered in the expectation, indeed the hope, that it would be spurned and it was – spectacularly so with the witness repeating the evidence which within minutes was to be destroyed by a genuine expert in the field of firearms and ballistics.

"I am putting to you that there never was a revolver shaped weapon in the box – never."

"Well, I saw what appeared to be a German automatic Luger revolver."

Joe Baxter left the witness box without ever being directly confronted with the patent inaccuracy of his testimony. It was left to the next night's account in the local newspaper of the evidence of the man from the Ministry of Supply, Home Office Section, Woolwich, to expose him to himself, as well as the wider readership in the town, as a discredited 'expert', a witness on whose word not even the proverbial dog would hang.

Hard on the heels of Joe Baxter into the witness box stepped the real expert, Dr. Horace Alfred Mayes, Master of Science and Doctor of Philosophy. The defence would not be putting in issue anything that he had to say. All of the bullets, he explained to the court, fired and unfired, recovered whether from the bodies of the officers, the crime scene, the tall boy in the bedroom or the heap of rubble in the farmyard were of the same 9 millimetre calibre. Those that had been fired had markings indicating that they had all been fired from the same weapon. Those unfired were capable of being fired from the same weapon. That weapon was a revolver, not an automatic, the barrel of which was too large for the bullets. Dr. Mayes went on to explain how he could authoritatively arrive at such precise conclusions. When a bullet leaves the cylinder of the rotating chamber of a revolver and enters the barrel of the weapon if the barrel and cylinder are not exactly aligned the bullet will receive a dent. These bullets had all received just such a dent. This simply would not happen with an automatic pistol where the bullet starts its journey in the barrel of the weapon. Not only was a dent to be found on each bullet but also striation markings, not of themselves remarkable except that these were not uniform but irregular in both position and direction. Dr. Mayes could think of but one explanation for the appearance of these markings – the bullets had not, during their split second of travel through the barrel of the gun, pursued the direct course that would have been expected in the event of a snug fit of bullet with barrel, but had, and here the expert deliberately used non-technical jargon, "rocked about."

Throughout the trial thus far Mr. Justice Pearson had exhibited judicial restraint in his few interventions; interruptions from the bench had been brief, to the point, aimed only at achieving clarification. At a time when judicial activism was rife and grounds of appeal drafted by counsel regularly complained that judges asked as many, sometimes more, questions than the barristers and with the effect, undoubtedly intended, of boosting the case against the prisoner, the conduct of this newly appointed judge was beyond reproach and indeed remained so during the evidence of the ballistics expert. However, the interventions increased in number as the judge, evidently unlike so many of his brethren not a shooting man, struggled to make a note intelligible to himself and from which, when the time came to sum up the case to the jury, would make sense to them as well. Judicial ignorance is too often played for effect and headline and questions such as 'Who are the Beatles?' and 'What is the internet?' can be guaranteed media coverage under the well-trodden but ever popular storyline that judges do not live in the real world. The point being made, and which to the quiet amusement of the judges concerned the Press invariably fail to appreciate, is that in a court of law nothing can be taken for granted and strict proof is required of everything but that which is truly notorious. With Mr. Justice Pearson there was nothing feigned about his ignorance of weaponry and no doubt the jury were grateful to have explained the differences between a revolver and an automatic, the definition of striations and just what was meant by "co-axial positioning of chamber and barrel."

When the discussion between counsel and expert moved from revolvers to the more precise ".38 revolver" the judge confessed to the court in terms of endearing frankness: "I am very ignorant. What is meant by a .38 revolver? Is that an army number?" The discussion that followed may have disabused the learned judge of his notion that '.38' was an 'army number' but otherwise was singularly unenlightening. In impenetrable terms it was explained that it means '.38 of an inch' but that was "only a nominal size not the actual calibre of the weapon". There the matter was left with probably few in court much the wiser. However, it really didn't matter; the murder weapon had never been recovered and the fate of the man accused of the crime was not going to turn on the enigmas of ballistic science.

Hylton-Foster's cross-examination of Dr Mayes extracted a number of useful concessions. The defence had been well served by their own ballistics expert, Major H. Pollard of Churchill Gunsmiths in Orange street, Leicester Square, London. At considerable expense he had provided for the defence a highly technical report, dated the 28 November 1951, which contained much useful information to enable an effective cross-examination of the Crown's expert. In his Brief to Counsel Ted Hutchinson had sought advice as to whether Major Pollard should be on stand-by to be called as a witness at the trial, pointing out that it would be well if this could be avoided as the witness was 'rather expensive'. The proceeds of sale of Whinney Close Farm were fast dwindling and the advice was that the written report would suffice for counsel's purposes.

Without qualification the expert agreed with Hylton-Foster that 9 millimetre calibre ammunition was the most common form of ammunition in the world, used in a wide variety of pistols, sub-machine guns and automatic weapons. Not merely was the calibre commonplace but nothing actually really turned on the fact that all the recovered bullets were of the same calibre because they were each capable of being identified as emanating from various sources and as having been manufactured on different dates; in short, none came from the same manufacturer's batch. The quietus to the evidence of Joe Baxter was finally administered when Dr Mayes confirmed that Luger, a German firm, had never manufactured a weapon which could be described as a revolver; their product was the heavy calibre automatic weapon.

The final prosecution witness was yet another expert, Lewis Charles Nickolls, Master of Science and Fellow of the Institute of Chemistry, formerly the Director of the Forensic Science Laboratory at Wakefield. By the time of the trial he held the same position but by now at the far more prestigious Scotland Yard in London. He had been summoned to the crime scene even before the farmhouse had been entered and the arrest of Moore effected. Within moments of that arrest he was at work. Doubtless today the Director of a Forensic Science Laboratory would be working behind a desk, managing his team, administering the work of his laboratory, signing off forms and ticking boxes to re-assure his masters at the Home Office that key performance targets were being met and risks to the health and safety of personnel the subject of thorough assessments. In 1951 he enjoyed no vast army of scenes of crime officers and was regularly to be seen at work where some high profile crime had been committed.

The first mystery of the night that Mr Nickolls had been requested to address was the puffs of smoke seen bellowing from the chimney into the night air shortly after the shooting. Asked about his examination of the fire grate and his findings he told the court that a fierce fire had taken place, paper material had been consumed but from the ashes it was possible to identify carbonised blocks of 2 ½ d postage stamps. Following earlier revelations it was a finding that came as little surprise to anyone. The inference that the smoke was the result of determined efforts to destroy evidence of criminal activity was inescapable.

Next for his scrutiny were a pair of men's shoes which, Mr Nickolls told the court, were wringing wet, encrusted with seeds in the welt and with remnants of light, shale soil on the soles. The seeds were similar to those to be found at the scene of the shooting. The prosecution had already proved with the unchallenged evidence of Charles Henry that Moore had been out on the fields and at or near the murder scene that night so neither the wet condition of the shoes nor the seeds were remarkable but the shale deposits, being similar to the exposed subsoil at one end of the farmhouse, tended to show, the jury were told, that the wearer had walked in that vicinity at some point *after* leaving the fields; any shale deposits on the shoes before walking on the wet fields would have been quickly removed by the effects of the moisture. It was not lost on the jury that a live bullet had been recovered from the heap of rubble in the farmyard.

None of the findings of Mr Nickolls were challenged by the defence. No explanation had been offered as yet by the defence to account for the shale deposits but the defence knew that one would shortly be available for the jury's consideration. Today the rules of procedure, designed to promote efficient and effective trial management, would require uncontested evidence to be adduced by a document, read into the record and placed before the jury, containing all the facts agreed by both sides. It is undoubtedly a convenient procedure, saving much court time and public expense, but it can diminish the impact of significant evidence and rob it of immediacy.

The forensic findings in relation to the shoes may have been of only limited significance by the time of trial but at the time they were made, some five months earlier, they were huge. They established that the wearer had been out and about shortly beforehand, very possibly at the time of the shootings; any defence contradicting that fact simply could not be true, was capable of being convincingly refuted and must, therefore, be a lie and lies are yet further evidence of guilt. It was not, of course, until he entered the witness box that Alfred Moore first told of his evening walk to Almondbury and back with his brother. Up to that point he had simply maintained that when the shootings occurred he had been in bed though, in the absence of any police questions directed to what he might have been doing at some point earlier than midnight (and there were certainly none), the failure to mention his earlier movements was not something to be held to his detriment.

From the findings at the crime scene questions turned to the later laboratory examination of the items of clothing being worn by the dead officers and the suspect. That of the officers indicated not merely bullet holes but bullets which had been fired at close range. Of itself hardly a significant finding but one which became so when taken with the solitary human hair recovered from Moore's gabardine mackintosh, described as a short hair complete with root, about three-quarters of an inch in length, white in colour and "could have been derived from a head similar to the sample of controlled head hair taken from the body of Inspector Fraser".

It was to the finding of the head hair that Hylton-Foster directed the thrust of his cross-examination.

"The difficulty with human hairs from a scientific point of view is that a wide range of hair has mutual resemblances?"

"You cannot say that one hair came from a certain head and from none other, no."

"This hair could have come from the head of Inspector Fraser but it is impossible to say that it did. It could have come from any similar head?"

"I cannot say it did.'

In other words looking at the two hairs they were of similar appearance no more than that, and the attribute of a reasonable measure of eyesight rather than necessarily the expertise of a forensic scientist sufficed to make the comparison. It was not evidence which had the conclusive precision of a fingerprint comparison - or anything remotely approaching it. Today, of course, any sample taken from the human body provides a conclusive genetic fingerprint, DNA. But this was a forensic development which lay many decades into the future.

Whilst the defence had undoubtedly limited the potential for the evidence of the head hair advancing the case for the prosecution, both by demonstrating its strictly limited weight and by raising a real possibility of cross-contamination, curiously the argument was never made that it was unlikely, if not impossible, for hair to be transferred as the prosecution were alleging had happened. There was no evidence of physical contact between the Inspector and his killer. The Inspector was wearing a hat. On all the evidence, when shot he fell backwards away from the gunman. The evidence of the head hair was in reality tenuous, of minimal value but obviously capable of being given in the eyes of the jury a weight that it simply did not bear. Its potential for prejudice was considerable. Today judicial discretion might well have been exercised to exclude it on the ground that its admission was likely to have an adverse impact on the fairness of the proceedings. In 1951, however, the test was relevance, not fairness, and plainly the evidence had relevance.

Mr Nickolls was the final witness for the prosecution and Hylton-Foster's cross-examination concluded with a minor forensic triumph for the defence. Unexpectedly, without warning, questioning turned to the right hand pocket of the gabardine raincoat, the pocket from which in his sworn deposition Jagger said that the gun had been taken. Confirmation that it had been forensically examined was sought, a safe question because if it had not been the thoroughness of the whole forensic exercise would have been called into question. The witness confirmed that the pocket had indeed been examined, adding incautiously "I have no note that I found anything that was of interest to me at that time." Hylton-Foster pounced: "It might not interest you but it might interest this court at this time; if you had found any gun oil ....? When you are doing a forensic examination you do not only busy yourself with things you are looking for; you busy yourself with things you find".

It was a well-directed rebuke. Mr Nickolls acknowledged that counsel was indeed correct. It took only four further questions to establish that no trace of gun oil, powder or gun rust had been found to be present in the pocket from which the murder weapon had allegedly been drawn, and that the pocket was one with crevices in the corner in which trace deposits of such material might well reside.

Hylton-Foster resumed his seat. The witness withdrew without further questions from the Crown. Mr Hinchcliffe formally closed the case for the prosecution. It would not be right to say that the onus shifted to the defence because the defence bear no onus of proving innocence – or anything. But, to use a homely metaphor, the ball was now firmly in the defence court.

21 – "I am going to shock everybody"

Alfred Moore approached the second day of his trial in the almost certain knowledge that he would take the stand that day and enjoy his first, and only, opportunity to give to the court his version of the events of the Saturday night and Sunday morning. That he would be a witness in his own defence was never an issue for his legal team though in many cases, at this time, the decision was one liable to cause defence lawyers sleepless nights. It was only just over fifty years earlier that a general right of a prisoner accused of a crime to give evidence was allowed by law at all. Prior to the Criminal Evidence Act 1898 the thinking was that evidence given by a person accused was worthless on the ground of bias, that with an interest, all too obvious, in the outcome of the proceedings it was not testimony on which any tribunal of fact might safely rely. It sounds quaint to the point of grotesque but in many cases it was a disability that acted as an immunity. It shielded the prisoner from the prosecutor's deadliest weapon - cross-examination; when the law was changed lawyers often said that more murderers lost their lives by giving evidence than had ever saved it by keeping silent. All too frequently the high point of the defence case was the close of the prosecution. The defence might have enjoyed a veritable field day with witnesses for the Crown but once the defendant went into the witness box it was all downhill.

There is no test of the truth so relentless as that of the witness box, deadly to the guilty but capable also of saving the innocent. After the Criminal Justice Act 1993, giving evidence is no longer an optional luxury. Failure to do so almost inevitably ensures that the defendant faces unfavourable comment from both judge and prosecutor that he has no answer to the charge, or none that would withstand cross-examination.

None of these, however, were dilemmas troubling Hylton-Foster, his junior or their instructing solicitor. The evidence available to the prosecution, whilst not without some glaring deficiencies, plainly amounted to a case for the defendant to answer. When the prosecution case closed later that day there would be no submission to the judge that the case should be withdrawn from the jury on the ground that the evidence was insufficient to found a safe verdict of guilty. To do so would be a hopeless waste of valuable court time and endear the defence to no-one, not least the judge. Maybe the prisoner had nothing to prove for, until his jury pronounced otherwise, he was an innocent man, but that was the theory of jurisprudence remote from the practical realities of a trial involving the senseless, cold-blooded killing of two police officers cut down in the prime of their lives whilst acting in the execution of their duty. Silence would be interpreted as a confession of guilt. There were issues as to whether to call witnesses in support of the defence but none as to Alfred himself going into the witness box – not to prove his innocence but simply to give evidence as a witness, like any other, for the jury to judge it for what they might consider it to be worth. It is a cliché of the courtroom, something as to which all juries are directed, that all witnesses, whether prosecution or defence, police or civilian, start equal. They do not, of course, all finish equal. With some their credibility is enhanced, with others it is undermined, and with some completely destroyed. These, of course, being exactly the sort of judgements that the jury are there to make.

No witnesses were intended to be called apart from Moore which denied the defence the opportunity to make an opening statement to the jury. So, on the announcement that that case for the prosecution was closed, and without interruption to the smooth flow of the trial, Hylton-Foster rose and quietly, simply stated "I call Alfred Moore". With this implicit acknowledgement that the prosecution case was at least sufficiently compelling to call for an answer to be made to it, Moore, escorted by two prison officers, made the short walk from the dock to the witness box to try to supply that answer. His feelings as he did so can, perhaps, be more easily imagined than described. Upon what he said, how he said it, depended the future course of his whole existence; both his words and demeanour would be subjected to unimaginable scrutiny. The recent experience of Joe Baxter was fresh in the memory of all and an antidote to any sense of misplaced over-confidence. This was Moore's opportunity to speak in direct terms to the jury, "twelve of his equals and neighbours, indifferently chosen and superior to all suspicion so that the liberties of England cannot but subsist" - in the words of Blackstone, the great eighteenth-century legal commentator.

In truth, the randomness of jury selection was in the appearance only; the reality was that juries in 1951 comprised property owning, rate paying, fully subscribing members of the middle-class, many of them with a background of distinguished, sometimes even heroic, service to their country in the recent conflict. In fact, just the sort of people unlikely to enjoy any natural sympathy with one seen to have shirked his duty and with a history of predatory behaviour towards the property rights of his fellow citizens.

Alfred took the oath in what the local newspaper later described as a 'clear, loud and determined voice', his eyes fixed firmly on the judge as he did so. Alice, sitting in the well of the court only a few feet away, watched him intently throughout his time in the witness box. His story was an essentially simple one to tell. He was offering for the consideration of the jury a defence of alibi. He did not shoot the officers. It was not him who had been confronted by Inspector Fraser and Constable Jagger. He may not have been miles away from the scene of the shooting but he was at the time, and had been for the best part of two hours, asleep in the matrimonial bed.

When, later the next day, Moore departed the witness box his evidence, clearly, cogently, given, remained largely unshaken. In its essentials it had withstood the test of cross-examination though, it has to be said, it was hardly, on this occasion, an acid test. However, the combination of sympathy for the dead officers and their families and condemnation of all that the burglar-deserter appeared to represent did not, in reality, require the prosecution to do much more than avoid a disaster. None was likely or foreseeable. What Moore was going to say was by now clear enough; no new revelations, no surprise developments in cross-examination were expected and, in the end, therefore, no-one was disappointed.

Moore began his evidence with a show of sensitivity for the future welfare of his young family that cannot but have done him some credit in the eyes of the jury and which shamed the lawyers, who had the knowledge at their disposal which the poultry farmer plainly did not as to the measures provided by the law to prevent the naming of young children in the course of court proceedings. It was Alfred who, having told the jury something of his personal circumstances immediately prior to his arrest and having named and given the ages of his four daughters turned to Mr Justice Pearson with the enquiry –

"May I request that these names are not published?"

"Certainly" was the unhesitating response of the judge. But it was not to be a formal order of the court, merely a politely framed request for restraint on the part of the media –

"I am sure the representatives of the press present will give effect to that wish."

With a slight bow of the head in acknowledgement Moore thanked the judge and, having established a brief mastery over the course of the proceedings, he doubtless felt more at ease than when he had stepped into the witness box moments earlier. Questioning by Hylton-Foster now turned, however, to the distinctly uncomfortable topic of his wartime service or, more accurately, the fact that he had in his own words "skipped it, just chucked it" opting to join the merchant navy instead. It was a topic that had to be covered, quite apart from anything else it laid the foundation for later submissions concerning the mugshot that would have been available to any police officer taking part in the surveillance of Whinney Close Farm. But it was not a topic to be dwelt upon and when Moore attempted once more to dictate the course of the questioning with "May I add that I was given ...." he was peremptorily cut off by Hylton-Foster, anxious to prevent any excursion into unknown territory with all manner of potential pitfalls.

Moore's criminal career by now well-established the next question took it for granted –

"Have you in all your career, honest or criminal, ever used violence to anybody?"

"No."

"Had you anything to do with the shooting of Inspector Fraser or Police Constable Jagger?"

"No."

"Do you know who shot them?"

"I have no idea."

"On the night when they were shot were you yourself concerned with any crime at all?"

"No."

"Did you either break in anywhere or attempt to break in anywhere?"

"No."

"Or contemplate breaking in anywhere?"

"No."

"Did you on that night at any time have in your possession any instrument of housebreaking or any stolen property on your person?"

"No."

Having established the total innocence, whether by action or in thought, of the accused on the fateful night, questions turned to a general overview of Moore's career in crime, first seeking to establish that it was only after the cessation of wartime hostilities that he had taken up crime. In a show of apparent total candour Moore told the court –

"I had been charged with being dishonest once."

Hylton-Foster chose not to explore further, even if he understood, this oblique reference to the proceedings in 1947 when Alfred had walked free from court, his innocence vindicated and the declamation of Mr. Eaton-Smith of the great wrong done to him resounding in his ears; as his next question pointed out –

"But that is not being dishonest!"

Alfred may have shirked making a total commitment to the national effort at time of war but at least he had waited until its cessation before turning to crime. What was his motivation for so doing? No startling revelations here; it was "to save face" he told the court, adding that his children were being "very well educated."

Counsel, pointing to the massive array of skeleton keys exhibited on a table at the front of the court, asked him:

"Are they yours?

The answer was obvious, there having been no challenge to the fact that the keys had been properly recovered from Whinney Close Farm, and were properly exhibited at court as the tools of the defendant's felonious activities. Somewhat unfortunately Moore did not bow to the obvious, engaging for the first time in evasion –

"Well, I would have to examine them closely to tell you."

To this fatuous answer, undoing much that the earlier questions had achieved in establishing the defendant as imperfect, but at the same time open and frank, Hylton-Foster testily responded:

"You need not trouble with that."

Questions proceeded on the assumption, wisely now accepted by Moore, that these were indeed his keys. He told the court how he had made a special study of the art of key filing and the science of lock opening and of his workshop and tools devoted to the task of creating skeleton keys. Without hesitation he acknowledged that the treasure trove of watches and gold cigarette cases were the proceeds of his crimes. He explained that whilst he had never possessed a weapon that could be described as a revolver or purchased 9 millimetre ammunition, he had possessed a number of 9 millimetre cartridge cases which he had picked up at Malvern in 1947 when performing his delayed military service. Reading the transcript today furnishes at least some insight into England's post-war austerity. Moore told the Court that he had taken possession of the spent cartridges to make into lipstick holders, a task which, however, he had not yet, even after four years, started. So far as he was aware the cartridge cases had been left in the tool box, mention of which led seamlessly on to questions relating to the discredited evidence of Joe Baxter. Moore described how the box fell apart and that it contained nothing more lethal than an air pistol and folded air rifle.

Having told the court about the removal of the tool box to Whinney Close Farm, Moore was asked general questions about the venture which had brought him and his family across the town from Honley to the isolated hill top farmhouse. Immodestly Alfred described himself as "very good at poultry" and the enterprise with a few hundred pullets ("one hundred layers and six at the point of lay") and three gilts ("two in pig") as prospering. He had every confidence that prosperous times for the Moore family lay ahead and, therefore, no motive to engage in further dishonesty. Since the move he had led a life as honest and law-abiding as it was industrious. With all the work that needed to be done renovating farmhouse and outbuildings he had not left the confines of the farm for something like three weeks before the decision to take the night air and accompany Charles Henry back to Almondbury.

Charles Henry had already told the court of his work at the farm on the Saturday and of how his brother had accompanied him almost, but not quite, to his home in Fernside Crescent. There was no need to go over the same ground again but what did benefit from being emphasised was the spontaneous, unpremeditated, virtually random, character of the decision to leave the house at all that night. Alfred told the court that until it was realised that Charles Henry had missed his bus not a thought had been given to leaving the farm and that when he left, as Charles Henry had already told the court, he told Alice to expect him back within the hour. The only incident of note on either the outward or homeward limb of the journey was that he had slipped on a stepping stone fording a stream on the walk to the farm and soaked one of the brown crepe-soled shoes being worn by him. Walking back up the fields to the farm he encountered nobody, was wholly unaware of any police cordon around the house – if, indeed, it was in place. Nor had he done anything and nor was he in possession of anything which might cause him to wish to avoid the attentions of the police. He estimated the time of his arrival back at the farmhouse at any time between 11-45 pm and midnight.

Before entering the house through the French window he secured a number of outbuildings, pausing as he did so at the pig sty to feel the beasts for signs that would mark the time for farrowing. By now one of his trouser legs was not merely soaked from its immersion in the stream but contaminated with pig slurry. They were taken off and placed in the washing boiler. Inside the bedroom there was a minor problem to be addressed. Pat, the ten year old, was "wanting to sleep with mummy" adding "they do from time to time, I would not let her that night........" Fearing, perhaps, an indelicate excursion into the intimacies of the marriage bed Hylton-Foster, for the second time, acted to suppress his witness:

"We do not want that."

Sleep followed and, after the exertions of the walk to Almondbury, it was a deep sleep but a short one. It was interrupted, not for him by the noise from outside in the fields but the reaction to it of Alice, sitting up in bed, demanding urgently of her husband:"What do you think it is Alfred?" He went outside to investigate having in mind, he said, that poultry thieves might be at work – and not for the first time.

"I am going to shock everybody" he then announced.

The mere forecast of a shock to come sufficed to shock. Some revelation was about to follow but it was not actually one that was going to address all those unanswered questions as to the true identity of the police killer.

"About that time, July and August, poultry had been put in cold store for Christmas, and point of lay pullets are ...." was the 'shock' announcement.

It was a shock announcement that was apparently turning into a digression concerning some of the finer points of choosing a bird for the Christmas table. It was, this time rightly, cut short by counsel.

Christmas, albeit just two weeks away, was the last thing on anyone's mind at Leeds Assizes that afternoon. The point of this evidence, but one probably lost in the excitement of the 'shock' announcement, was simply to explain the shale deposits found on the shoes in the course of forensic examination.

Re-assured that all was well at the poultry houses Alfred returned to the bedroom still, he claimed, unsuspecting that the activity in the fields involved police officers. Sleep, however, was to be denied him for Alice "kept bobbing up in the bed and looking through the window." As light began to dawn in the sky, and with it a dawning realisation that whatever was happening outside did involve the police, his thoughts turned to the proceeds of his past misdeeds, the incriminating evidence of that lifestyle now put behind him. What could not be burned was "shunted" into any convenient crevice, of which in a dilapidated building undergoing renovation there were many, and what could be burned in the grate, the dollar bills and stamps, were the subject of attempted, but as the court already knew, not entirely successful incineration. For a full fifteen minutes the activity was frantic until, as Alfred told the jury, "I realised I was being a bit silly; I thought what is the reason for it all? why do it?"

And so, with all now apparently quiet outside, instead of returning to the matrimonial bed he sat and smoked a cigarette. His attempt at relaxation from the unexpected exertions of the night was, however, again short-lived and disturbed by Alice informing him – "there's someone calling out."

Alfred went on to describe his arrest in terms not factually at all different from the account given earlier by police witnesses. But it was an account stripped of all the implications of a guilty mind with which the police account was redolent. He had no reason to believe, he said, that an officer had come to harm that night and whatever guilt he might feel it was not in relation to firearms. He did not deny being behind the door when it was opened by Alice but that was not him hiding but simply putting on his Wellington boots so that he could join the police outside in order to address whatever their concerns might be. His recollection of what was said was that in addition to questions about poultry he was also asked if he had been out that night shooting foxes because there had been an accident and someone had been injured. Although denied by police witnesses these questions made some sense both in the context of what had occurred and as a device for seeking some, at least limited, admission that Moore had earlier been out and about in the fields armed with a gun. On being suddenly handcuffed and arrested and asked by Alice if it was "something serious" he did acknowledge that it was "*something* serious" but that, he claimed, was a reference to all the possible implications for his family of the police discovering stolen property and his burgling kit of skeleton keys on the premises. It was by no means an unreasonable explanation given that, despite his best efforts, both were there to be discovered and, in the light of what was happening, an imminent search was surely inevitable. It was, however, hardly an explanation justifying the uncharacteristic lyricism with which the poultry farmer sought to embellish it:

"When you have something like this in the house, it is a sort of undercurrent, shall I say, washing away the banks."

His evidence turned to events at the police station that Sunday morning with a ready admission that he had lied when asserting that once in bed he had "never got up again." But once more this was an attempt, one which he acknowledged was 'a long shot', to escape the consequences of his criminal activities.

With one eye on the clock Hylton-Foster turned to the judge.

"My Lord, I shall necessarily have to go on a bit longer."

There followed that elegant *pas de deux* so often marking the end of the day's business in court with neither judge nor advocate wishing, for some reason, to be seen as being responsible for bringing proceedings to a close.

"Entirely at your convenience" responded the judge.

"This really would, I think, be a convenient moment. I cannot quite finish tonight."

Day two concluded with Mr Justice Pearson briefly reminding the jury of his exhortation to them the previous day not to discuss the case away from court with others. Moore, who had spent the final hour of the day's proceedings in the witness box, was taken to the cells below to await his return to the hospital wing at Armley Gaol. It was to be the last night he would spend there.

In the short journey from prison to court the next morning Alfred Moore was in no doubt that before the end of the day the months of anguished waiting would be at an end. A decision was going to be made which would determine whether he was to die imminently or return to Huddersfield, to his family, to his dream of prosperity on the proceeds of honest to goodness poultry farming, a dream the flame of which had burned brightly until his arrest and the enforced sale of the farm. The prison hospital records detailing anything of significance in his time on remand and chronicling every nuance of mood presented a consistent picture of confident optimism and there is no reason to think that he approached the third and final day of his trial with that confidence in any way dimmed. Not many shared that confidence.

Day three began with Moore taking his place on the witness stand for the final time. He remained there for the next 1¼ hours. He was questioned first by Hylton-Foster about the events at the bedside of the dying constable. Moore told the court that he did indeed both request and actively wished for legal advice and representation from a solicitor. Today the absence of that representation would be considered a fatal flaw, denying the defendant his inviolable right to a fair trial, resulting in the exclusion of the evidence of identification – which in the context of this trial, where it was the sole and decisive evidence of guilt, would inevitably bring the prosecution to an end. But to Hylton-Foster it was nothing more nor less than a circumstance of the case, unfortunate no doubt but certainly nothing to dwell upon unduly or to make it a vehicle for anything that might be thought a criticism of the police.

"In fact" he stated to Moore and the court "it was not possible for you to have one."

Evidently Moore had no wish to brush to one side his denial of representation and before Hylton-Foster could draw breath and move on to the next topic he began an answer:

"Well, I shall have to go into a little detail, Sir, ..."

"No, you will not" commanded the voice of the advocate so long accustomed to dominating courtrooms and witnesses.

Instead, questions about the identification parade concentrated upon Moore's state of mind concerning the outcome and his confidence, notwithstanding the absence of legal advice, that it could not be other than favourable to his interests.

"Had you any fear of P.C. Jagger picking you out?"

"None whatsoever, Sir."

"Was it a dire shock to you when he did?"

"Yes."

The examination-in-chief of Moore concluded with a short series of safe questions and predictable answers:

"Have you done what you can to think of anything which would help to track down the killer of these two police officers?"

"I have done all I can, Sir."

"Is it true that you said that you yourself were entitled to be believed as much as P.C. Jagger?"

"I may have said words to that effect, Sir."

"Do you desire here on oath to protest your innocence of this shooting?"

"I do, Sir."

With an expectation that the next half hour or so might produce, if not exactly fireworks at least an end to an exercise of one bland question after another predictably answered but actually furnishing not the least clue as to where the truth of it all was to be found, those present in court watched Raymond Hinchcliffe, one of Her Majesty's Counsel learned in the law, rise to his feet, fix Moore with a stare and ask what turned out to be a question as bland and innocuous as any that had gone before. The most important questions in cross-examination are the first and the last. The first sets the tone of what is to follow and if it both seamlessly follows from the last answer of the witness and requires pause for breath and thought before being answered then the witness is wrong-footed and made to appear shifty and evasive – the whole objective of the exercise after all. Often the best opening question in cross-examination is simply 'why?' or even better still 'why not?' Hinchcliffe's first question was:

"Do you recall clearly when Mr Metcalfe came to your farmhouse at 4-40 on the morning of the 25th of July?"

The purpose of the question was to set the scene for questions arising from Moore's earlier assertion that he had no sense of guilt in relation to firearms when the officers attended. Each of the firearms recovered by the police were itemised in the questions that followed and it was pointed out that when asked at the police station about the firearms he possessed he had avoided the question by complaining that his head was 'bad'. None of these weapons, of course, had anything remotely to do with the shooting of the officers; they were wholly irrelevant to the crime charged on the indictment. If there was purpose in the questions it could only have been to deflect attention away from the one weapon conspicuous by its absence from the trial.

Next, the evidence of the discredited Joe Baxter was, without shame or apology, put to Moore who denied that there was anything apt to be described as a revolver to be found in the tool box.

"Of course" asked Hinchcliffe "if there should happen to have been a revolver in that black box, it was taken to Whinney Close Farm was it not?"

It was a statement of the obvious, hardly deserving a response, and serving only to confirm that this was not going to be remembered as a classic in the art of cross-examination. And it continued to fail to delight. Question after question did no more than recite the case for the prosecution with Moore wearily but respectfully answering along the lines of: "I believe that is the evidence, Sir" and "I believe that is the suggestion, Sir" or more curtly "That is what was said". A clash as to whether the cash box containing the dollar bills had been recovered from under the bed or from the top of the tallboy, even involving on Hinchcliffe's part a tone of stern incredulity that Moore should seek to put in issue the integrity of the police evidence on the point, excited no-one.

Questions about the late night walk, proved of course by the evidence of prosecution witnesses, evoked feigned incredulity – "a queer time to take a walk did you not think?" the question which followed had some potential for making a valid point indicative that Moore, whatever else, was up to no good that night.

"I am interested to know Moore why you went out of your way to ask your brother what time it was that you left him?"

Moore had a ready answer –

"For the simple reason that I had already walked further than I intended."

Questioning intended to reveal to the jury at least a hint as to where the truth of it all might lie does rather depend upon the witness being off guard, taken by surprise. This was hardly something that was going to be achieved following the announcement – "I am now going to ask you some questions about motive". With that Hinchcliffe asked Moore to look at the numerous skeleton keys, exhibited in the case and mounted on boards for display purposes. Moore acknowledged both that they were indeed his handiwork and that he had no wish that either they, or any stolen property, should be discovered by the police in the farmhouse. A motive for concealment was confirmed but there was an absence of logic in alleging anxiety about keys and dollar bills being found in the farmhouse as the motive for doing that which would inevitably bring about a police search of every nook, cranny and cavity wall.

What Moore was unable to explain was the live round found within the pile of rubble in the farmyard, a yard which he accepted visiting during the course of that night. It was an account which necessarily involved as well a repeat of his earlier acknowledgement that his first account of his alibi, that he had gone to bed at midnight and "never got up again, lad", involved a lie. He was now saying that he had. In seeking to explain the lie Moore contrived to dig himself into a yet deeper hole by praying in aid the caution that he was not actually obliged to say anything at all. As Hinchcliffe was quick to point out this was an excuse merely for silence, not lies.

Moore's crass attempt to explain his lies by reference to the caution represented the high point of the cross-examination. For the next half hour or so Hinchcliffe did no more than take the witness on a whistle stop tour of the prosecution case inviting assent to its essential accuracy which was, for the most part, forthcoming and just occasionally denied. When it came to the police evidence about what Moore had allegedly said at, and following, his arrest he declined to accept that it was necessarily word perfect accurate – understandable, perhaps, given that he had made no note of the conversation and even the police record was hardly contemporaneous. But at a time when the word of any police officer tended to be accepted uncritically for counsel to tease out even a hint of criticism represented a minor triumph. When Moore was asked whether he had any complaint about a particular interview he responded:

"I have no particular complaint" incautiously adding "it's what you expect in the hands of the police."

Not only did this sound very much like a criticism but one borne out of past experience of being interviewed by the police.

"What do you expect at the hands of the police?" he was asked.

Appreciating that his last answer had done him no favours, Moore parried with –

"To be questioned" adding, not unreasonably, "but I would have liked my solicitor to be there."

Finally, questioning turned to the *piece de resistance* of the prosecution case, P.C. Jagger's sworn deposition, with Moore being asked to confirm that which needed no confirmation at all, namely, that according to this evidence the man whose actions were being described by the officer, or as Hinchcliffe with heavy sarcasm referred to him "this other man", had "worn a raincoat", had "whipped out a revolver" and had had "police torches shone in his face". Hylton-Foster rose to object, observing not unreasonably –

"How can the witness answer any of this when his whole case is 'I was not there' "

For once the intellectual incisiveness of Mr Justice Pearson failed with a response that was contradictory, bordering on the incoherent:

"Yes, I think it is a matter of argument; but I do not think there is anything to object to in this line of cross-examination because the witness is saying 'I do not know, I was not there'. One can see a possible objection, I think. Go on, Mr Hinchcliffe."

If the questions were argumentative, as plainly they were, they were not properly the subject of cross-examination. However, whilst Mr Hinchcliffe did, as invited, 'go on' he moved from the fields surrounding Whinney Close Farm to a venue where Moore undoubtedly was present – the hospital bedside.

"Who did P.C. Jagger pick out?" he asked.

"Me, Sir."

"Were you given the opportunity to cross-examine him?"

"Yes."

"Was the question you put 'are you quite sure?' "

"It was, Sir."

"And was the answer, 'I am quite sure'?"

"Yes."

It was a series of 'soft' questions, based on an assumption that identification evidence, especially when given by a police officer and however difficult the circumstances, provided evidence of guilt beyond the power of questioning to doubt. It was an assumption accepted at the time but which a sorry trail of later miscarriages of justice based on undoubted misidentifications convincingly established to be false. Today any conviction based on evidence of identification where the jury has not been warned of a special need for caution when evaluating the evidence will be quashed almost automatically.

In 1951, however, Hinchcliffe resumed his seat with quiet satisfaction as Hylton-Foster rose and, with a nimble display of footwork and gallows humour (of the worst, and in the context of this trial most literal, kind), swiftly established Moore's ineptitude as a cross-examiner. Having ascertained that this was Moore's debut effort at the art, he asked –

"The next time you will not ask that question, will you?"

"Most certainly not, Sir" replied Moore, entering into this rare moment of levity.

The final questions asked in the course of the evidence at this trial established that whilst where the officers were shot might properly be described as a track leading to the farm, it was also a public footpath leading beyond the farm to Cockley Hill Lane.

As Alfred Moore was led back to the dock Hylton-Foster announced:

"My Lord, that is the case for this man."

Counsel resumed his seat. There was to be no further evidence. That had been decided long ago. In counsel's brief was a proof of the evidence that might be given by Alice Moore which, in its essentials, supported the alibi put forward by Alfred but with ominous portents that the account given by her to the police might actually not be quite so supportive with all the potential that may offer for cross-examination of the most devastating kind. In the defence proof of her evidence she refers to the fact that she spent a number of hours at the police station on that Sunday morning making no less than two statements, each written down as she responded to questions asked, neither of which she was permitted to read before signing and with her requests for a solicitor to be present brushed aside as unnecessary. In addition to the hazard that the statements might fail to support, possibly even contradict, Alfred's evidence as to the time that he arrived home, there were also in what Alice had told the defence clear indicators that her police statement contained material concerning her husband's reprehensible conduct towards his family whose welfare he was asserting was his paramount concern causing him to engage in criminal activity. Alice had told Ted Hutchinson that the police officer directing the taking of her statement at the police station had instructed the scribe "put down her husband has knocked her about" with her protest "but he hasn't" met with "we know he has, put it down." Little wonder that at the conclusion of the copy of Alice's statement in counsel's brief Hylton-Foster made a pencilled note, still faintly decipherable today – 'it may be useful to have Mrs Moore's recollection of Patricia's statement and of her own 2 statements'.

There were a number of undoubted elephant traps involved in calling Alice as a witness and it may be that the defence calculated that even if her evidence was unimpeached it would carry very little weight; that it would inevitably be dismissed by the prosecution, and ultimately the jury, as neither more nor less than the testimony a devoted wife might be expected to provide to support a husband in mortal peril.

The defence had, of course, been denied the opportunity to consider the statements made to the police by Alice it being an accepted legitimate tactic for the prosecution simply not to play trump cards in advance of trial, or, in modern parlance, make disclosure to the defence of 'unused material' (evidence, that is, collected in the course of the investigation but not relied upon in support of the prosecution case). It was a tactic apt to ambush the defence into calling a witness to support the defence only to find the witness cross-examined about a statement made to the police, signed and solemnly declared to be the truth, flatly contradicting the evidence given moments earlier. Some might still consider this to be a perfectly proper tactic in the interests of uncovering the truth. Where it became objectionable was when material was withheld which either seriously undermined the case for the prosecution or provided material support for the defence case. Justice miscarrying was inevitable and when the bitter fruits of this tactic came to light in the 1980's and 1990's something had to be done and the ground rules were changed.

And so the jury would have to reach their verdict, in accordance with their oath, on the basis of what was now before them. The hazards involved in calling more evidence were all too evident and to do so anyway would lose the defence the right to have the last word with the jury.

No time out was afforded to counsel to prepare their final submissions and there was to be no break to ease the mounting tension within the courtroom and mark the fact that the trial, now inevitably to end that day, was moving into a wholly different phase. Mr Hinchcliffe rose to address the jury.

22 – Burglar not murderer

Predictably Mr G. Raymond Hinchcliffe K.C. told the jury that the evidence they had heard should lead them irresistibly to the conclusion that it was the prisoner who had shot and killed Inspector Fraser. It being a convention of advocacy that no reference should be made in a murder trial to the dreadful consequences of a guilty verdict lest, of course, squeamishness should sway a calm, dispassionate appraisal of the evidence, counsel simply invited the jury not to "shrink from your duty." Whilst support for capital punishment was overwhelming at this time there were no doubt many citizens called upon to do jury service who, whilst favouring it in principle, might wish to step back from the personal responsibility involved in a guilty verdict. The convention of advocacy was one that Hylton-Foster would, later that day, take to the very boundaries of permissibility.

Mr Hinchcliffe told the jury that they now knew that which they did not know when he had opened the case to them two days earlier - that Moore was a burglar, adding "a fairly successful burglar at that." But, he told them, "do not convict the prisoner of murder because he has been a burglar." It might be thought to indicate a low regard for the system of trial by jury that they could even be considered as capable of following such a thought process; however, the submission served to establish the prosecutor as a 'minister of justice' intent not upon a conviction at all costs but concerned for a fair and just outcome. In the same vein the jury were exhorted to give "careful and anxious consideration to the evidence called not only on behalf of the Crown but also the evidence the prisoner himself has given."

The true relevance, argued Mr Hinchcliffe, of Moore's career as a burglar was not to explain his actions in destroying and concealing evidence but to supply the motive for the shooting of the officers. Pointing out that the prosecution could not have introduced evidence of Moore's criminal career he suggested that the jury might, up until hearing that evidence, have been puzzled as to why an apparently respectable poultry farmer should suddenly shoot and kill two police officers; indeed, might have considered the prosecution case an improbable one. Now, however, all was clear, the jury had before them plain evidence of motive "to avoid or postpone arrest, to give time to dispose of stolen property that was in the farmhouse that night, to destroy a quantity of stamps, to hide a quantity of valuable pieces of jewellery, to hide live and discharged cartridge cases."

These were cogent points well made but necessarily reference to evidence of concealment in general, and cartridge cases in particular, raised once more all those questions which had haunted police and prosecutors since the search for the murder weapon had been called off. The issue had to be addressed by counsel and this was the point at which to do so. Recalling that Hylton-Foster's cross-examination had "elicited that a very prolonged search had been made, that the army had been called in, that many police officers had been engaged in this search for fourteen days" Mr Hinchcliffe declined to make any apology:

"You may think, and rightly so - it would be a poor day for this country if police officers are to be shot and killed in the execution of their duty and the police failed to take every conceivable and reasonable practicable step to obtain the weapon that fired such shots; the prosecution make no apology that the search for the weapon was an extremely thorough one."

Counsel's efforts appear to miss the point entirely and spectacularly. No criticism had been made that the search was a thorough one. If apology was appropriate it was for the failure of the search to yield up the weapon; better still, an explanation as to how Moore, if the killer, could have concealed so effectively the weapon when all his admitted efforts at concealment of evidence should have proved such a lamentable failure. But for this failure neither apology nor explanation were to be forthcoming.

Turning to the evidence of the police cordon counsel reviewed, first, that which related to 'opportunity' to commit the crime, asserting that the evidence established beyond sensible doubt that the cordon was in place by 11-40 pm and that Fraser and Jagger were "more or less astride the footpath leading to the farmhouse owned by the prisoner and along which one would not expect to find in the early hours of the morning any stranger to the district unless such a stranger was going to Whinney Close Farm." It was a fair point but then to describe the footpath as "little used except by persons going to or coming from that farmhouse" was arguably less than fair, there being absolutely no evidence before the court concerning the extent to which this footpath was in fact used. Therefore, submitted counsel, on the prisoner's own account of his movements he must have encountered the cordon; rhetorically he asked "how did he get through those two experienced police officers without being seen?" And, supplying the answer to his own question, "the overwhelming probability is that the prisoner was returning by that footpath to his farmhouse, not at midnight, but at 1-55 in the morning when he was seen and spoken to first by Jagger, then Fraser."

In telling the jury "you will have to make up your minds as to what you think of the evidence that was given by Mr Joe Baxter" there was at least an implicit acknowledgement that here was evidence open to more than one view. Nonetheless, counsel prayed in aid the naval experience of his witness and asked how he could conceivably have mistaken an air pistol for a revolver with a rotating cartridge. Even the head hair found on the gabardine mackintosh was prayed in aid as "another point; not an immaterial one."

Joe Baxter and the solitary white hair were, however, make weights; mere straws blowing in the wind, not proof in themselves of guilt but serving to lend support to the evidence of what had occurred at the hospital bedside of the mortally wounded Constable. With an apology to the jury for having "detained you too long", rather more a forensic stratagem than heartfelt, Mr Hinchcliffe proceeded once more to read out the material passage in the dying deposition, following it with his final rhetorical question of the day; if the man who shot and killed Inspector Fraser was not Moore, why did he answer to the name of Moore? The answer might very well be of course that the man was not Moore but it suited his purposes that night to be mistaken for Moore. Rhetorical questions, however, do not allow of answers, certainly not by jurors to counsel in the forum of the courtroom.

Before resuming his seat Mr Hinchcliffe concluded as he had begun, not with an unadorned request for a guilty verdict from the jury, but with a bold submission that "the evidence in this case should lead you irresistibly to the conclusion that it was the prisoner who shot and killed Inspector Fraser."

Once more at a point in the proceedings which today might well signal the opportunity for a mid-morning comfort and refreshment break there was to be no respite for this jury. As Hinchcliffe sat down Hylton-Foster rose. His speech was a marathon by the standards of the time, lasting in all some one-and-a-half-hours, not concluding until the afternoon session at 2-40pm. No one present in court to hear it, no one reading the account of it which appeared in the late edition of the *Huddersfield Daily Examiner* that afternoon could have guessed that its eloquence was belied by an unshakeable faith in the guilt of his client and a readiness, without qualm or conscience, to perform, if called upon, the act required to launch Alfred Moore into eternity.

The speech began with formal words of tribute to the assistance given to him by his junior "here and elsewhere" and a reminder that up to this point in the trial he had occupied the jury for very little time, the suggestion being of course that he had not needed to do so because of the paucity of the evidence available to the prosecution. As Hinchcliffe had done earlier he opened his resume of the evidence with the theme 'burglar not murderer' but this time with a claim that credit should be given to the defence "for seeking to introduce some reality into this case" as well as a profession of having far too much respect for the jury even for it to cross his mind that they might "convict this man of murder because he is a burglar".

Advocates (and judges) regularly exhort juries not to leave their common sense behind when they enter the jury box. Here, revelations volunteered to them by the defence about the past history of the prisoner served to tell the jury only and no more than they would have deduced for themselves through the application of 'common sense'; the very fact of the police cordon around the farmhouse, said Hylton-Foster, belied any thought that Alfred Moore was "a respectable, innocent West Riding farmer". Having introduced this evidence it was open to the prosecution "then and there to prove, if it be true, that some place was broken into that night, so that it could be said that the accused on his return home was in possession of stolen property". There was no such evidence and, therefore, no such motive.

The evidence might appear to the jury at first sight to be strong but in reality it was, and had never been anything other than, a case of suspicion. It was a case built upon the assertion of P.C. Jagger 'that is the man' but it was a case where the death of the witness so shortly afterwards was "a very great misfortune not only in human sympathy but in the wider interests of justice". Being far more generous to the tactics of the investigating police officers than was deserved, but with the understandable intent that the defence should not appear to be mounting an attack upon police integrity, Hylton-Foster told the jury that "it was not anybody's fault that the accused was not able to have the assistance of any person trained in my task in life just to ask a few questions". What was known, however, was that Alfred Moore was a stranger to Jagger increasing the likelihood of mistaken identification. It was a fair point and one that today would require something more to commend it than the argument of counsel – nothing less than a direction from the judge that witnesses who are convinced that they have got it right on an issue of identification, and who are, therefore, honest and convincing witnesses, have been shown, on occasions, to have got it wrong with the result that justice has miscarried.

The point, however, that then had to be made by counsel involved the suggestion that perhaps, after all, the farmer was not altogether unknown to the policeman.

"Supposing you are a group of police officers brought together for this rather tedious job, would you not ask: what is it all about? If that was asked would you not then expect the response 'here you are' and out of the files a photograph."

That was the question that needed to be asked and would have been asked by any self-respecting advocate. If a photograph had been shown to officers taking part in the cordon it robbed the evidence of identification of much of its cogency. The identity of the person expected to approach the farmhouse was known making it more likely that a male person doing just that would be mistaken for Moore. Furthermore, the later identification parade became a worthless charade with its inevitability that Moore, the person in the photograph, would be picked out. The circumstances of this identification could hardly be less reliable.

Turning to the cartridge cases, the jury were reminded that the evidence had been that they were manufactured at different times, in different places:

"Can you really imagine this wicked smallholder – incidentally no suggestion of violence in his record – buying revolver ammunition for some nefarious purpose and getting it in such funny shapes that he got two bits made in England in 1942 and one bit in America in 1943? .... It is rather a pity that nobody smelled them, but do you suppose that any police officer would have missed the smell of burnt powder if it were there? And if it was not, does it not just go to confirm that they were stale scraps?"

From cartridge cases counsel moved on to timings and the prosecution's suggestion that on the farmer's account he could not have avoided hitting the cordon. Was the cordon in position at the time alleged? Hylton-Foster's answer was – "the best laid schemes of mice and policemen ...." Reminding the jury that the clock at the home of Charles Henry and Alice Mahala was correct, or so it was claimed, to three minutes, counsel embarked upon a minute analysis of all the evidence that had been heard concerning times with an oblique reminder to the jury of the inevitable consequences of a guilty verdict, something which the conventions of advocacy in hanging cases forbad but which, on this occasion, was accomplished with a subtlety which defied objection.

"I suppose, as I am being tried on a capital charge, that I am entitled to claim at least three minutes grace of you to test these things."

Pointing out that "the margins are so narrow" and the possibility that Jagger, on taking up his position, might have decided to "take the tiniest walk round not expecting to get anything in the net till much later on, that would be quite sufficient for a man in crepe-soled shoes to go by at that moment without him being aware at all."

It is in the nature of a circumstantial case that it involves flitting between many separate and disparate topics. Counsel was about to move from timings to something completely different. The clock in the court room showed 12-55pm. There followed the ritual of barrister and judge each deferring to the other as to whether this was or was not a convenient point to break. The formalities over the court rose for its mid-day adjournment. Alfred Moore was led to the cells below for what he, at least, believed would be his last meal courtesy of His Majesty's Prison service.

When the business of the court resumed Hylton-Foster turned his attention to the solitary strand of hair recovered from Moore's gabardine mackintosh. As the strand had not been anything like definitively identified as that of Inspector Fraser, "why as against this man should you assume that it was? - I do not know and I hope you will not." But even if it was, there was a real possibility that it had been transferred innocently from P.C. Hopping, one of the officers who had stretchered the body of the Inspector, onto the clothing of Sergeant Sadler when the two of them were together stripping the bed in the farmhouse and from the Sergeant onto the gabardine when he transferred it from the farmhouse to the police station "unwrapped, unparcelled." A tortuous, perhaps, but undoubtedly feasible route. It is precisely to avoid the possibility of such innocent cross-contamination that today would require, on pain of evidence being ruled inadmissible, the strict quarantining of exhibits in bags provided for the purpose. The submission concluded that "the value of the hair as a pointer any way at all in this case is just precisely nothing." It was a powerful submission, leaving open only the question of why counsel had not argued from the outset that valueless evidence is irrelevant evidence and the law does not permit the introduction of irrelevancies. Before leaving the gabardine mackintosh counsel made the further point that its recovery at 5-15 am "bone dry" when the evidence was that there had been a heavy downpour after midnight did rather tend to support Moore having returned home when he claimed rather than at the time that the officers were shot.

Returning to the theme 'burglar not murderer' counsel agreed with the prosecution that Moore's assertion, following his arrest, that having gone to bed he had not got up again was not the assertion of an innocent man. That, however, merely begged the question: innocent of what? His guilt of burglary explained just about everything that needed to be explained both as to what he said and what he did. When he said, on being handcuffed, that it was serious "it meant nothing as between on the one hand possession of keys, possession of stolen property and on the other the much, much graver matter of this shooting; of course it was serious, as serious as it could be."

As to the dispute between his client and Superintendent Metcalfe concerning whether, just before the handcuffs were applied, the officer had attempted to distract Moore by a question about whether he had been out shooting foxes, a series of rhetorical question were posed (which by definition could not be answered but as to which in truth there was no answer that could have withstood scrutiny):

"How could it help this man, on trial here before you on this serious charge, to say that at that time Mr Metcalfe mentioned foxes? How does it make it better for him in any way? What is the object of saying it unless it is true? If Mr Metcalfe was prepared to say that he talked to him about his chickens at first in order to distract his attention, to get his mind off the approaching thing, is it very surprising if the conversation went further and got as far as shooting foxes?"

Dealing with the conversation in the police station cell, a few hours later, and Moore's response "don't talk about it" Hylton-Foster invoked Moore's unqualified right to remain silent – one of the few aspects of the criminal process more liberal in 1951 than today. The prosecution were taken to task for urging the jury to regard that answer, in response to the question concerning firearms held at the farm, as proof of guilt.

"What is the point of cautioning a man, setting a trap for him, and then coming here to complain that he did not answer? That is not fair comment as against this man."

Having the previous day undermined totally the credibility of Joe Baxter counsel had evidently decided that this was not the time for overkill. The point had been made. It did not require to be hammered home that this was a witness who was as opinionated as he was wrong. And so, with restraint and feigned respect, the jury were told:

"I do not desire to suggest in any way that Mr Baxter has not come here to tell you the truth as best he believed it to be. But did you notice, curiously – I really do not desire to use offensive words, but I have to indicate to you what I mean – how strangely opinionated Mr Baxter was; you remember the impertinent reaction about the German Navy? He did not mean to be rude but that is a portrait of a man who feels very confident about himself."

Inside the velvet glove was the clunking fist. Reminding the jury of the numerous times that Joe Baxter had confidently described what he asserted he had seen in the tool box as a Luger revolver Hylton-Foster stated simply – "there is no such thing; it does not exist; there never has been a Luger revolver and never will be; Luger do not make revolvers. If he saw a Luger that was not the weapon used in this case because the weapon used in this case was revolver; if he saw a revolver it was not a Luger."

Returning to the suggested motive, that the shooting of the officers was so that Moore might return home in order to conceal or destroy stolen property, counsel castigated it as "absurd, preposterous"; having been in possession of the proceeds of his crimes "since the Honley days, all the month of May, all the month of June and half the month of July: do you think he was wandering round the country with a revolver in his pocket waiting to shoot any policeman who might be going to arrest him before he could get back home and dispose of that property?" Nor did any alternative motive, such as Moore returning home with the proceeds of an offence committed that night, hold good: "nothing had been stolen that night, all the thefts were old, it will not do."

Finally, reserving the best for last, the search of the farmhouse, outbuildings and surrounding fields. In meticulous, remorseless, telling detail the jury were reminded of just how thorough that search had been, the number of persons involved in it, the period of time that it covered, the numerous small objects that it uncovered. Far from the search having failed, declared Hylton-Foster, it had been a resounding success "in establishing Moore's innocence, by showing that it is true that he had not got a weapon of that kind because, if he had, it would by now have been found; it shows that whoever it was who killed those two policemen took the weapon not towards Whinney Close Farm but out of the area in the direction in which everybody knows the accused did not go – he was inside the cordon right up to the time of arrest."

The peroration of counsel's address of course reminded the jury that the burden was not upon Moore to prove his innocence and that, echoing Moore's own words following the identification of him months earlier at the hospital bedside, he was as entitled to be believed as Jagger. He concluded:

"A ghastly, callous, brutal crime has been committed which would fill every decent citizen with a sense of horror. But, the more horrible the crime the more important it is, not the less important, to see that no-one is wrongly convicted of it."

Counsel resumed his seat, his job well-done, perhaps even slightly persuaded himself by the force of his own eloquence that there was at least a nagging doubt as to the guilt of his client. Moore's fate now rested with judge and jury.

23 – The last word

Following his brief enquiry of the prosecution to confirm that the name of "the prisoner" was 'Alfred' not 'Albert' Mr Justice Pearson began his summing-up of the case. It was to be the last word that the jury would hear before retiring and, almost certainly, the first summing-up of a criminal trial they had ever heard. For that matter it was also the first summing-up, at least in a murder case, that the judge himself, newly appointed to the bench and with no experience of crime at the bar, had ever heard. One of the lesser anomalies of the workings of our criminal justice system is that serious crime is tried by Justices of the Queen's Bench Division of the High Court of Justice who are in the main recruited from the ranks of those with practices at the bar in the fields of banking and commerce, libel and slander. The theory being that the intellectual stamina required for practice in such esoteric fields provides more than sufficient qualification to pick up at a stroke the more simplistic concepts involved in criminal law, evidence and procedure. This was 1951 and the criminal law was simple and straightforward; the rules of evidence were easily understood, simply stated and only rarely gave rise to controversy in the trial process. The last major piece of criminal justice legislation had gone onto the statute book three years earlier in 1948 and it was not until 1968 that there was to be another. In the modern age, with politicians of all hues intent on establishing their tough law and order credentials, not a year goes by without at least one major piece of criminal justice legislation passing through Parliament – and sometimes more. The criminal trial is no longer an arena for the novice to learn the rudiments of judge-craft.

All that said, no one in the assize court at Leeds on that day, listening to the summing-up, would have rated it the efforts of a novice. It began with a brief, but entirely adequate, reminder to the jury that they were the sole judges of the facts and that "the case should be approached and considered and decided as a question of fact simply, uninfluenced by any sentimental considerations on the one side or the other." Explaining this further –

"You should not say that this man is guilty of murder because he is a self-confessed burglar and of course you should not be misled into any adverse verdict by indignation at the horrible crime or by sympathy with the deceased police officers and their wives and families or by sympathy with the police force as a whole. On the other side, of course, you should not be misled the other way by any feelings of mere sympathy for the accused man or his family."

Again briefly, but adequately, the summing-up dealt with the burden and standard of proof in a criminal trial. No words were wasted on the legal definition of the crime of murder for as the judge told the jury –

"You will have no doubt whatever that Duncan Alexander Fraser was shot at and killed by somebody."

The issue for the jury to decide was: "Are you sure beyond any reasonable doubt that Alfred Moore is the man who shot and killed Duncan Alexander Fraser in the small hours of that Sunday morning?"

What then followed was an analysis of the evidence that had been heard by the Court which was a model of clarity and, certainly by the standards of the time when so many such exercises amounted to little more than a second speech for the prosecution, largely fair. This was to be no idle reading out of that which had been recorded in the judicial notebook devoid of any effort to marshal the evidence into a coherent structure. This judge had worked hard on his task and, as he told the jury "I put the facts before you as disclosed by the evidence in the order in which they happened."

The obvious place to begin was at Honley and the criminal activities of Alfred Moore whilst living there. Both sides of the argument were placed before the jury for their consideration:

"It is a fact on which the prosecution rely as showing that the accused had or may have had some motive for committing the crime. It is relied on by the defence as affording an explanation of why he made certain apparently incriminating statements."

Next came the move from Honley and the evidence of Joe Baxter. Having reminded the jury of the expert evidence "that there was no such thing as Luger revolver", the weapon that Baxter claimed to have seen in the tool box when it broke open, the learned judge speculated – and uncharacteristically fell into error which ought to have been but was not, on this occasion, corrected by counsel:

"There are several possibilities. He may not have seen anything at all. He may have seen one of those two exhibits and mistaken it for a revolver. He may have seen a revolver which was not a Luger *or he may have seen a Luger revolver and it has disappeared since.*"

Seamlessly the summation of the evidence moved on to the events of the 14 July and the evidence of Charles Henry Moore and his wife. The evidence concerning the time at which the brothers parted and that at which P.C. Jagger took up his position on the cordon was rehearsed and the conclusion argued for by the prosecution balanced by a reminder of the defence submission that Moore might have passed through the cordon without being observed or him being aware of the cordon. It may have seemed to the jury at the time a far-fetched submission. In the light of what is known today – but wilfully concealed from the defence at the time – as to the instructions given to the officers forming the cordon it was in fact a submission underpinned by a firm foundation.

Following a reminder of the positions of the various officers on the cordon Mr Justice Pearson turned to '1-55 am'. Although the jury had heard the sworn deposition read to them twice it was read again.

"I will" said the judge "read it very slowly. It is direct evidence on the question you have to consider."

Only briefly were the jury reminded that there had been no effective challenge by way of cross-examination of this evidence and nothing at all was said concerning the possibility of mistaken identification. It was a possibility hardly countenanced in 1951. If an eye witness to a crime, giving patently honest, and therefore convincing, evidence pointed the finger at the accused, what better evidence of guilt could there be? Why should any tribunal of fact doubt such evidence? On this occasion it was the potential strengths of Jagger's identification which were emphasised: it was made by a police officer of experience whose object that night it was to observe "anyone going out or coming in" and it was aided by the torchlight shone onto the face of the killer.

Today, even on the highly unlikely assumption that the case would ever have reached a court of trial or, if it had, that it would have survived the inevitable submission of no case to answer at the close of the case for the Crown, the way in which such evidence would be dealt with by the judge would be very different and replete with hazard warnings about the dangers of placing reliance upon it as evidence of guilt. First, because it was the sole and effective evidence of guilt, untested by cross-examination and which the defence would have wished to challenge but had no opportunity to do so. Secondly, because the experience of the courts was that witnesses, convinced that their identification of an accused was correct, had been shown on occasions to be mistaken with the calamity that justice had miscarried. There is today an obligation upon a trial judge to remind the jury not only of what might be considered the strengths of an identification but also the weaknesses as well. In this case that would require specific reference to the fact that this was a fleeting glimpse of a stranger in the hours of darkness. Without such warnings any resulting conviction would be quashed by the Court of Appeal.

Having dealt with evidence that, the judge told the jury, was "central, direct and vital" he turned to other evidence which was relevant only to the extent that the jury might consider that it corroborated the correctness of Jagger's identification of Moore as the killer. The evidence concerning the arrest of Moore and the subsequent events of that Sunday, at police station and hospital, was placed before the jury with little or nothing by way of comment either way. On the failure to recover the murder weapon Mr Justice Pearson simply observed "you have heard arguments to and fro from learned counsel." Comment would not have gone amiss that the search had been as thorough as could be imagined; that it had unearthed, uncovered and revealed a veritable mountain of other evidence and that the failure to recover that which was crucial strongly pointed not towards but away from Whinney Close Farm. However, in some detail the evidence was rehearsed which underpinned the defence submission that the single strand of white hair either was not definitively identified as coming from Fraser's head or, if it had, it had been accidentally transferred onto Moore's clothing via the medium of P.C. Hopping. Somewhat lamely the saga of the solitary white hair concluded "but of course there does remain the fact that there was a white hair on the raincoat and that Fraser had white hair and a comparison of the two from a technical point of view did not reveal any dissimilarities."

The jury were reminded fully of the evidence given so recently by the defendant and without comment save to remind the jury of something which had almost certainly crossed their minds already -

"Two people living today, Mrs Moore and his daughter, know the time when he arrived at his house. They were not, of course, called as witnesses so they cannot assist you in this matter."

The summing-up concluded with a brief reminder of the main points made to them earlier by both sides, an exercise intended no doubt to assist but which from a judicial perspective was fraught with the hazard that brevity might result in some inaccuracy marring an otherwise unimpeachable effort. The mind of the learned judge was evidently tiring and for the second time he fell into error when reminding the jury of the evidence of Joe Baxter.

"For the defence you know what is said about Mr Baxter that he was wrong in saying that he saw a Luger weapon. Of course, it does not actually follow that Mr Baxter might have been wrong. *There might have been a Luger revolver there*, even if it was not ...."

For counsel to interrupt the summing-up of any judge, let alone one of the Queen's Bench of the High Court, was almost unheard of but, on this occasion, with that presence with which Hylton-Foster was wont to dominate the courtroom, he rose to his feet.

"With great respect, the evidence is that there cannot be a Luger revolver."

There was no arguing with that. Seldom can the word 'grovel' be applied to a response from the bench to a member of the bar – though where that position is reversed it might. On this occasion it would seem entirely apt.

"I beg your pardon. You are perfectly right. I had mentioned it before. You are absolutely right. I am very much obliged to you, Mr Hylton-Foster."

The attempt at saving some face which followed was inept, incoherent.

"The evidence is that there cannot be such a thing as a Luger revolver and, therefore, he cannot have seen a Luger revolver. Of course he may have seen ...."

At this point the thought processes of the learned judge as to just what Joe Baxter might have seen failed and after a few seconds of embarrassing silence he concluded unconvincingly.

"Well, it is a matter for you to consider whether he may nevertheless have seen *some* revolver."

Before the invitation to retire the jury were once more reminded of their proper approach to the task of evaluating evidence in a criminal trial.

"You will remember the burden of proof and therefore the proper way to look at the question whether you are satisfied beyond reasonable doubt that Alfred Moore was that man who shot the deceased inspector."

To the final charge to the jury to "consider your verdict" the learned judge added "if you wish to retire you may do so." The notion that in a capital case the jury, having listened to extensive evidence over three days, might feel able to turn to each other in the jury box and within the moment announce a life or death verdict seems quaint to say the least although one hundred years earlier juries regularly did exactly that. Centuries before, of course, at the trial of Thomas Moore, the celebrated charge to the jury of Master Cromwell was – "Retire! I do not think you need to retire in such clear a case."

The jury bailiffs were sworn to 'keep the jury in some private and convenient place and to suffer no person to speak to them concerning the trial this day save to ask them if they are agreed upon their verdict.' It was at 4-21 pm that the jury retired, a time at which if a jury were being asked to retire and deliberate today would give rise to, inevitably successful, grounds for an appeal that pressure as to time was being placed upon the jury to reach a verdict. It was not until 1992 that the Court of Appeal (Criminal Division) held that the latest time at which a jury should be asked to begin its deliberations was 3-00 pm. No-one present in court, however, with the possible exception of the reporter from the *Huddersfield Examiner,* anticipated a lengthy retirement and no-one, apart from the reporter, was to be disappointed.

24 – The reporter's gaffe

As the jury deliberated Moore paced anxiously from wall to wall of his cell in the Victorian Bridewell below the courtroom. The show of confidence that he had maintained during the weeks of his remand was by now in tatters as the denouement of his trial loomed. Those owing him a duty of care would have offered him refreshment but whether, by now, he had an appetite to satisfy must remain doubtful.

Ted Hutchinson strongly advised Alice Moore to leave the building and not return until the outcome be known. He had every reason to fear an emotional display marring the dramatic ritual which would follow an unfavourable outcome to the deliberations of the jury. It was arranged that Alice would remain with her friends, Mr and Mrs Norris Bennett, just outside the building in their car and that Ted's son, Arthur, would be the messenger bringing news of her husband's fate. For a young lad it was an unenviable task and as the minutes ticked away it was not only Alfred Moore who prayed that sufficient doubt had been raised to return him before the day's end to his wife and daughters.

The local crime reporter, with his vast experience of these things and possibly a thirst to be satisfied, appears to have calculated that the capital nature of the charge and the jury's need to be seen to be giving nothing less than anxious consideration to the evidence, meant that he was safe for the next hour. His apparent absence from court at the point of sentence suggests at least the possibility that he retired across the road to that favoured watering hole of the journalistic classes, the Town Hall Tavern – or as it was, indeed still is, more shortly known 'the THT'. As with all those able to view the proceedings with detachment he did not expect a particularly lengthy retirement, harbouring few doubts that the deathbed identification of Moore as the killer would prove decisive in the thinking of the jury, though even he failed to judge just how little time the jury would take to deliberate and reach their verdict. The last edition of that day's *Examiner* had long been 'put to bed' so this was a story that might be written and the climax savoured without the pressure of a deadline. Already the words in which the drama of the black cap were to be painted for readers the next day were forming in his head. Weeks earlier the editorial decision had been made that the expected outcome of the trial would be accompanied by a special feature recalling multiple murders in and around Huddersfield over the past couple of centuries.

It was at 5-12 pm, nine minutes short of an hour since the jury retired, that they filed back into a hushed and crowded court. During the course of the afternoon, as it became clear that the trial would end that day, the courtroom had gradually filled and during the jury's retirement few without reserved places, such as the local reporter, had left. For any observer of the legal scene the ultimate experience was to witness the donning of the black cap and the utterance of the words of doom. It was standing room only with just one empty place on the reporters' bench.

What followed was as brief as it was dramatic. Moore was brought up into the dock for the last time looking strained, drawn, ill at ease, no longer sporting that ruddy complexion signifying an outdoor life spent on the land. He was plainly terrified at the prospect of what the next few minutes might bring.

The Clerk of Assize addressed the jury:

"Would one of you please stand up and act as Foreman and answer this question? Members of the jury are you agreed upon your verdict?"

One of their number, selected by them to preside over their deliberations and act as their voice, rose.

"We are."

"Do you find Alfred Moore guilty or not guilty of murder?"

All eyes in the courtroom were now upon Moore who contrived to remain impassive as the jury foreman spoke the one word.

"Guilty."

"Is that the verdict of you all?"

"That is the verdict of us all."

The preliminaries to sentence being passed were not yet complete. The ritual of asking the prisoner if there was any reason why the court should not give judgement against him had to be observed. It was a ritual centuries old, with real justification when representation by counsel was exceptional, and gave to the accused one final opportunity to urge anything – such as in the case of a woman pregnancy – which might operate as a ground for respiting judgement. By the time of Alfred Moore's trial it was no more than a hollow ritual allowing one final protestation of innocence to be made.

Turning from the jury to the dock the clerk of the assize addressed Moore.

"Alfred Moore, you stand convicted of wilful murder. What have you of yourself to say why sentence of death should not be passed upon you?"

With, for the first time, a noticeable catch in his voice, Moore spoke –

"My Lord, I protest my innocence. I am not guilty."

The judge's clerk stood to place upon his judge's short bench wig the square of cloth known as the black cap, an essential of the macabre ritual of pronouncing sentence of death. It was the judge's first murder trial since his elevation to the bench shortly before and his practice at the bar had done nothing to prepare him for the task that lay ahead. As he began to speak Mr Justice Pearson was visibly moved, as much if not more so than the prisoner.

"Alfred Moore, you have been convicted of murder by the verdict of the jury. The sentence of the Court upon you is that you be taken from this place to a lawful prison and thence to a place of execution and there suffer death by hanging and that your body be buried within the precincts of the prison in which you shall have been last confined before your execution. And may The Lord have mercy on your soul."

The Chaplain, another necessary player in the ritual, intoned "Amen." Moore was gripped firmly on the arms by the two prison warders performing prisoner escort duties that day and, without further protest or show of emotion, led smartly down the steps and out of public view for the penultimate time. Simultaneously Mr Justice Pearson was assisted to his feet by his clerk and led from the bench, his formal bow to the court on this occasion little more than a perfunctory nod. The words of the Clerk of Assize formally to close the court were not spoken that day.

What had occurred following the return of the jury to the courtroom had taken no more than a couple of minutes. It just didn't seem that way to any of those present. The main players having left the stage there was a collective, almost palpable, sigh of relief as the crowds in the well of the court and public gallery silently dispersed.

The local reporter, who had missed the drama, arrived breathless at the door of the court to receive from his fellow scribes a sufficient account of what had just taken place to write his copy. It had all the makings of a good story for not only did it involve a show of emotion on the part of the condemned man, which was to be expected, but a no less dramatic display on the part of a judge passing his first death sentence.

The reporter did not of course need to be told the words of the death sentence for he had heard it all before but it was his reporting of those words that gave him away. In the next evening's *Examiner* it was reported that Moore was told that his fate was 'to be hanged by the neck until you are dead.' Those may have been the words uttered when the reporter was last in court to hear sentence of death pronounced but were not the words spoken on this occasion. The pronouncement 'hang by the neck until you are dead' was one hallowed undoubtedly by centuries of use but dating back to an age before 'the drop' when death by hanging involved asphyxiation and where powerful neck muscles or a particularly resistant windpipe often led to slow strangulation or even the executed man coming back to life after being cut down. The Royal Commission on Capital Punishment had been sitting since 1948 and one of its earliest recommendations was that the wording be changed to 'suffer death by hanging' in deference to the supposedly – there being necessarily a dearth of first-hand evidence – swift and merciful efficiency of modern methods.

It remained only for young Arthur Hutchinson to break the news to Alice, an unenviable task and one that caused him to question whether he really did wish to follow in the footsteps of his father. With what words he did so he no longer recalls, perhaps a sombre expression and the words 'I'm sorry' were capable of saying all that needed to be said. The local reporter anxious to make amends for his earlier lapse remained on duty in the building and was able to add to his report that Alice Moore was to be seen entering the building in great distress and, having been allowed to see her husband in the cells, leaving it to be assisted into a waiting car in even greater distress. In much the same condition in fact that she had been reported as leaving the magistrates' court months earlier on the occasion of her husband's first court appearance.

As part of the death sentence Mr Justice Pearson had directed that Moore should be taken to a place of lawful execution. Leeds Prison was so designated. There had in fact been no execution at Leeds since March the previous year. Up until then the execution shed was located a distance 40 metres across the open prison yard from where the condemned cell was situated in A wing. Such a distance for the condemned man to walk to his doom was commonplace in Victorian times but by the mid-twentieth century was an anachronism and so for the eighteen months prior to the arrival of Alfred Moore work had been taking place to construct within the grounds of the prison a new purpose-built execution suite. It housed not merely the execution shed and adjoining condemned cells but also the visiting area and the quarters where the executioner and his assistant were housed on the night before the event. Whilst this work was ongoing prisoners condemned to death in Leeds were sent to Manchester's Strangeways Gaol for execution. Moore was the first prisoner to enjoy the amenities of Leeds' newly opened execution suite. Although the new facility housed two condemned cells, one on either side of the execution shed, even this was insufficient to cope with the four men condemned to hang at the 1953 Leeds Winter Assize. None were reprieved and two of the four met their end across the Pennines.

Following the abolition of the death penalty in the 1960's the execution suite was re-designated as an administrative centre, housing also the prison's dog unit.

Although there was to be no change of venue for Alfred Moore the circumstances of his incarceration would now take on a curiously kinder and more solicitous face. At this time the capital punishment debate raged and a Royal Commission had spent years considering the evidence and arguments. In its final report it described in chilling, clinical, fascinating detail life in the condemned cell.

"Immediately a prisoner sentenced to death returns from court, he is placed in a cell for condemned prisoners and is watched night and day by two officers. Amenities such as cards, chess, dominoes, etc., are provided in the cell and the officers are encouraged to – and in fact invariably do – join the prisoner in these games. Newspapers and books are provided. Food is supplied from the main prison kitchen, the prisoner being placed on hospital diet, with such additions as the medical officer considers advisable. A pint of beer or stout is supplied daily upon request and ten cigarettes or half an ounce of pipe tobacco are allowed unless there are medical reasons to the contrary. The prisoner may smoke in his cell as well as exercise. It is the practice for the Governor, medical officer and chief officer to visit the prisoner under sentence of death twice daily, and the chaplain or minister of any other denomination has free access to him. He may be visited by such of his relations, friends and legal advisers as he desires to see and as are authorised to visit him by the visiting committee and the Commissioners and he is given special facilities to write and receive letters."

This show of humanity can have done little to mitigate the sheer terror of the experience, the mortal fear of what the brief future held. What motivated Alfred Moore during those final terrifying days was knowledge of his innocence and a residual, though by now seriously diminished, faith in the best justice system in the world to right a terrible wrong. For hours each day he 'worked' on his appeal, writing screeds of material highlighting all those reasons why the verdict of the jury was wrong, his innocence not merely 'non-proven' but positively vindicated by all that had been placed before that jury at the recently concluded assize.

His faith was not shared by his legal advisers. They were too well aware of the limitations of the appeals procedure and of how the exercise of the Home Secretary's power to reprieve operated in the case of convicted police killers. Above all they were aware of the personalities and 'track records' of the two figures who now stood between Alfred Moore and his appointment with the hangman.

25 – Goddard and Kilmuir

In the days following Moore's conviction the press reported that Ted Hutchinson was making repeated visits to the prison and that an appeal was being 'considered' and later 'almost certain'. An appeal was in fact as inevitable as death and taxes. Following sentence an announcement was made that January 3rd had been provisionally fixed as the day on which Moore's execution was to take place, calculated by reference to the convention which permitted the condemned man three Sundays in which to prepare for his death and make peace with God. Once an appeal was lodged the date was automatically vacated and the intervention of the period between Christmas and the New Year, when the machineries of Government and Justice pause, did rather more to lengthen the span of Alfred Moore's earthly days than the efforts of any of his advisers could realistically ever have achieved.

In capital cases, unless the prisoner was actively looking to end his or her life (as was the case with Ruth Ellis, the last woman to be hanged in Britain) an appeal was automatic and the requirement of leave to appeal a formality. This generous dispensation too often led, however, to judges in the appeal court approaching their task on the basis of 'just another appeal in just another murder case' and did not fight shy of saying so. None of those professionally involved in Moore's defence believed for one moment that giving notice of appeal would produce any effect other than to postpone the inevitable and a feat of some imagination was required even to draft grounds that appeared faintly arguable.

An appeal was not (still is not) a re-hearing of the case, merely a review of the safety of the conviction and the basis on which an appeal might be considered are so strictly limited that few are brought and very few actually succeed. There had to be either a material irregularity in the proceedings in the court below (plainly these proceedings were entirely regular); or misdirection of the jury by the judge on a matter of law (the only issue in this case was one of fact) or that the conviction was unsafe and against the weight of the evidence. By definition, where a case has reached the stage of a jury verdict either the judge will have ruled that there is a case to answer or he will not have so ruled simply because the defence have accepted that there is a case to answer. 'Fresh evidence' is another possible gateway to the quashing of a conviction but one requiring various hurdles to be surmounted. The evidence has to be 'fresh' in the sense of not capable of being adduced at the trial because either it did not then exist or was not capable of being discovered by the exercise of due diligence. It is also required to be cogent and with a potential to cast real doubt on the validity of the conviction.

The case for an arguable, let alone successful, appeal would have been tenuous in any age. At this time the obstacles were actually more than merely procedural. They were personal. Rayner Goddard, holder of the office of Lord Chief Justice of England and Wales, presided over the proceedings in the Court of Criminal Appeal and personally took charge of all appeals in capital cases. His humour was of the gallows variety and often he would tell an audience that he had never seen a man to whom hanging had done any harm. He was an enthusiast for the rope, for flogging, for sternness in fact tempered only by severity, and when it came to the word of a police officer his presumption that it was the truth and nothing but was irrebuttable. In the conduct of his court he enjoyed a reputation for expedition in the despatch of his daily list of cases which took precedence over the needs of justice or the conventions of ordinary courtesy.

The division of labour between leading and junior counsel conventionally required that the task of drafting documents fell to the junior. The task set for Ray Dean to put on paper grounds on which at least his leader might rise to his feet and address the Lord Chief Justice was an unenviable one. No less enviable was that of Ted Hutchinson in seeking support for a petition for clemency should the appeal fail. The very fact of the conviction had dissipated any residual sympathy that the predicament of the poultry farmer might have attracted. The only persons likely to be interested in putting their names to a petition to reprieve a double police killer were close friends and family and ardent abolitionists. In 1951 there were few of the latter about. The exercise of the Royal Prerogative of mercy was obviously that of the, failing, Monarch - George VI. But it was one exercised entirely upon the recommendation of the Home Secretary of the day and herein lay yet a further impediment to an outcome that might have saved Alfred Moore's neck – David Maxwell-Fyfe, later, as Lord High Chancellor, Lord Kilmuir.

Whilst the lawyers busied themselves with the task of doing what little they could to prolong the life of their client Moore himself settled into the routines of life in the death cell, every day following the invariable pattern of timed visits from family, timed periods of exercise in the prison yard, bouts of furious writing about his case and why his conviction was just plain wrong and ought to be quashed, interspersed with light entertainment in the form of dominoes and chess (Alfred's particular favourite) with his guards. In other circumstances it would have been a routine of boredom writ large but by now every second of mere existence was precious and every waking moment overshadowed with thoughts of how it all might shortly end.

For Alice and the girls, by now living in rented accommodation at Birkhead Street in Heckmondwike under the assumed surname Hirst, preparations for the festive season were muted if not altogether put on hold. The worst of post-war austerity may have been consigned to the history books but for this family there was nothing to celebrate and the New Year that beckoned hardly one to anticipate. The best that could be said of their predicament is that they were able to maintain a low profile with the press keeping a respectful distance, there being none of the intolerable media intrusion into their daily lives that would almost certainly occur today with a family imminently to be violently bereaved.

Their new neighbours had of course read about the trial and conviction of the Kirkheaton farmer but failed to make the connection with the single parent family newly moved into the street. Alice's absence from the home each afternoon, occasionally accompanied by her eldest daughter Pat, raised no more than mild curiosity. Patricia Moore had been spared nothing of the realities of it all and was a regular visitor to the prison at Leeds with her mother.

On the day following the conviction an article about the case appeared in a now long-forgotten national newspaper – the *Daily Dispatch.* It contained an interview with Ben Stafford and his wife, residents of Cockley

Hill Farm and near neighbours of Alfred and Alice. It was an interview eulogising the late Inspector Fraser with whom the Staffords claimed to have been on friendly terms. So friendly in fact that he had popped into their house for a chat on the night of the shooting immediately before taking up his position on the cordon. If this was right then it represented a significant breach in the prosecution case that all the officers involved in the exercise had assembled at the West Riding Police Headquarters in Huddersfield, travelled together in convoy to the brickworks at Kirkheaton and from there straightaway taken up their positions on the cordon *by at the latest 11-45 pm.* The time was critical to the prosecution case. If what the Staffords were saying was right and given that it was, as Ted Hutchinson instructed counsel in the handwritten supplemental Brief for Counsels' appearance in the Appeal Court, a 15 to 20 minute walk from their farmhouse to Fraser's position on the cordon it placed his arrival on the cordon significantly later than had been claimed at the trial. In short it lent credence to Moore's assertion that he had walked up the fields to his home without being aware of a police presence.

Ted Hutchinson was by now a very anxious solicitor. Not, perhaps, entirely convinced of the innocence of his client but with sufficient doubts as to the evidence on which he had been convicted that, whatever his personal views on the hanging issue, he was desperate to avoid losing him to the hangman. He was spending much time in and around Kirkheaton and not just pacing out the walk from the Stafford's farm to where the shooting occurred but, as a convivial man, listening out to any gossip, of which there was plenty, about the case. According to his brief to counsel an informant, who was prepared to do no more than provide information but otherwise insisted on remaining anonymous, had told him that the Staffords had been saying in and around the village that it was midnight before Fraser left their house. This was potentially useful in nailing any suggestion that the *Daily Dispatch* article referred to a visit much earlier in the evening but in fact worthless because it represented hearsay upon hearsay and could not be admitted as evidence.

The real problem, however, with this evidence was that it was known only too well where the sympathies of the Staffords lay and it was not with their former neighbour. Any approach to them for a statement would, it was feared, be met unfavourably. The only course open was to serve on them a *subpoena* to attend and testify at the Appeal Court should leave be granted to admit fresh evidence. It was a high risk strategy because even if called they could not be cross-examined – you cannot cross-examine your own witness, only that of your opponent – and, without a statement, there was no way of knowing what they might say and every reason to think that they would adopt whatever stratagem they could to avoid lending oxygen to the case for Alfred Moore.

Problem it might have been but it was certainly not a dilemma. Evidence from the Staffords certainly represented fresh evidence of which the defence could not previously or reasonably have been aware by the exercise of due diligence. Where a case is not going well strategies that in other circumstances would be regarded as replete with risk may be taken in the sure and certain knowledge that the case is not going to get worse and might, just might, improve.

A problem of an entirely different kind was posed by the other witness against whom Ted Hutchinson had served a precautionary and actually unnecessary *subpoena.* Unnecessary because this was not an unwilling witness. Quite the reverse. This was a witness not merely ready but positively eager and willing to have his day in court, take the stand and proclaim not merely the innocence of Alfred Moore but the justice of his own cause.

It was only a few days after conviction and sentence that Tom Holdsworth of 1, Bryan Place, Rastrick made himself known to Ted Hutchinson with information that on first telling appeared cogent and compelling. Only a few days before the shooting, he told Ted, police officers who were to form links in the cordon, and in particular one by the name of Garnett, had spoken to him concerning recent local burglaries and shown to him a photograph of Alfred Moore. This, of course, was what the defence had suspected all along but had been unable to establish and, if it was right, meant that Jagger's identification of Moore was, arguably, not so much recognition of the killer but of the features on a photograph with which he was all too familiar.

Ted, however, was well aware that notorious cases regularly attract the attention of those with but a tenuous grip on reality and this particular clock whilst chiming twelve sound and convincing notes chimed also, on closer questioning, a distinctly crazy thirteenth stroke. Holdsworth claimed, first, to have been himself under suspicion, because of his employment as a night watchman, for the very burglaries now admitted by Moore. Then to be a police informer who had given much useful information to the police in the past, in particular concerning Alfred

Moore's responsibility for burglaries in and around Huddersfield. That was at least plausible, as was the fact that he claimed to have been shown a photograph of Moore only days before the killing and asked the question: "is this the man?" He had also, he claimed, told the police that he was "confident Moore was not guilty of murder and wished to help him." The basis of this confidence lay, and lay entirely, in his psychic powers. He went on to claim to be a member of a wealthy Huddersfield family "of the same name" and his ramblings soon revealed that this witness was unhinged and acting in pursuit of some grievance arising from his claim to be a sufferer from silicosis and the victim of a conspiracy by the medical profession to deprive him of compensation to which he was justly entitled.

Notwithstanding clear indicators that Tom Holdsworth was at best far from well and at worst unhinged Ted instructed counsel that he 'was impressed by Holdsworth's apparent sincerity and felt it his duty to mention it to Mrs Moore who has instructed him to have Holdsworth available if counsel wishes to call him.'

The grounds of application for leave to appeal drafted by Ray Dean were the best that could be devised in the circumstances but were never likely to persuade a case-hardened Court of Criminal Appeal presided over by Goddard that there was anything either wrong or unsafe about the conviction. A number of niggling complaints concerning errors in the trial judge's summation of the evidence were put forward, the tone of which was set by the first paragraph of the draft grounds – the judge had told the jury that the raincoat was recovered from the tallboy "when in fact it was found in a different and separate piece of furniture in that bedroom."

Not much better really was the complaint that the summing-up got it wrong when the jury were told that the accused's explanation for his lie that he did not get up after midnight was because he had been told that someone had been hurt and was "trying to cover up" whereas in fact what he had said in evidence was "I know why I had been up and I was trying to cover up." The fact was that he had lied – for whatever reason.

The grounds went on to criticise Mr Justice Pearson's observation that if Moore had been "inside somewhere" on the night of the shooting between the hours of midnight and 2-00am then of course the raincoat would have been dry, a comment that trumped the defence assertion that given the rain that had fallen that night it would have been wet – assuming that Moore had been out and about at the time. It was a good defence point but the comment made by the judge, and when summing-up judges are entitled to make comment, was plainly within permissible bounds. On the prosecution case Moore was not indoors at Whinney Close Farm between those hours. The borderline between speculation and guesswork on the one hand, which is not permissible, and legitimate inference from facts admitted or proven by the evidence can be a fine one. But here was evidence on which a jury might legitimately conclude that Moore was not at home and, if he was elsewhere but was not for saying where he was, a legitimate inference was that he was under cover somewhere. Judicial comment at this time, undermining the defence, was to say the least robust and on occasions bordered on the outrageous; this comment by the judge was never ever going to be regarded other than as falling within acceptable bounds.

The 'Albert/Alfred' problem also enjoyed a run out in Ray Dean's grounds of appeal with a complaint that the summing-up failed to mention that the person who committed the crime had acknowledged his name to be 'Albert' Moore. A trial judge is not required to remind the jury of every single piece of evidence. To do so would be a tedious and unprofitable exercise and this was a piece of evidence the jury were unlikely to have overlooked and equally unlikely to have given it any weight at all in the absence of there being an Albert Moore there or thereabouts in the vicinity of Kirkheaton who might, even just possibly, be a candidate for the role of double police murderer.

In short, these were just the sort of grounds likely to be testily and peremptorily dismissed by an irascible Lord Chief Justice anxious to move on to the next case in the court's list.

Accompanying these flimsy grounds of appeal was Form XXVI, an application to call evidence not available at the trial and *subpoenas* were duly served on the Staffords and Tom Holdsworth. Technically the hearing that was to take place was one for leave to appeal and permission had to be sought for Moore to be present. It was granted as it always was in these cases.

All that could be done had been done to prepare for an appeal in respect of which none of those professionally involved entertained the faintest hope that it might succeed. But for the Moore family at least it kept hope alive over an otherwise gloomy festive season and utterly dismal New Year.

On Sunday 20th January 1952 Moore was taken from Leeds to spend the night at a London prison for the hearing the next day in the magnificence of the court of the Lord Chief Justice in the Royal Courts of Justice on the Strand.

Promptly at 10-30 am the next day the case was called on and Moore, for the final time, brought up into the dock. Throughout the proceedings he was reported as looking 'strained' – as well he might. Apart from the Barristers also present in court were Alice Moore who waved to her husband as he entered the dock, her loyal friend Mrs Norris Bennett and, of course, Ted Hutchinson. Neither then, nor at any stage during the hearing, did the prisoner acknowledge the presence in court of his wife.

The Crown were evidently confident not only that the outcome of the appeal was a foregone conclusion but also that their own advocate was not even likely to be troubled to take to his feet and address the court. Leading G. Norman Black on this occasion was the glamorous Rose Heilbron KC whose name was widely recognised at the time well beyond the ranks of the criminal Bar. During the recent hostilities and the enforced absence from practice of so many of her male colleagues she had carved out a reputation for herself as a defender in murder trials on the strength of which she had taken 'silk' (short hand for appointment as one of His Majesty's Counsel learned in the law and so named because of the silk gown worn by those of that elevated rank). She was in fact the first woman to be appointed King's Counsel, the first woman to lead in a murder case, the first woman Recorder and the first woman to sit as a judge at the Old Bailey. When in 1974 she was appointed a judge of the Family Division of the High Court of Justice, she was only the second – on this occasion - woman to be appointed as a Justice of the High Court. Unsurprisingly she was the envy of male colleagues denied this recognition and regularly the subject of sexist comment that her success owed as much to her physical attributes as it did to her forensic skills. She died in 2005.

Evidently G. Raymond Hinchcliffe KC had more pressing duties to discharge and the calculation that it mattered not who led for the Crown because he (or she) would not be troubled to respond to the appeal proved all too accurate.

The 'Chief' sat with Mr Justice Byrne (later to enjoy brief fame as the judge in the 'Lady Chatterley Trial') and Mr Justice Parker (Goddard's eventual successor as Lord Chief Justice) as his 'wingers' or, as the other two members of the court are sometimes less respectfully referred to by the Bar, 'book ends'.

Hylton-Foster rose to address the court. His submissions began with a recital of the further evidence the defence wished the court to hear. From a newspaper interview, published after the trial, it appeared, the court was told, that Inspector Fraser had spent part of the Saturday evening at the home of Mr and Mrs Stafford. Not of itself of any great moment; however, "Mrs Stafford has told some person unknown, who communicated it to the appellant's solicitors, that it was midnight before Inspector Fraser left the house." He continued:

"Assuming that proposition to be true, and assuming Mrs Stafford could prove it if she were called, I submit it would go as far as this – the Stafford's house would be fifteen to twenty minutes' walk from the scene of the crime, where according to the evidence Jagger had been posted by Fraser. Of course, if that were true it would completely destroy the prosecution's submission that Jagger was posted there at 11-37 or 11-38 pm."

The logic of it was unassailable and Hylton-Foster paused for at least a response (he did not exactly anticipate encouragement) from the bench. He waited in vain. Goddard and his brother judges were too experienced to launch a broadside upon a submission from which they could only retreat having underlined its cogency. They sat stony-faced and counsel was forced to conclude, somewhat lamely:

"That is the substance underlying the application."

There was now, said counsel, a second application to call fresh evidence "from a man named Holdsworth who has made a statement that one of the West Riding detectives was in possession of a photograph of Moore some ten days before the crime." Whilst it was known at the trial that the police, as a body, were in possession of a photograph of the prisoner, here was an identified officer who, what is more, was a member of the cordon. If he was in possession of a copy of the photograph, did not that make it more likely that Jagger also had had access to the photograph? And, if he had, did not that circumstance alone raise questions as to whether Jagger's identification of Moore was really an identification of the killer? Might it not have been no more than a recognition of someone seen in a photograph a few days earlier?

Counsel waited in vain for a response. To respond would inevitably prolong the proceedings and the court had a list of cases to get through of greater importance than consideration of the safety of a conviction in a capital case.

Turning to the complaints of jury misdirection, knowing that his best shots had been fired and failed and that what was to follow were duds, counsel drew to the court's attention the evidence that rain had fallen that night between midnight and the time of the shooting and that Moore's raincoat when recovered was dry; those facts suggested that when it rained Moore had, as he always claimed, been indoors - and at home. Whilst he had made no secret of his activities in the past, and at that the recent past, as a burglar he denied that on the night of the shootings his temporary absence from home was for anything other than an innocent purpose and as to that the prosecution had not sought to challenge what he had to say. The comment by the trial judge that if Moore had been inside 'somewhere' between the hours of midnight and the time of the shooting his raincoat would have been dry carried the implication that he may have been 'somewhere' other than at home.

"There was" argued Sir Harry "no justification in the evidence for suggesting that the appellant was inside anywhere except his own home at the material time. The comment was unfortunate for the appellant's interests because the inference was not justified upon the evidence that Moore had been inside anywhere in the sense in which the jury would understand the meaning of 'inside'."

Hylton-Foster paused. Once more no response. Even unfriendly comment would have facilitated an exercise in pursuing the argument, perhaps underlining its logic, just possibly even in sowing the proverbial mustard seed of doubt. But response was there none. Not even a slightly raised eyebrow. The Court was evidently wholly unpersuaded.

What followed was a classic example of a coded exchange between bench and bar which they alone understood. From the outset counsel had harboured no illusions as to the outcome. Now the futility of the exercise had been laid bare. Some words by way of conclusion seemed to be called for.

"I have been through this case with the greatest possible care and it will be of confidence to the appellant's relatives to know that this court has had it wholly under review."

In other words – *I've done what I had to do, that which Mrs Moore, who is sitting at the back of the court, wished me to do and has paid me to do. I know perfectly well there is nothing in it at all and I know that you know there is nothing in it. But there it is.*

The suggestion that, even in an age of far greater deference to authority than today, anybody could have departed that hearing with confidence that what had taken place was a fair and open-minded review of the safety of a conviction in a capital case was risible.

As Hylton-Foster resumed his seat Rose Heilbron KC made a token half movement in the direction of a standing position, all the while her eyes fixed on The Chief, anticipating the very words that followed and confirmed, at least to the professionals present, that this conviction would stand – though it hardly needed confirming.

"We need not trouble you Miss Heilbron."

Without reference to his brother judges, Goddard, in characteristic pose with elbow on bench and head resting on outstretched left hand cupped below the chin, gave the judgement of the court. It was brief, delivered without reference to the three volumes of transcripts of the proceedings at the Assizes and hardly an exercise capable of being described as 'reasoned'. As the hanging of a man would shortly follow it was better that not even a scintilla of doubt be allowed to cloud the judgement of the court. So what followed was an acclamation of the guilt of the appellant delivered in nothing less than robust, absolutist terms.

There was, in the opinion of the court, he began, no misdirection of the jury at all, the trial judge had not unfairly stated the evidence in the smallest possible matter and the new evidence it was suggested should be heard had no bearing on the case at all. Fortunately, for the interests of justice, P.C. Jagger had given a deposition before he died in which he gave evidence, in the most clear and convincing way, as to how he shone a torch in the prisoner's face and saw and recognised him as the man who produced a firearm and shot Inspector Fraser dead and then turned the revolver upon him and shot him as well. He concluded:

"There is nothing in this case at all except that it was a particularly brutal murder and the application is refused."

And that was it. No comment concerning the bedside identification, the circumstances of the subsequent recording of the critical evidence of P.C. Jagger or the possibility that an honest and convincing identification might just be mistaken. Nothing about the fairness of a trial where the defence had enjoyed no opportunity to challenge effectively the sole and decisive evidence of guilt. The whole proceedings had taken less than thirty minutes.

Moore had listened intently as judgement was delivered, evidently believing to the end that all was not lost. At its conclusion the full implications seemed, for the first time, to strike home. His face contorted with anger and he could be seen uttering words which failed to carry across the courtroom. The dock officers acted promptly to quell any further protest and he was taken hold of by both arms, smartly turned around and removed, for the last time, from public view to begin the journey back to the north and the death cell at Armley Gaol. Passing through the prison gates those words about his body being buried within the precincts of the prison in which he had last been confined told him that, for the remaining few days of his life and for the whole of eternity, he would not be moving more than a very few yards.

As for Goddard, he lived on to a ripe old age, dying in 1971 just short of making it to a century, with a reputation fraying at the edges but still largely intact. It was, however, later in the same year that he perfunctorily dismissed Alfred Moore's appeal that he presided over a trial that half a century later was to lead to a devastating reappraisal of the man. At the trial of Christopher Craig and Derek Bentley he had ensured the conviction of 19 year-old Bentley, a feeble-minded youth who had been under arrest for all of twenty minutes at the time of the fatal shooting of a police officer by his co-accused, by inviting the jury to prefer the word of "conspicuously brave" police officers to that of a defendant whose word was tainted for no reason other than that he "stood in mortal peril." When, in 1999, the Criminal Cases Review Commission referred Bentley's conviction to the appeal court not only was it posthumously quashed but Goddard's reputation posthumously revised. It now stands at a level commensurate with the devastating characterisation of his summing-up as "denying Bentley that fair trial which was the birthright of every British citizen."

26 – Last days

Only one man now stood between Alfred Moore and his appointment with the hangman, fixed on the day following the dismissal of his appeal for Wednesday 6 February. That man was the Home Secretary, Mr Maxwell-Fyfe. It was popularly quipped of him at the time – "There's nothing nearer to death in life than David Patrick Maxwell-Fyfe." There were plainly no compassionate grounds on which to recommend the Monarch to exercise the Royal prerogative of mercy, these were, as Goddard had rightly said, two brutal killings of police officers acting in the execution of their duty. As a matter of practice, a sentence of death was sometimes respited where though the evidence proved guilt beyond reasonable doubt – the fact of conviction left open no other interpretation – there remained, nonetheless, some residual scintilla of doubt rendering it expedient not to exact the ultimate, irreversible penalty. The logic of the approach was questionable to say the least and it was a discretion hardly admitted to exist and only exercised sparingly in exceptional circumstances.

No doubt some Home Secretaries did conscientiously take another look at the evidence in these anxious cases. There was no prospect, however, of this Home Secretary doing so in the case of Alfred Moore or any other hapless condemned prisoner. His faith in the justice system always to deliver the right answer was as unswerving as it was naive. Just a few years earlier, in 1948, he told the House of Commons:

"There is no practical possibility of an innocent man being put to death. Of course, a jury might go wrong, the Court of Criminal Appeal might go wrong as might the House of Lords and the Home Secretary: they might all be stricken mad and go wrong. But that is not a possibility which anyone can consider likely."

Just a year on from his deliberations on the issue as to whether Alfred Moore should live or die, and in the teeth of a popular groundswell of public revulsion at the idea of Derek Bentley hanging, he declined to recommend mercy.

No one, not even Moore himself, entertained hope that a reprieve would be forthcoming though Ted Hutchinson continued his efforts to recruit signatures for a petition to be submitted to the Home Office. There were few subscribers. When submitted it spoke eloquently that the public verdict was overwhelmingly that Moore should pay the price. Nor was the emotional letter from Alice Moore pleading for the life of her husband and the father of her girls to be spared likely to sway the decision. Such appeals, after all, were an invariable circumstance in these cases. They were always made and never carried any weight.

Monitoring of Moore's mental health continued with continuing confirmation being sought that he was not a criminal lunatic, it being considered contrary to good conscience to execute judgement of death upon a man not in a condition to make his peace with God. Two days before the date set for his execution Moore was told by the Prison Governor of the Home Secretary's decision on the plea for mercy. It came as no surprise. Once again the wording was as ritualised as the sentence of death itself. 'The law must take its course.' Explanations were rarely offered by the Home Office as to why some murderers were reprieved whilst others were not though in the case of the killing by an admitted burglar of two police officers taking part in an exercise to seek to bring him to justice an explanation was hardly required.

With this last chance of life denied the countdown to the fierce and sickening climax of execution morning began.

On the morning of Moore's last full day of life he was visited for the final time by Ted Hutchinson. No longer was there any point in discussing the case, considering strategies, even contemplating the future. They engaged in what had become Moore's favourite pastime during his weeks in the condemned cell. They played chess.

In the afternoon Alice Moore and Patricia paid their last visit. The memory of that visit is an abiding one for Patricia. There were tears to be shed but this was not the time to shed them. In fact it was a time during which it was the condemned man who kept up the spirits of his visitors rather than the other way round. A promise was made that if ever the occasion arose to put right the wrong that was to be done in a few hours' time it would be taken. It never did arise during Alice's lifetime. Patricia, sitting on daddy's knee and eating the sweeties which the prison guards had provided for Alfred to give to his little girl, was asked to promise that she would be a good girl for her mummy and look after her little sisters. It was a meeting charged with emotion but not until the separation following the final embrace did the dam burst on either side.

As the visit was taking place the executioner, Steve Wade, and his assistant, Harry Smith, slipped unnoticed into the prison with strict instructions not to leave its confines until the execution had been carried out.

For the past several decades the counties of Lancashire and Yorkshire had been the exclusive source of public executioners. Steve Wade was a Doncaster motor-coach dealer. Though only the Deputy to Chief Executioner, Albert Pierrepoint, he was a man with a mission. He had first applied for the job of executioner on leaving the army at the age of 19 in 1921 because, as he candidly acknowledged, he hated murder and murderers. It was twenty years before he was finally accepted for training. "I was never nervous" he once said. "It's a job which needs a special type of temperament. You're either fit to do it or you're not. And you soon find out." Undoubtedly Steve Wade had the necessary temperament. In an interview given by him to his local newspaper he spoke of the numerous executions performed by him, some of them "virtually my own neighbours". The occasion of the interview was the vote in the House of Commons in 1948 to suspend the death sentence for an experimental period. With no attempt to disguise his fury at the decision he told the reporter:

"Don't think that because I am now out of work my view has been influenced. Not a bit! This job has been a sideline, but I know these desperadoes; they are a menace to society and should be made to pay the penalty. I know the prison officials are against abolition. The ordinary criminal under sentence of two or three years creates enough trouble for them as it is and every day there are assaults of one kind or another. So think of all the trouble a murderer could cause during his 15 to 20 years of 'life' at the end of which he will be free to repeat his crime."

He need not have worried. The experimental period did not run its course and hanging was resumed after a brief lull and remained the mandatory sentence for all forms of murder until 1957 when it was restricted to murders classified as capital - which included murder by shooting, double murder and the murder of a police officer. The killings at Whinney Close Farm would have qualified for the rope under all three heads!

Moore may not have been greatly comforted to be told that Pierrepoint, in his recent evidence to the Royal Commission, had described Wade as "a good, reliable man."

Pierrepoint, himself, a man who began a schoolboy essay on 'What I Should Like To Do When I Leave School' with the words 'When I leave school I should like to be the official executioner' was presumably engaged in practising his craft, as he proudly termed it, elsewhere; for him one of the attractions of the job was, he told the Royal Commission, the opportunity that it gave him to travel. Wade was to succeed Pierrepoint as Chief Executioner in 1955 but retired within months on health grounds and died the following year at the age of 59.

Following Alice and Patricia's visit Moore would have been invited to take his daily exercise. This was not prompted by concern for the well-being of the condemned man. It was in order to provide Wade with a discreet opportunity to size up the physique of his victim from what the Royal Commission grotesquely described as 'some vantage point' and both make those calculations necessary to ensure that the business of the next morning was despatched with efficiency and expedition and to test the equipment in the execution shed without being overheard in the condemned cell next door. Moore was a man short in stature and the 'drop' calculated was a commensurately long one. The last task of Steve Wade before retiring to bed was to fill a bag with sand to the approximate weight of the condemned man and suspend it from the rope overnight in order to stretch it to its maximum extent.

The 'long drop' had been perfected by the Victorian executioner William Marwood. A cobbler by trade, from Horncastle, he was a man who took pride in his work. He believed himself to be a humane man and would often speak contemptuously of his predecessor in office, William Calcraft:

"He *hanged* them. I *execute* them."

By a combination of experience and experiment Marwood had developed a technique, aimed at producing instantaneous death from a fracture between the 2nd and 3rd cervical vertebrae, by dropping the prisoner at the end of the rope into a pit below the scaffold. The drop would be between seven and ten feet according to the height and build of the condemned man. No one, of course, knew whether death was ever quite literally instantaneous or whether the appearance of a humane technique represented the reality of what actually happened. Certainly the heart continued to pump blood and the pulse to beat faintly after the drop – sometimes for as long as twenty minutes. And as for the hood placed over the prisoner's head that was more a concession to the susceptibilities of the necessary spectators than those of the condemned man. When a short drop was used the head of the victim would not pass below floor level. The contorting face of the suspended body would have provided the most compelling evidence of all that the drop was not quite as instantaneous as its supporters claimed. Perhaps the best that can be said is that the technique was an improvement on the slow strangulation and death by asphyxiation of the past.

During his last night Moore slept but it was a fitful sleep during which it was reported that he cried out the name Alice. When awake he continued to protest his innocence and rail against the iniquity of what was shortly to happen. Whether he partook of that 'hearty breakfast', supposedly the fare of the condemned, history does not record. What is known, however, is that in the hours before the arrival of Steve Wade and the rest of the execution party in his cell Moore was scribbling. He was determined to place on record for posterity the enormity of the injustice that was about to take place. In those last hours it was not terror that dominated the mind of Alfred Moore nor solemn contemplation of the hereafter but fury that a determination to avenge the deaths of two serving police officers had resulted in evidence being skewed, manipulated, falsified to bring about his own death. Without thought as to when or by whom his letter might be read, if indeed ever at all, he wrote steadily requesting only that his letter be taken by the Prison Governor and placed with the record documenting his stay at Armley, first as a remand prisoner, latterly in the condemned cell. The Governor gave his word and was true to his word but it was to be more than half a century later before Moore's final testimony was to see the light of day again.

Moore knew full well that his protestations of innocence would, as the minutes ticked away, avail him not at all. That which was to be would be. If he was a man of any faith at all this was a time to open his conscience and, if he was indeed guilty of the crime of which he stood condemned, make true confession in the hope that at least the mercy denied him by the Home Secretary might be found in a court of superior jurisdiction.

It was not, however, penitence but defiance that took over. This was not only Alfred's final but his definitive statement of innocence. It was a case very different to that put at his trial by counsel anxious that a head on confrontation with the evidence of police witnesses would serve only to antagonise a middle class jury with unswerving faith in the total integrity of officers of the law.

In this final testimony all the material police witnesses are denounced but with especial bile reserved for the evidence given by Superintendent George Metcalfe. His evidence of what was said at the point of arrest was 'entirely a figment of his imagination, untruthfully supported by Cleaver.' It was Superintendent Metcalfe who made suggestions to him such as 'you are confused Albert! You can't think Albert! You don't like the police Albert, do you?' Having made to him these assertions they were later written up in the pocket books of the officers as his words – 'I need time to think. I never did like the police.' Police malpractice was not confined to the fabrication of incriminating evidence but extended to a denial of his basic rights as a suspect under arrest at the police station: 'I continually asked for legal aid and received only abuse' he wrote. 'I was systematically obstructed from getting a solicitor for about 12 hours before the identity parade.' Adding 'I did not say Heaton (sic) Smith can't help me now – this is typical of the way Superintendent Metcalfe talked that day.'

The letter concludes on a calmer, more rational, note with an explanation, proffered neither at the trial nor it would seem to his legal advisers in his pre-trial instructions, for the finding on the farm of the 9 mm cartridge cases. These may, he suggested, 'have been picked up by children in and around the outbuildings .... there were bullet holes through the bedroom window in the unfurnished part of the house when we first bought it as an unfinished structure, because of this I feel there is some person near Kirkheaton who has been into the farm building whilst it was unoccupied for a considerable period. Mr Markham of Messrs Heap Ltd Builders, Chapel Hill, Huddersfield can vouch for what I say about bullet holes in the windows.'

If Alfred Moore had any suspicions as to the true identity of the killer – and if he was innocent as he claimed he must have had his own thoughts as to who the armed man approaching his farmhouse in the middle of the night might have been – he was not seemingly minded to commit them to paper for the future consideration of posterity. He concludes simply – 'The above statement is true. Alfred Moore 6/2/52.'

As part of the ritual of the day Moore would have been joined for the final hour of his life by the Prison Chaplain whose duty required him to be present at the execution to read the funeral office during the final moments of the condemned man's life. Plainly there was to be no last minute confession and the defiant tone of Moore's last letter suggests that spiritual consolation was far from his mind as the minutes ticked away to the fateful hour of 9-00.

The events of the morning of an execution followed an unvarying pattern. A key player was always the High Sheriff of the County, usually some land-owning member of the gentry who served for just a year in the job after his, or occasionally these days her, name had been picked from a list presented to the Monarch. He is now largely a ceremonial functionary whose responsibilities include proclaiming the accession of a new sovereign. Of rather greater everyday practical utility he has the duty of ensuring that writs and orders of the High Court are *executed*. It was his duty to commission and pay the hangman and also, nominally at least, to provide what the Royal Commission described as 'the necessary apparatus': in practice this was usually done by the prison authorities. On occasions such as this the duty of witnessing the *execution* of the order of the court has an undoubted literal ring attaching to it. No doubt all but the most atavistic of High Sheriffs were relieved to be able to delegate the task to their Under Sheriff, a full-time professional official.

In accordance with tradition 20 minutes before the appointed time the Under Sheriff, Mr Benjamin Dodsworth, arrived at the prison. Only a small gathering awaited him outside. Capital punishment may have been the subject of angry debate but there was to be no mass protest such as that which was to accompany the hangings later that decade of Derek Bentley and Ruth Ellis. No account was ever publicly given of how any particular condemned man met his end save for the most bland and formulaic assurance that there had been 'no hitch'. Once more the Royal Commission provides graphic detail as to the general process:

> "The executioner and his assistant wait outside the condemned cell, with the chief officer and officer detailed to conduct the prisoner to the execution chamber. On a signal given by the Sheriff they enter and the executioner pinions the prisoner's arms behind his back. He is escorted to the drop with one officer on

> either side. The Sheriff, the Governor and the medical officer enter the execution chamber directly by another door. The prisoner is placed on the drop on a marked spot so that his feet are directly across the division of the trap doors. The executioner places a white cap over the prisoner's head and places the noose round his neck, while the assistant pinions his legs. When the executioner sees that all is ready he pulls the lever."

Not all executions were carried out with textbook precision. When giving evidence before the Royal Commission Pierrepoint was asked:

"What happens if a prisoner faints at the last minute?"

"They carry him to the scaffold."

"But what happens if he gets on to the scaffold and then faints?"

"He has to go just the same. They pull the lever and away he goes".

It is unlikely that before the opening of the door to the execution shed Moore even realised that he had spent those weeks since sentence of death was passed upon him no more than ten paces from the gallows on which he was to hang.

Pierrepoint prided himself on a time lapse of nine to twelve seconds between first entering the cell and the drop. No more than moments after the executioner and his assistant entered his cell Moore experienced his last earthly sensation as he dropped into space. The savage public will had been done and with it Moore denied either pity or the hope of redemption, at least on this side of the grave.

There has been no finer account of the atmosphere inside a prison at the time of an execution than that of Major Frederick Wallace Blake, a humanitarian Prison Governor who served at Pentonville during the 1920's. Blake witnessed numerous executions and saw only too clearly the dehumanising effect it had on all involved. He wrote -

> "Why is it that we feel a horror, as if we are about to commit a crime, when a man is going to be hanged? Why is it that we feel something unholy, something not clean? It is not only my own feelings; those of the warders, who have to assist in the hanging, are the same. They are given spirits to help them pull themselves together. I shall be glad when this awful form of punishment no longer exists. It is frightful suffering, because one feels deeply the mind of the stricken man, and his thoughts seem to vibrate

> through the prison and give us some of the terror through which he is passing. And every prisoner in his cell seems to look white and lined; his nerves are on edge. There is not a sound in the prison until the wretched man has found his last home and gone to a higher Judge."

It was not until 1965 that the rope finally disappeared from the darker annals of English penal history. Whilst the English had been for centuries, and many still are, enthusiasts for the rope in the unproven, and unprovable, belief that it acted as a deterrent, they were also rightly ashamed of the whole ghastly business. Any euphemism would do - "topping," "despatching," "paying the supreme penalty," "launching into eternity" - to avoid calling it what it was, killing. Ironically, the defining opposite of death, namely life, was substituted as the mandatory penalty for murder following abolition.

Pierrepoint, after a 24 year career as public executioner in which he conducted some 400 executions, concluded in his autobiography – ".... executions solve nothing and are only an antiquated relic of a primitive desire for revenge which takes the easy way and hands over the responsibility for revenge to other people. All the men and women whom I have faced at the final moment convince me that in what I have done I have not prevented a single murder." By the end of the century Britain's position as a signatory of the European Convention on Human Rights and Fundamental Freedoms put the spectre of the return of the rope beyond rational debate.

As Alfred Moore was being launched into eternity the wretched Alice stood before the clock at home, her arm around Patricia. Pat has a vivid recall that as the clock struck nine her mother dissolved into uncontrollable weeping. She had hoped for some miracle over the past terrifying and desolate days; it was hope rather than optimism but at least it sustained her during the ordeal of waiting for this moment. Now that waiting was over, all hope utterly extinguished, her status in life that of the widow of an executed notorious criminal.

The debate about Moore's conviction and the probity of the evidence upon which it was based continues over sixty years later. If he was innocent of the crime of which he stood indicted and convicted what took place that morning was no less an atrocity than the crime itself. If he was guilty then he was responsible for a brutal callous crime – yet, in the words of Oscar Wilde 'Fate will use a running noose for the best man and the worst'.

The pulling of the lever was not quite the final act of the unholy ritual. As the lifeless body of Alfred Moore swung at the end of the rope, its neck broken and the side of the head lolling against the shoulder blade, the Chaplain intoned the prayer reserved for these occasions whilst those present stood, heads bowed, in respectful silence.

"Into Thy hands, O Lord we commend the spirit of this thy servant. O Lord, we beseech Thee, mercifully hear our prayers, and spare all who confess their sins unto Thee; that they whose consciences by sin are accused, by Thy merciful pardon may be absolved; through Christ our Lord. Amen."

The solemnities concluded the practicalities commenced. The medical officer proceeded to the pit where life was formally pronounced extinct, although with wicked barbarity the body was left to hang for one hour before being taken down by the executioner as the last of his duties. At 9-15 a.m. a prison official came through the wicket door in the main gate and posted the two required official notices. The first was signed by the Under Sheriff, the Governor of the prison, Captain E. C. Tunnicliffe, and the Chaplain, the Reverend K. Fawcett, as witnesses to the deed. It read: 'We, the undersigned, hereby declare that judgement of death was this day executed on Alfred Moore in His Majesty's Prison at Leeds in our presence.' The second was signed only by Dr. James Walker, prison medical officer: 'I this day examined the body of Alfred Moore, on whom judgement of death was executed in the said prison and on that examination found that Alfred Moore was dead'. The process of doing this man to death required representatives of the Monarch, the Church, the Law and the medical profession to be present.

The handful of morbid individuals who had attended outside the prison to derive some vicarious satisfaction from being in the near presence of violent, premeditated death had been kept at a distance of 150 yards from the prison but, on the posting of the notices, they were permitted to approach and file past.

The statutory inquest held later that morning in the prison was a formality but one that, nonetheless, required eight jurymen, presided over by the local Coroner. It returned the inevitable verdict: the medical evidence was fracture of the cervical vertebra, duly translated into legal jargon as "death by judicial hanging." As inevitable as the verdict was the evidence that the execution had been carried out “expeditiously and without a hitch.” No doubt everything was done that could be done to ensure the minimum of suffering to the victim but some measure of scepticism may be permitted that even if a hitch had occurred the outside world would have been allowed to know of it via the coroner and his jury.

John Ellis, who carried out numerous executions between 1901 and 1924, once told an interviewer who asked him if he had ever bungled an execution. “We don’t make mistakes nowadays, it’s all taped and worked out, and even if there should be some slight mishap, the whole government machine goes all out to save the hangman’s face. *They have to.*”

Burial in an unmarked grave within the confines of the prison followed. No member of the family was permitted to be present, only the Governor if he chose to attend, the prison officers selected to dig the grave and fill it in afterwards and, of course, the chaplain, fresh from his participation in the violation of the sixth commandment, to read the burial service. The use of quicklime to obliterate all trace of the mortal remains had mercifully been discontinued by Home Office Circular in 1922.

That evening the local newspaper briefly reported the proceedings of the day. This was a ‘routine’ hanging, attracting nothing in the way of national notoriety, and that was how these things were reported. In fact on this day there was a far bigger story to report and it dominated the front pages of evening newspapers throughout the land. During the night the King had passed away. A new Monarch had been proclaimed. The prison referred to in the official announcement of Moore’s execution as ‘His Majesty’s’ was in fact wrongly so described. No one had thought to correct the pro forma wording. For the Sheriff of the County it had been an eventful day.

The normal routine of the prison was resumed after the mounting tension of the previous days. Until, that is, the arrival of the next man condemned to enjoy the facilities of Armley’s newly purpose-built condemned suite.

27 – And still the argument rages.

Over half a century on from that bleak February morning when the nation awoke to the proclamation 'The King is Dead; Long Live the Queen' and Alfred Moore went angrily to the scaffold, protesting his innocence and railing against the injustice of his conviction, the story of the Kirkheaton police killings refuses to go away. It is a story with a seemingly enduring potential for some aspect of it to feature in the local newspaper on those days when news is otherwise sparse.

The main focus of attention with these stories has always been the burglar-farmer, whether he was justly hanged and the mystery of the missing gun. The slain officers have been relegated to the role of minor characters in the drama.

It was not until 1997, 46 years on from the tragedy, that the fallen officers were officially commemorated in the town and even then not in a manner which was likely to catch the public imagination. Their memorial is a brass plaque inside the police station at the Civic Centre. It was generously paid for from the proceeds of a book on the history of policing in Huddersfield written by former local police sergeant Steve Holberry. His timely reminder of the events of 1951 prompted the demand for a permanent memorial and local serving police officers paid up willingly to buy the book and fund this long overdue mark of recognition of the ultimate sacrifice made by the two officers in the line of duty.

A commemoration no more accessible to the people of the town is the National Police Memorial to be found at the corner of Horse Guards and the Mall in London, inspired by the shooting in April 1984 of W.P.C. Yvonne Fletcher at the Libyan Embassy Siege. This memorial, tirelessly campaigned for by film director and television personality Michael

Winner, was unveiled by the Queen in April 2005. Included among the names of 1600 officers recorded are those of Duncan Fraser and Gordon Jagger.

The many members of the Moore family still living in the town do not relish reminders of their notorious relative. Particularly so when the reminder of the past is generated by another relative living on the other side of the world and not even bearing the stigma of the Moore surname. In August 2006 a nephew, David Schofield, living 11,000 miles away in New Zealand, was reported as launching a sensational attempt to clear his uncle's name. The headline this time: "Farmer Should Never Have Been Hanged."

From Timaru on the country's South Island he told the *Examiner* – "I have within me a real sense of injustice". He would do that which generally represented the last refuge of the desperate for it was never going to illicit, if anything at all, more than a polite, wholly non-committal, response; he had determined that he would write to the Prince of Wales and the Prime Minister.

As a counter-weight the newspaper lifted a quote from former P.C. Carl Tipling, one of the few surviving members of the team of West Riding police officers who searched the fields surrounding the farmhouse in the days following the arrest of Alfred Moore. He had told the newspaper a couple of years earlier, when some other aspect of the controversial trial of Alfred Moore briefly became headline news again, that he was personally in no doubt that the right man had hanged. Drawing on his personal knowledge and recollection of one of the murdered officers he protested:

"P.C. Jagger knew there was no hope for him and he was dying – he was a God-fearing man and an excellent policeman. He would only have picked out Moore if he was sure it was him that night. He would never have done it just to get a conviction. He would only have picked out Moore if he was sure. They got the right man."

Adding for good measure: "Moore was evil."

This posthumous commendation of the piety of the long dead officer appears to have prompted almost instantaneous doubts in the mind of the far distant nephew for the next day and under the headline – "Claims Of Innocence Do Not Tally with Evidence At The Time" David Schofield, his burning sense of injustice reported the previous day having apparently cooled, told the *Examiner* reporter that his understanding of the case was admittedly heavily reliant on what he had been told by his Aunt

Mary, widow of another Moore brother, Alan, and that perhaps it was not wholly and entirely accurate. But, nonetheless, he would welcome anyone with in-depth knowledge of the case coming forward.

It is, however, the failure to find the murder weapon, despite the best and most strenuous efforts of police and army and the failure of the prosecution to explain how this squared with the guilt of the poultry farmer who was confidently said to have fled immediately from the scene of his crime to the shelter of his farmhouse, that continues to fuel lurking doubts as to the safety of the conviction.

In the *Examiner,* for the 7 January 1998, appeared a photograph of a seriously corroded lump of metal still vaguely recognisable by its shape as a handgun. It was said to have been discovered at Lane Side Quarry, Kirkheaton by a local man using a metal detector. Extensions to the quarry had been made in recent months and it was thought the disturbance of the ground might have had the effect of bringing nearer to the surface this obviously long buried artifact. It's location, 200 yards from the murder scene, and rusty condition certainly qualified it as a serious candidate for being the murder weapon. Although sent off to the police firearms forensic laboratory at Huntington the result of tests to anyone acquainted with the case was a foregone conclusion. What was clearly to be seen attached to the barrel of this rusted relic was a silencer. The shots fired on the night of the tragedy rang out loudly, piercing the night air – unmuffled by any silencer. Forensic tests confirmed that this was not the murder weapon.

Almost two years on from the excitement of the finding at Lane Side Quarry, local furniture dealer John Mead, then aged 50, caught yet further headlines and once more excited public interest in the case with a sensational claim to have discovered the murder weapon when playing out with other children back in 1956 when he was 7 years of age. He, his brother Barry and two friends had discovered a gun hidden in the cavity of a dry-stone wall near to his father's scrap yard at Stafford Hill, Kirkheaton. "We took the gun" he told the local reporter "to my father Clifford Mead but he went white, took it from us and told us never to tell anyone what we had found. He said it would cause a lot of trouble if we ever revealed the truth."

Clifford had died the previous year and his mother shortly before this revelation was made to the town's newspaper. John claimed that he had asked his mother many times about the day when, as a boy, he had brought home a gun. She remained, however, tight-lipped, promising only that on her death she would leave behind for him all the information that he wanted to know. But all that she had left that was relevant to the hanging of Alfred Moore and her son's finding of a gun was an old cutting from the *Examiner*, about the case certainly but unenlightening as to the provenance of the rusty gun.

So nothing there to be submitted for forensic examination but a story, if true, suggesting that he and his pals had indeed discovered the murder weapon and the vital clue to the innocence of Moore, for, as Mead pointed out with undeniable logic:

"If this was indeed the murder weapon, and I am convinced as far as I can be that it was, then there was no way that Alfred Moore could have been the killer. He could not have got from his farm, a mile and a half away, and back again to hide the gun with all those policemen about. They had the house surrounded. It would have been impossible."

The *Examiner* clearly thought the lead was one worth following. Were you one of the boys, it asked, who stumbled upon the weapon with Mr. Mead? If so, call Jenny Parkin at the *Examiner* on 437769. No one answered the invitation and this particular story went no further.

What was of as much interest as the alleged finding of the murder weapon was the reported reaction to it of Clifford Mead and his wife. The counter balance to doubts raised by the failure to find the murder weapon had always been – if not Alfred Moore, then who?

Clifford Mead, born in 1920 and just over 30 years of age when the murders occurred, lived in Kirkheaton with his wife Joyce and their young family. He earned a legitimate income as a scrap metal dealer, supplemented by the proceeds of crime. He was known to police intelligence as someone ready and willing to 'fence' stolen goods and as an associate of Alfred Moore. But he shared none of Alfred's easy-going charm. He was a gun-obsessed, menacing character with a sadistic streak. Patricia recalls him as a regular visitor to Whinney Close Farm and before that to the family home at Honley and as someone who invariably wore a white scarf. During the war and post-war years of austerity he was a man you could rely upon to provide what were euphemistically described as 'essential supplies'. Even before Moore's trial rumour was rife as to Clifford Mead's knowledge of the events of that night – if not indeed his own involvement in them – and the hanging of Moore did nothing to dispel those rumours.

In 1971, when Clifford Mead was under police surveillance on suspicion of being involved in a series of tie-up robberies and burglaries at isolated farmhouses in and around Kirkheaton, information was received that at a drinking party attended by a select group of like-minded associates he had brazenly brandished a gun which he described as “the gun that killed two coppers in 1951 at Kirkheaton”. There was, however, no appetite in 1971 to pursue an enquiry possibly impugning the validity of the conviction and judicial execution of twenty years earlier and Clifford Mead died in 1998 untroubled by further police interest.

Even the most self-confident and skilled burglar needs associates. Someone to ‘fence’ criminal property is indispensable to the burglar and without someone to assist in the disposal of stolen property the efforts of the burglar are to no avail. That is why the sentence imposed on the receiver is sometimes as high, occasionally in fact higher, than that on the thief. As Judges often remark when passing sentence: without receivers there would be no thieves or burglars. All that is known about Clifford Mead is consistent with him being a visitor to the farmhouse for a nefarious purpose in the middle of the night with no desire to submit to police questioning and who, following a confrontation, would have fled away from the scene - taking with him any weapon that might have featured in that confrontation. And someone who if asked if he was Alfred – or Albert – Moore would almost certainly have agreed with alacrity; his reply would not have been “No: I am Clifford Mead”. The prosecution point that the killer answered to the name of Moore was not merely a bad point it was actually a very silly one.

If indeed the real killer was a ‘fence’ coming across the fields at dead of night by prior appointment to collect Moore’s cache of stolen goods it goes a long way towards explaining the otherwise semi-irrational actions of Moore in seeking to obliterate by fire the proceeds of his past criminal endeavours.

However, to describe Clifford Mead as a prime suspect is about as high as it gets or will ever get. His guilt of the crime is now incapable of proof. Suspicion is not proof. Suspicion, which must equally attach to Alfred Moore, ought not to have been mistaken for proof of his guilt. Moore had the opportunity, compromised though it may have been, to defend himself. Clifford Mead no longer has any such opportunity.

In the course of writing this book I have been asked innumerable times whether I believe Alfred Moore to have been innocent. Actually I do but it is, perhaps, the wrong question to ask. The real questions are: was the available evidence sufficient on which to hang the man? did he receive a fair trial? is there today any further evidence available to cast doubt on the safety of this conviction? At the very least that which is known about Clifford Mead raises issues as to whether the wrong man was hanged. Such evidence as points towards Mead as the killer tends towards pointing away from Moore.

Leaving aside then speculation about Clifford Mead, into the category of new evidence is the testimony of one Rex Hallas. In 1951, just 16 years of age, he had spent the day haymaking at nearby Stancliffe's farm. Shortly after midnight he walked across the fields leading to Whinney Close Farm on the way to his home in Cockley Hill Lane having first accompanied his friend and fellow toiler in the fields that day to nearby Houses Hill. After the shooting of the officers and even before the arrest of Moore officers were knocking on the doors of nearby dwellings and rousing the occupants either to alert them to the siege at Whinney Close or, perhaps, to glean further evidence relevant to the murder investigation. One such door was that of Rex Hallas who recalls that when told that a posse of police officers had been keeping watch on the nearby farm he responded: "you couldn't have been, if you had been why didn't you approach me?" The police had indeed located a material witness but one with an account inconsistent with the lynch pin of the prosecution case – the secure cordon being in place comfortably before midnight and where the operational order clearly required that anyone approaching it be stopped and challenged. Young Rex was told – "keep your trap shut and go to bed". And he did – for many years.

A desire to avenge the senseless killing of two brave police officers is entirely understandable but does not begin to justify the extraordinary steps taken to suppress evidence. A consistent theme characterising convictions where justice is later shown to have miscarried is the failure of police and prosecution to make available to the defence not only the evidence alleged to prove guilt but all of the material gathered during the course of the investigation – the so-called 'unused material'. Today that responsibility is enshrined in law with particular reference to material which might either support the case for the defence or undermine that for the prosecution. Central to the case against Moore was that had he returned home at the time he claimed he would have been stopped and challenged. It is not only the late evidence of Rex Hallas that throws this assertion into doubt, if not indeed give the lie to it; the evidence of Rex Hallas is convincingly confirmed by a police memorandum discovered within a file of papers at the Public Record Office at Kew. Admittedly written subsequently to the murders but well in advance of the trial, it states: "The police officers were instructed that any person seen *after say 12-30 am* should be stopped ....." The italics are of course mine with apologies to the intelligent reader for placing emphasis on what is obviously significant.

The dying declaration of Gordon Jagger with its reference to a white silk scarf was never disclosed to the defence no doubt because no white silk scarf was ever recovered from Whinney Close Farm. Had one been found there can be little doubt that the statement would have been served and strenuous arguments advanced that it be allowed in evidence notwithstanding the constraints of the rules against hearsay.

To be added to the charge of suppression is that of manipulation, the massaging of the available evidence to present it in its most favourable aspect and with a view to ensuring that any potential for inconsistency was addressed in advance of, rather than during, defence cross-examination. How else is to be explained the fact that all of the statements of police officers in the cordon were taken by one senior officer, Detective Chief Inspector Jenkins? Police officers at all levels are experienced statement-takers, the most basic of police tasks, and would ordinarily be expected each to make their own statement. What occurred here was unprecedented; to describe it as an attempt to pervert the course of justice would be going too far but it was undoubtedly a premeditated exercise in ensuring that the flow of justice did not depart from pre-ordained channels and that any potential for inconsistency, and therefore doubt, was scotched in advance of the trial.

To all this is to be added that the trial proceeded without the least appreciation of the dangers inherent in reliance on evidence of a fleeting glimpse identification in darkness of a witness the defence enjoyed no opportunity effectively to question. Similar flaws today would all but guarantee an acquittal, that is in the unlikely event of a trial taking place at all. There were questions to be asked of Gordon Jagger which to any criminal lawyer cried out to be asked but were nothing like as obvious to the poultry farmer. Had he seen a photograph of Moore during the briefing for his role in this exercise? (In the light of Moore's history one would undoubtedly have been available and to have shown it to those officers tasked with confronting the prime suspect would not of itself be a cause for criticism; it would, however, be relevant to any fair assessment of the reliability of the later bedside identification). Even had he not been shown a photograph in advance, had one been shown to him whilst he lay in his hospital bed? Just why was the individual who approached the officers addressed as 'Albert' Moore? His fitness to give evidence at all would no doubt have been gently probed: how was he feeling? had he fully recovered from the effect of the anaesthetic?

Assuming both an effective opportunity to challenge the evidence of Gordon Jagger and the disclosure to the defence of his dying declaration, neither of which the defence were of course allowed, the discrepancy between the deposition suggesting a face-to-face confrontation with the killer and the dying deposition 'saw man going up field and went after him' could, and would, have been emphasised and later brought to the attention of the jury.

None of these questions were ever asked because Moore was denied the most basic right of legal representation at the most crucial point in the investigation. It resulted in a trial that was unbalanced, unfair and with a clear potential for an unjust outcome.

Leaving altogether aside all that is <u>now</u> available to suggest that an innocent man was hanged, was the available evidence at the time cogent or sufficient on which to exact the ultimate penalty known to the law? The failure to find the murder weapon, the absence of the so-called smoking gun, remains the most striking singular feature of the case crying out that the killer fled the scene of his crime, away from the farmhouse, away from the cordon, taking with him his gun, not towards the farmhouse where his eventual apprehension was as inevitable as the recovery of the murder weapon itself.

This deficit in the prosecution case might just have been compensated for by other evidence – direct, circumstantial or forensic – that Moore had either carried or fired a gun that night. There was no such evidence. Nor was there any credible explanation for the failure of a search carried out over weeks, occupying the time of countless officers and volunteers, and which yielded up so much to yield up the one object that was its focus.

Why did the jury fail to see all of this? The answer lies in the mindset of that era. Respect for the institution of the police was unquestioned. When a police officer fell in the line of duty it was something to be avenged and the police did not charge and the prosecution did not prosecute innocent men and women – or so it was naively thought. It was a mindset that resulted shortly afterwards in a Lord Chief Justice and Home Secretary bringing about the execution of three-quarter witted 19 year old, Derek Bentley, for uttering the ambiguous words to his co-accused in possession of a gun 'let him have it'. It was in fact the same mindset that clouded the brilliant mind of the top KC, paid handsomely to defend Moore, and which caused him to declare on the eve of the trial his willingness to pull the lever that would instantaneously break the neck of his client. The jury could hardly be blamed.

And finally: what befell the widow and daughters of Alfred Moore who had fled Huddersfield within days of the shooting. They moved again shortly after the execution. In fact they moved many times over the following years with at least the solace that each move served to tighten the shroud of merciful obscurity over their true identity and history. It was the only solace. Patricia recalls what she describes as a "hellish childhood" and for her alone of the sisters the trauma of guilt, without justification but easily understandable, that her evidence contributed to the conviction and execution of her own father. At over 70 years of age it is a pain that does not go away.

Poverty and destitution as well as pain and trauma characterised the childhood of all four sisters. After the substantial legal costs of solicitor, top QC, junior counsel and ballistics expert the proceeds of sale of Whinney Close Farm were exhausted. At the worst of times Tina and Sandra were placed in orphanages for the State to provide at least for their basic needs.

Within the family the events at Kirkheaton were a taboo subject. If what had occurred needed to be referred to at all it was only as 'the incident' and punishment swiftly followed whenever the girls' hushed tones were overheard discussing the events which had rendered them fatherless.

Alice spent the rest of her life on valium, even following her re-marriage some years later resulting in the birth of three more children. She died in 1990 at the age of 72 and is buried at the picturesquely named Marston Mortaine near to Milton Keynes. Bron, Tina and Pat live on. Sandra died a number of years ago. Charles Henry and Alice Mahala Moore divorced shortly after the trial but did later reconcile and moved to Wareham where Charles Henry died in 1960. For those that survive there can be no closure on what occurred. When justice miscarries the victims are many and the effects life-long.

Lightning Source UK Ltd.
Milton Keynes UK
UKOW031239310812

198323UK00001B/50/P

9 780755 214846